Understanding tranquilliser use

Understanding tranquilliser use

The role of the social sciences

Edited by Jonathan Gabe

ROUTLEDGE

Tavistock/Routledge
London and New York

First published in 1991
by Routledge
11 New Fetter Lane, London EC4P 4EE

Simultaneously published in the USA and Canada
by Routledge
a division of Routledge, Chapman and Hall Inc.
29 West 35th Street, New York, NY 10001

Typeset by Input Typesetting Ltd, London
Printed and bound in Great Britain by
Biddles Ltd, Guildford and King's Lynn

British Library Cataloguing in Publication Data
Understanding tranquilliser use: the role of the social sciences.
1. Tranquillisers. Social aspects
I. Gabe, Jonathan
363.1943

Library of Congress Cataloging in Publication Data
Understanding tranquilliser use: the role of the social sciences / edited by Jonathan Gabe.
p. cm.
Includes bibliographical references.
1. Tranquilizing drugs—Social aspects. I. Gabe, Jonathan.
RM333.U53 1990
306.4′61—dc20 90–8436
CIP

ISBN 0–415–03080–3

For Liz

Contents

Figures and tables

Contributors

Cesario Bellantuono Lecturer, Department of Psychological Medicine, Institute of Psychiatry, University of Verona.

Lisa Bero Research Fellow, Institute for Health Policy Studies, University of California, San Francisco.

Anthony Clare Professor and Medical Director, St Patrick's Hospital, Dublin.

Jonathan Gabe Lecturer in Sociology, Section of Epidemiology and General Practice, Institute of Psychiatry, and Department of Social Policy and Social Sciences, Royal Holloway and Bedford New College, University of London.

Susan Golombok Lecturer in Psychology, Department of Social Sciences and Humanities, City University, London.

John Horder Department of Clinical Epidemiology and General Practice, Royal Free Hospital Medical School, University of London.

Helene Lipton Associate Professor of Sociology, Institute for Health Policy Studies, University of California, San Francisco.

Michael Montagne Associate Professor of Social Pharmacy, North-eastern University, Boston.

Jane Prather Professor, Department of Sociology, California State University, Northridge.

Larry Ray Lecturer, Department of Sociology, University of Lancaster.

Alan Shiell Research Fellow, Institute for Research in the Social Sciences, University of York.

Paul Williams Honorary Senior Lecturer, Institute of Psychiatry, University of London.

Foreword

Margot Jefferys

This book combines in one volume statements about the contributions which various social science disciplines have made to an understanding of the very recent phenomenon of long-term, legitimized use of drugs with acknowledged addictive properties – tranquillisers – and evaluative critiques of those statements by distinguished individuals whose opinions are likely to influence professionals and administrators. The editor and disciplinary contributors are to be congratulated on the combination, because participation in such a collection exposed them to the risk of an in-house, as it were, negative appraisal of the value of their disciplines from those on the metaphoric firing line.

In the event, the disciplinary contributors have not escaped totally unscathed. The evaluators, with long interest and experience in general practice, psychiatry, and social policy analysis, are critical of some of the theoretical propositions, prior assumptions, and interpretations of the findings of some of the empirical research reported. Moreover, the evaluators point to researchable issues which could well profit from appropriate social or behavioural scientific attention but have not so far been satisfactorily tackled.

Nevertheless, their general verdict, with which I wholeheartedly concur, is that each one of the disciplines represented in this book has already made a valuable contribution and, potentially, has still more to offer to an understanding of one or other aspect of the long-term use of minor tranquillisers by significant numbers of the adult populations of both developed and developing countries.

Wherein do the contributions mainly lie? Not, as yet perhaps, in pointing to specific techniques for practitioners to help withdrawal by those who resent their dependency on a drug or whose cognitive capacity has been demonstrably affected by it. The contribution of clinical psychologists is most likely to yield clues of this kind. The contributions lie more, perhaps, in indicating to manufacturers and distributors (including advertisers) as well as to the prescribers and consumers of the drugs in question that their activities have a significance far beyond the simple pharmacological effect on the individuals who take them: and that single fact should give them all reason to reconsider the justification for their current practices.

What is particularly valuable in the collective enterprise of aligning in one book the various contributions of psychologists, sociologists, anthropologists, economists, political economists, and communication scientists or semiologists is the clear emergence of an over-arching message. It is that the whole process of manufacturing, distributing, and consuming minor tranquillisers on the present global scale has economic and social repercussions which ripple out beyond individuals and touch ultimately, as several of the contributors to this volume show, on profound issues related to contemporary moral values.

The contributors do not point to ready answers to the dilemmas which their analyses disclose. Their merit is that they enhance the consciousness of social context and social meaning involved in transactions which, in the hurly burly of everyday life, we often seek to reduce to purely technical considerations.

Foreword

Michael Shepherd

In an earlier book, entitled *Tranquillisers*, Jonathan Gabe and his co-editor assembled sixteen chapters, twelve of them published previously, to present an overview of the social, psychological, and clinical aspects of tranquilliser use. Their stated objective was to demonstrate that 'the biomedical perspective cannot provide an adequate framework for a comprehensive understanding of this phenomenon. What is required, we believe, is an approach which places tranquilliser use within a *social* context' (Gabe & Williams 1986).

This book extends the argument of its predecessor. All ten of the chapters are original contributions and, taken as a group, they reinforce the ways in which the social sciences can illuminate the complex issues associated with the long-term consumption of the drugs involved, especially the benzodiazepines. The phenomena under discussion clearly lend themselves to analysis in terms of the concepts associated with a variety of disciplines, including psychology, anthropology, sociology, and economics.

At the same time, however, it is necessary not to lose sight of the fact that this cannot constitute the whole story. In his own chapter on the sociology of long-term tranquilliser use, the editor, contrasting the medical with the sociological outlook, identifies the former with the 'biomedical model' (see Chapter 2). Medicine, however, is more than applied pathophysiology, and the biomedical model is fast being superseded by the biopsychosocial paradigm (Engel 1977). The philosopher Gilbert Ryle regarded medicine as little more than 'the name of a somewhat arbitrary consortium of more or less loosely connected inquiries and techniques' (Ryle 1949), a view strongly supported by the sociologist Robert Merton who described the situation more graphically:

> Medicine is at heart a polygamist, becoming wedded to as many of the sciences and practical arts as prove their worth. . . . As the burden of work plainly becomes more than can be managed by the present members of the household, they become ready for new accessions to help carry the load of what needs to be done.
>
> (Merton 1957)

It was with such considerations in mind that in my foreword to *Tranquillisers* I referred pointedly to the need for a 'medico-social perspective' if a rounded view of the topic was to be attained (Shepherd 1986). Most of the contributors to this book might prefer to speak of a 'socio-medical' rather than a 'medico-social' perspective but the form of the adjective is less important than an acknowledgement of its compound nature. The facts and theories presented here should help practising physicians to deepen their understanding and render their professional activities more effective.

REFERENCES

Engel, G. (1977) 'The need for a new medical model: a challenge for biomedicine', *Science* 196: 129–36.

Gabe, J. & Williams, P. (eds) (1986) *Tranquillisers: Social, Psychological and Clinical Perspectives*, London: Tavistock.

Merton, R. K. (1957) 'Some preliminaries to a sociology of medical education', in R. K. Merton, G. G. Reader & P. Kendal (eds) *The Student-Physician*, Cambridge, Mass: Harvard University Press.

Ryle, G. (1949) *The Concept of Mind*, London: Hutchinson, p. 323.

Shepherd, M. (1986) Foreword, in J. Gabe & P. Williams (eds) *Tranquillisers: Social, Psychological and Clinical Perspectives*, London: Tavistock, pp. ix–x.

Preface

Much of the literature on long-term minor tranquilliser use has been written from a clinical perspective. As I have argued elsewhere (Gabe & Williams 1986), however, it has become clear in recent years that the biomedical model cannot provide an adequate framework for a comprehensive understanding of this phenomenon. Rather, we need an approach which places long-term tranquilliser use within a social context. With this in mind representatives from a broad range of social science disciplines have been invited to write about how their disciplines can enhance our understanding of this issue. In addition, clinicians from general practice and psychiatry and health policy analysts have been asked to respond to these authors and reflect on the practical relevance of these disciplines.

Many of those contributing to this book attended a conference on 'A Multidisciplinary Approach to Long-Term Tranquilliser Use' held at the Institute of Psychiatry in London during 1987. Others have been invited in order to increase the number of disciplines represented and to reflect the work of scholars from elsewhere in the world.

To my knowledge no other book has attempted to consider systematically the role which the different social sciences can play in increasing our understanding of the long-term use of minor tranquillisers. The few academic books with a social science content that have considered this issue have either done so within the context of a discussion of psychotropic drugs in general and from the standpoint of one social science discipline (Bruun 1983), or included it in a general analysis of drug prescribing (Mapes 1980; Melville & Johnson 1982), or treated it as one of a number of issues relating to the broader topic of tranquilliser use without focusing on the contributions of particular social science disciplines (Smith 1985;

Gabe & Williams 1986). There would therefore appear to be a need for a book, concerned with placing minor tranquillisers within a social context, which offers a multidisciplinary approach. Moreover, no other social science book on this subject has involved practitioners who have commented on its practical relevance. It is hoped that such an approach will appeal to health administrators, social workers, clinical psychologists, general practitioners, and other clinicians as well as to researchers, lecturers, and students with a social science or medical background.

REFERENCES

Bruun, K. (ed.) (1983) *Controlling Psychotropic Drugs: The Nordic Experience*, London: Croom Helm.

Gabe, J. & Williams, P. (eds) (1986) *Tranquillisers: Social, Psychological and Clinical Perspectives*, London: Tavistock.

Mapes, R. (ed.) (1980) *Prescribing Practice and Drug Usage*, London: Croom Helm.

Melville, A. & Johnson, C. (1982) *Cured to Death: The Effects of Prescription Drugs*, London: Secker & Warburg.

Smith, M. (1985) *Small Comfort: A History of Minor Tranquilizers*, New York: Praeger.

Introduction

Jonathan Gabe

Tranquillisers can be divided into two categories: major tranquillisers, drugs used in the management of psychosis, and minor tranquillisers, used primarily in the management of anxiety and insomnia. This edited collection is not concerned at all with major tranquillisers, and subsequently the term 'tranquilliser' will refer only to minor tranquillisers. At the present time the most frequently prescribed minor tranquillisers in Britain and other industrialized countries are the benzodiazepines: drugs with trade names like Ativan, Dalmane, Mogadon, and Valium. New anti-anxiety drugs like buspirone are coming on to the market but clinical trials indicate that they may not be an adequate replacement for benzodiazepines among long-term users (*Lancet* 1988), the category of tranquilliser user with which we are concerned here.

Long-term tranquilliser use has been chosen as the focus of this book because of the current concern in lay and medical circles about the risk of physical dependence among those who have been prescribed these drugs on such a basis.[1] The latter condition has been defined by the WHO (1974) as 'an adaptive state that manifests itself by intense physical disturbances when the administration of the drug is suspended'. There is, however, no consensus about what 'long-term' means. For some it refers to regular and frequent use for three months or more (e.g. Busto *et al.* 1986) whereas for others it means those who have been taking their tablets daily for over a year (e.g. Balter *et al.* 1984). And yet others prefer to see the duration of use as a process rather than as a static criterion (e.g. Williams 1983). A similar lack of consensus can be found among the contributors to this book. Even so, there is a need for at least a working definition, so I will use the term to denote the regular use of minor tranquillisers for a year or more.

TRANQUILLISER USE IN A HISTORICAL CONTEXT

Anxiolytic drugs have been taken by men and women throughout history. There is evidence that opium was used by lakeside dwellers as far back as prehistoric times (Stimmel 1983), and its medicinal use was later encouraged in Ancient Greece by Hippocrates and Dioscorides and in Rome by Pliny and Galen (Olivieri *et al*. 1986). Also at this time healers were identifying and listing the sedative and hypnotic properties of the leaves and roots of a wide range of other plants and encouraging their therapeutic use (Belloni 1957).

During the Middle Ages knowledge of medical botany was developed further by Arab scholars like Avicenna who brought together the drug lore of many different countries (Parascandola 1977). In the sixteenth century Paracelsus, the Swiss physician, encouraged alchemists to isolate the 'quintessence' of botanical substances by chemical processes such as distillation and extraction (Parascandola 1977). His unorthodox ideas however found little favour until the seventeenth century when chemically prepared remedies were at last included in the pharmacopoeias of Europe. Even so, it was only in the nineteenth century that the therapeutically active ingredients of many medicinal plants were identified and extracted.

Between the sixteenth and nineteenth centuries 'sleeplessness' and 'nervous restlesness' continued to be treated with preparations based on opium in its traditional plant form (Berridge & Edwards 1981; Porter 1989). Of these perhaps the most famous was laudanum, a mixture of opium, distilled water, and alcohol. Thomas Sydenham, the renowned seventeenth-century London physician regarded this preparation as 'the most universal and efficacious remedy available to man' (Olivieri *et al*. 1986) and his name became indelibly linked with it, thereby enhancing its popularity (Guthrie 1960). Other opium-based preparations found listed in textbooks and on sale by the nineteenth century included Battley's Sedative Solution and Dover's Powders.

With the widespread use of opium during this period for medicinal reasons and for pleasure, dependence was known but rarely discussed in Britain (Berridge & Edwards 1981). It was only during the nineteenth century that public concern (especially regarding the drug's popularity with the working class) became so widespread that the British government was forced to legislate. In 1868 it passed the Pharmacy Act in an attempt to regulate the marketing and use of opium and opium-containing preparations. Even so, laudanum continued to be found in pharmacists' shops at the end of the century.

It was during the nineteenth century too that therapeutically active ingredients were isolated and chemically extracted from opium. The alkaloid morphine, named after the Greek god of sleep Morpheus, was isolated in 1805 but was marketed commercially only in 1853. It was hailed initially as a major therapeutic breakthrough but it soon became apparent that those treated with it were likely to become addicted.

In 1826 bromide, one of the first synthetic drugs, was discovered. Like morphine it was marketed only after a considerable time lapse, in 1850, and it too was greeted with enthusiasm by clinicians, as a valuable sedative. Indeed, bromide was so widely accepted that it was possible to buy it over the counter without difficulty (Hollister 1983). Evidence of the abuse potential of this drug was first published in 1877 but with little effect (Olivieri *et al.* 1986). As a result many patients became addicted.

In the 1860s chloral hydrate was produced and marketed as a hypnotic and anaesthetic. It too was well received to start with and many doctors saw it as a replacement for opium. However, cases of dependence soon started to be reported and disillusionment set in, prior to a more judicious evaluation of the drug's comparative worth: a cyclical pattern of response which has been witnessed with other synthetic tranquillisers before and since (Cohen 1983).

The twentieth century has witnessed the rapid development of anti-anxiety drugs as a result of advances in organic chemistry (Lader 1978) and the marketing activities of the pharmaceutical industry, driven by the need to maximize its profits in the market (Rabin & Bush 1974). The first such drugs to be manufactured were the barbiturates, starting with barbitone (Veronal) in 1903. Approximately 2500 barbiturate compounds were synthesized over subsequent years and about fifty were marketed (Lader 1978). By the 1930s they had replaced bromide and chloral hydrate in the doctor's armamentarium on the grounds that they were 'safer'. Cases of abuse or dependence on short-acting barbiturates were reported at this time but it was only in the early 1950s that the risks involved were widely acknowledged (Hollister 1983). Thereafter people became apprehensive about the use of these drugs and the search began for a suitable alternative.

The first replacement was meprobamate, a sedative and muscle relaxant which was marketed under the name of Miltown, after the New Jersey town in the United States where the pharmacologist who discovered the drug worked (Smith 1985). When introduced in 1955 it was widely acclaimed and widely used, although some sceptics referred to it as 'the rich man's phenobarbital' because it was considerably more expensive than the barbiturates that it replaced (Hollister 1983).

Its reign was only short lived, however. In 1960 the first of the benzodiazepines, chlordiazepoxide (Librium) was introduced, followed by diazepam, its more successful stable-mate, in 1963 (Cohen 1970). The product of an atmosphere of commercial competition (Smith 1985), this group of drugs quickly made meprobamate obsolete, once it had become accepted that they were safer and more effective in alleviating anxiety (Lader 1978).

Between 1965 and 1970 prescriptions for benzodiazepine tranquillisers in England and Wales rose by 110 per cent compared with a 19 per cent increase for all psychotropic drugs (Parish 1971), and a similar pattern was found in the United States (Silverman & Lee 1974). Over the same period barbiturate hypnotic prescriptions fell by 24 per cent while non-barbiturate hypnotic scripts (mainly for Mogadon and Mandrax) increased by 145 per cent. In 1965 under five million prescriptions for the three main benzodiazepines (Librium, Valium, and Mogadon) were dispensed in retail pharmacies in England and Wales: by 1970 the number had increased to nearly 12.5 million (Parish 1971). The 'benzodiazepine era' had thus arrived (Hollister 1983: 13).

During the early 1970s prescriptions for benzodiazepines continued to rise in Britain and elsewhere (Marks 1983). However, growing concern about these drugs' overuse and misuse seemed to have some effect, as prescribing subsequently levelled off.

TRANQUILLISER USE IN THE 1980s

Since the turn of the decade there has been a decline in the number of prescriptions for minor tranquillisers dispensed in Britain (Taylor 1987). In 1979, 30.7 million benzodiazepine prescriptions were dispensed compared with 25.7 million in 1985 – a 16 per cent decline in six years (Scrip 1988). And the latest figures for 1987 show a further modest fall to 25.5 million prescriptions (Scrip 1989a). Moreover, a similar pattern has been found in other industrialized countries (Marks 1983). Even so, prescriptions for these drugs still represent a significant proportion of all drugs prescribed in the United Kingdom and, despite the 'limited list' which was introduced to restrict the prescribing of drugs like the benzodiazepines primarily to reduce the NHS drugs bill, their estimated cost in 1987 was still more than 30 million pounds (Scrip 1989b).

According to Williams (1987) a prime factor in the decrease in tranquilliser prescriptions has been the reduction in new prescribing, rather than the wholesale discontinuation of treatment by long-term consumers. This suggests that there is a cohort of patients – perhaps as many as 1.3 million in Britain alone (Balter *et al.* 1984; Taylor 1987) – who are still receiving and taking tranquillisers on a long-term basis. Furthermore, it appears that these 'users' are twice as likely to be female as male (Ettorre 1985), paralleling the sex difference in the overall consumption of these drugs in Britain (Parish 1971; Lader 1978) and elsewhere (Cooperstock & Parnell 1982). Recent epidemiological research using representative samples of benzodiazepine users and control groups (Tyrer *et al.* 1981, 1983; Rickels *et al.* 1983) has also found that between 27 per cent and 45 per cent of long-term users are dependent on their drugs. If this is so it represents a substantial number of people, given the estimates for long-term users.

This account of contemporary trends raises a number of important questions. Why are so many prescriptions for minor tranquillisers still being written given this risk of dependence? Why is there such a sex difference in consumption? And what can be done to help those long-term users who want to come off benzodiazepines but are having difficulty in doing so? In order to address these questions we need to draw on a range of social science disciplines. Only within such a multidisciplinary framework will a comprehensive social understanding of this phenomenon be achieved.

A MULTIDISCIPLINARY APPROACH TO LONG-TERM TRANQUILLISER USE

The role which a multidisciplinary approach can play in developing our understanding of long-term tranquilliser use can be illustrated by drawing on Williams's (1979) distinction between an 'area of study' – a set of topics to be comprehended and resolved – and a 'mode of thinking' – the disciplinary conventions and theories – which may be brought to bear on such topics. Applying this distinction to long-term tranquilliser use, it can be conceived as an area of study involving a range of topics (e.g. the characteristics of the drug users, the factors causing the prescribing and use of these drugs, its meaning to doctors and their patients, the consequences of such tranquilliser use and the process of withdrawal) which can be made sense of by means of a variety of disciplines. The disciplines with which we shall be concerned in this book are psychology, sociology, anthropology, epidemiology, health economics, communication studies, and political economy.

Clearly some of these disciplines have more to say about certain topics than they do others. Thus anthropology and sociology have a particular contribution to make to our understanding of the meaning of tranquilliser use, whereas health economics and psychology have most to say about the consequences of such drug use.

At the same time it should be noted that each of these disciplines has its own distinctive body of concepts, ways of reasoning, and criteria for determining what represent acceptable forms of evidence and this can lead to conflict regarding how a particular phenomenon is best explained (Armstrong 1987). Moreover, mutual suspicion between social science disciplines has traditionally been enforced by a lack of communication between them. This stems in part from the fact that the dissemination of research findings is generally restricted to those single discipline journals which are most likely to be read by an author's peers (Rogers 1987). It is also the result of institutional pressures within academic settings which have reinforced disciplinary boundaries (Fitzpatrick *et al.* 1983).

The likelihood of interdisciplinary conflict should not, however, stand in the way of the various disciplines using constructs and data from 'across the boundary' for purposes evidently within the tradition and object of study of the parent discipline (Spruit & Kromhout 1987). Moreover, greater exposure to other disciplines may yield insights which may feed back into the process of intellectual discovery in the mainstream of a researcher's discipline (Culyer 1983). There is certainly evidence of the former in the chapters in this volume with, for example, sociological findings being drawn upon in the chapters on anthropology, epidemiology, and political economy.

The book is divided into two sections, concerned with the contribution of various social sciences to understanding long-term tranquilliser use and their evaluation by a general practitioner, a psychiatrist, and two policy analysts. In the first of the social science chapters Susan Golombok focuses on the *psychology* of long-term tranquilliser use and pays particular attention to the causes and consequences of such drug use and the treatment programmes to help people stop their medication. She argues for a multifaceted approach which acknowledges that dependence stems from behavioural and cognitive factors, and utilizes these insights to develop treatment packages which provide patients with alternative coping strategies as well as a gradual withdrawal programme.

In the next chapter Jonathan Gabe offers a *sociological* account of long-term tranquilliser use. He considers four issues: the reasons for the long-term use of these drugs; their social meaning for patients and their doctors; the history of tranquilliser use as a social problem; and the extent to which these drugs function as a form of social control. He argues that the first two of these topics demonstrate the role which sociology can play in enhancing our understanding of 'personal troubles' while the latter two highlight its contribution to understanding 'public issues of social structure'. Throughout the chapter consideration is given to the gendered nature of tranquilliser use and how this can be explained. Thus the reasons for drug taking are discussed in terms of sex role theory, with its emphasis on differences in consulting behaviour and doctor stereotyping, the meaning of tranquilliser use is related to other unequally distributed resources which women can call on to manage their lives, and the issue of social control is explored in terms of the medicalization of women's social problems.

The third chapter, by Michael Montagne, highlights the value of an *anthropological* approach to long-term tranquilliser use. He focuses on the societal and subcultural differences in norms and values which allow or prohibit the use of these drugs. Also considered are the metaphorical and symbolic aspects of long-term tranquilliser use and issues of medicalization and social control discussed by Gabe. Like Gabe he also pays attention to the reasons for gender differences in benzodiazepine use, concentrating on the role which gender ideologies play in the diagnosis and treatment of anxiety. His conclusion is that no society or culture has developed well-defined rituals and social sanctions to direct and control the prescribing and use of tranquillisers, and that such sanctions are needed if we are to limit or prevent the long-term use of these drugs in future, in both the developed and developing world.

This is followed by a chapter from Paul Williams and Cesario Bellantuono on the *epidemiological* aspects of long-term benzodiazepine use. They outline the contribution which this discipline has made to understanding the characteristics of long-term users in terms of sociodemographic (for example gender) and health indicators, and consider trends in the extent of the long-term use of these drugs and the relationship between prescription and consumption. They then review research which has established the factors which predispose people to long-term use and consider the implications of their analysis for the planning and monitoring of health services. In particular, they argue that the identification of risk factors for long-term use is of paramount importance if this pattern of tranquilliser use is to be minimized in future. From the studies they review, women reported by their GP to be suffering from social problems and the less educated would appear to be most at risk.

The fifth chapter, by Alan Shiell, describes the contribution which *health economics* can make to understanding tranquilliser use on a long-term basis. Attention is given first to ways of measuring the costs and benefits of these drugs, after which a literature review is undertaken to establish their effectiveness when compared with counselling. It is argued that while counselling may accelerate relief from distressing symptoms, reduce long-term dependency on tranquillisers and be preferred by patients, the symptomatic relief achieved tends to be short lived and the benefits gained are expensive. For Shiell the most cost-effective way of treating new cases of psychological distress is for the GP to offer simple reassurance and advice, but he concedes that this alone will do little to reduce the level of long-term use.

In the next chapter Jane Prather highlights the role which *communication studies* can play in understanding tranquilliser use through a review of the literature on psychotropic drug advertising. After considering advertising as one of a number of drug promotion strategies for the pharmaceutical industry in the developed and developing world, she looks at two approaches to studying drug adverts – content analysis and semiotics. In this context, content analysis involves rigorously comparing adverts in order to discover patterns of similarity and difference, whereas semiotics concentrates on decoding the messages conveyed by adverts. Reflecting concerns of earlier chapters about gender differences in tranquilliser use and medicalization, she argues that both forms of analysis suggest that these adverts have reinforced stereotypes about the role of women and their need for tranquillisers in the eyes of physicians (even if such images are less common than they were) and have helped promote the medicalization of everyday life.

The eighth and final chapter on the contribution of the social sciences to understanding long-term tranquilliser use concerns *political economy*. Here Larry Ray reviews the activities of pharmaceutical companies in the developed and developing world with regard to prescribing and use of these drugs. In particular he focuses on the strategies adopted by the companies to maximize their profits, the attempts of governments to regulate the price charged, the growing pressure in the developed world to make the industry publicly accountable for the dependence caused by long-term tranquilliser use and the ideological effects of the drugs' promotion. As regards the latter, attention is again drawn to the role which advertising has had in reproducing a patriarchal ideology (confirming women as 'help seekers', dependent on male authority) and encouraging medicalization.

In the remaining chapters of the book the practical relevance of these disciplines is assessed by clinicians and policy analysts. John Horder, representing *general practice*, evaluates the disciplines in terms of three key questions of concern to his colleagues. Are benzodiazepines effective? Should long-term use be avoided? And is effective alternative treatment available and practical? He suggests that they have a contribution to make regarding each of these issues, and that doctors for whom the medical model incorporates illness as well as disease will find the insights generated particularly useful.

Next, Anthony Clare provides an assessment from the standpoint of *psychiatry*. As a clinician he too is concerned with what the social science contributors have to say about the effectiveness of these drugs, the costs and benefits of use, and the alternatives which are available. However, he also draws particular attention to the answers they provide to questions about the causes of long-term use and the characteristics of those who take them. He suggests that the authors have something of value to say about each of these topics and, furthermore, have shown that the prescribing of these drugs is a complex cultural and social process with political, economic, and moral as well as medical implications.

Finally, Helene Lipton and Lisa Bero consider the relevance of the book for *health policy*. They argue that the multidisciplinary perspective offered highlights the need for both further research and policy change. As regards the latter they propose that it should be targeted at the level of the individual (physician and patient) and of society (government, pharmaceutical manufacturers, and health professional organizations). Thus they advocate, among other things, increasing doctors' and patients' knowledge of drug-free therapies as alternatives to benzodiazepines, by changing medical school curricula and running national educational campaigns; the funding of additional treatment programmes for combating long-term tranquilliser use which incorporate psychological (i.e. 'coping' skills) as well as medical components; and stronger regulation by national governments of tranquilliser approval and marketing.

As far as these practitioners are concerned, then, the social sciences do have an important part to play in helping us understand long-term tranquilliser use and in providing insights which are of practical value. At a time of mounting public and medical concern and sensationalist media coverage of this issue it is hoped that this book will encourage a broadening of the debate and provide a basis for rational discussion.

ACKNOWLEDGEMENTS

I am grateful to Paul Williams and Mike Bury for their comments on an earlier draft of this chapter.

NOTES

1 This book is not concerned with the non-medical use or abuse of benzodiazepines which occurs at modest levels relative to their widespread medical use. For a discussion of such abuse in the United States see the report of the Committee of the Institute for Behavior and Health (1988).

REFERENCES

Armstrong, D. (1987) 'Theoretical tensions in biopsychosocial medicine', *Social Science and Medicine* 25(11): 1213–18.

Balter, M. B., Manheimer, G. D., & Uhlenhuth, E. H. (1984) 'A cross-national comparison of anti-anxiety/sedative drug use', *Current Medical Research and Opinion* 8(Suppl. 4): 5–20.

Belloni, L. (1957) 'The Mandrake', in S., Garattini and V. Ghetti (eds) *Psychotropic Drugs*, Amsterdam: Elsevier Publishing Company.

Berridge, V. & Edwards, G. (1981) *Opium and the People: Opiate Use in Nineteenth Century England*, London: Allen Lane/St Martin's Press.

Busto, U., Sellers, E., Naranjo, C., Cappell, H., Sanchez-Craig, M., & Sykora, K. (1986) 'Withdrawal reaction after long-term therapeutic use of benzodiazepines', *New England Journal of Medicine* 315(14): 854–9.

Cohen, I. (1970) 'The benzodiazepines', in F. J. Ayd & B. Blackwell (eds) *Discoveries in Biological Psychiatry*, Philadelphia: J. B. Lippincott.

Cohen, S. (1983) 'Current attitudes about the benzodiazepines: trial by media', *Journal of Psychoactive Drugs* 15: 109–13.

Committee of the Institute for Behaviour and Health (1988) 'Abuse of the benzodiazepines: the problems and solutions', *American Journal of Drug and Alcohol Abuse*, 14 (Suppl. 1): 1–69.

Cooperstock, R. & Parnell, P. (1982) 'Research on psychotropic drugs: a review of findings and methods', *Social Science and Medicine* 16(12): 1179–96.

Culyer, A. J. (1983) 'Introduction', in A. J. Culyer (ed.) *Health Indicators*, Oxford: Martin Robertson.

Ettorre, E. (1985) 'Psychotropics, passivity and the pharmaceutical industry', in A. Henman, R. Lewis, & T. Maylon (eds) *Big Deal: The Politics of the Illicit Drug Business*, London: Pluto Press.

Fitzpatrick, R., Hinton, J., Newman, S., Scambler, G., & Thompson, J. (1983) *The Experience of Illness*, London: Tavistock.

Guthrie, D. (1960) *A History of Medicine*, London: Nelson.

Hollister, L. (1983) 'The pre-benzodiazepine era', *Journal of Psychoactive Drugs* 15(1–2): 9–13.

Lader, M. (1978) 'Benzodiazepines – opium of the masses?' *Neuroscience* 3(2): 159–67.

Lancet (1988) 'Buspirone – a radical advance in the treatment of anxiety', *Lancet* 1(8589): 804–6.

Marks, J. (1983) 'The benzodiazepines: an international perspective', *Journal of Psychoactive Drugs* 15(1–2): 137–49.

Olivieri, S., Cantopher, T., & Edwards, J. G. (1986) 'Two hundred years of dependence on antianxiety drugs', *Human Psychopharmacology* 1: 117–23.

Parascandola, J. L. (1977) 'A brief history of drug use', in A. L. Wertheimer and P. J. Bush (eds) *Perspectives on Medicines in Society*, Hamilton: Drug Intelligence Publications.

Parish, P. (1971) 'The prescribing of psychotropic drugs in general practice', *Journal of the Royal College of General Practitioners* 21(Suppl. 4): 1–77.

Porter, R. (1989) *Health For Sale*, Manchester: Manchester University Press.

Rabin, D. L. & Bush, P. J. (1974) 'The use of medicines: historical trends and international comparisons', *International Journal of Health Services* 4(1): 61–87.

Rickels, K., Case, G., Downing, R. W., & Winokur, A. (1983) 'Long-term diazepam therapy and clinical outcome', *Journal of the American Medical Association* 250(6): 767–71.

Rogers, T. F. (1987) 'Improving the fit between social science and health care practice: suggested next steps for the researcher', *Social Science and Medicine* 25(6): 689–96.

Scrip (1988) 'UK campaign against tranquillisers', *Scrip* 1291: 2.

— (1989a) 'UK benzodiazepine scripts 1983–86', *Scrip* 1378: 4.

— (1989b) 'More parliamentary questions on UK benzodiazepine prescribing consumption', *Scrip* 1410: 5.

Silverman, M. & Lee, P. R. (1974) *Pills, Profits and Politics*, Berkeley: University of California Press.

Smith, M. C. (1985) *Small Comfort: A History of Minor Tranquilizers*, New York: Praeger.

Spruit, I. P. & Kromhout, D. (1987) 'Medical sociology and epidemiology: convergences, divergences and legitimate boundaries', *Social Science and Medicine* 25(6): 579–87.

Stimmel, B. (1983) *Pain, Analgesia and Addiction*, New York: Raven Press.

Taylor, D. (1987) 'Current usage of benzodiazepines in Britain', in H. Freeman & Y. Rue (eds) *Benzodiazepines in Current Clinical Practice*, London: Royal Society of Medicine Services.

Tyrer, P., Rutherford, D., & Huggett, T. (1981) 'Benzodiazepine withdrawal symptoms and propranolol', *Lancet* 1(8219): 520–2.

Tyrer, P., Owen, R., & Dawling, S. (1983) 'Gradual withdrawal of diazepam after long-term therapy', *Lancet* 1(8339): 1402–6.

Williams, A. (1979) 'One economist's view of social medicine', *Journal of Epidemiology and Community Health* 33(1): 3–7.

Williams, P. (1983) 'Factors influencing the duration of treatment with psychotropic drugs in general practice: a survival analysis approach', *Psychological Medicine* 13(3): 623–33.

Williams, P. (1987) 'Long-term benzodiazepine use in general practice', in H. Freeman & Y. Rue (eds) *Benzodiazepines in Current Clinical Practice*, London: Royal Society of Medicine Services.

World Health Organisation (1974) *Expert Committee on Drug Dependence Twentieth Report*, WHO Technical Report Series No. 551, Geneva.

Part I

The contribution of the social sciences

1 The contribution of psychology to understanding long-term tranquilliser use

Susan Golombok

Drug dependence has traditionally been considered to result from underlying physiological mechanisms, a view which presents the drug-dependent individual as having no control over the situation and as unable to use his or her own efforts to become drug free. In recent years, however, an increasing amount of attention has been paid to the view that psychological factors are also important in the development and maintenance of drug dependence, and that psychological approaches to treatment can be helpful for a wide variety of addictions including behaviours which do not involve the use of drugs such as compulsive gambling or eating. In fact, it is the striking similarity in behaviour between individuals whose addictions are not to drugs and those who are drug dependent which is partly responsible for the upsurge in interest in psychological approaches to the understanding and treatment of drug dependence.

Since the early 1980s when it became apparent that large numbers of individuals had become dependent on benzodiazepines, psychologists have been actively involved in investigating both the causes and the consequences of long-term tranquilliser use, as well as in developing treatment programmes to help people stop their medication. This chapter will examine each of these areas in turn with an emphasis on what is known about the psychological processes involved.

ORIGINS OF LONG-TERM TRANQUILLISER USE

In an attempt to shed light on the causes of benzodiazepine dependence, a number of studies of factors associated with the long-term use of benzodiazepines have been carried out. From these studies it seems that both sex and age are important determinants. Twice as many women as men become long-term benzodiazepine users

(Cooperstock 1976, 1978; Curran & Golombok 1985) and older people are more likely to be chronic users than younger people (Mellinger *et al.* 1984). Williams (1983) has also shown that for women the presence of social problems is related to prolonged medication. In addition to demographic factors, personality characteristics have been implicated in long-term benzodiazepine use. Tyrer (1989) argues that both anxious patients with borderline personality disorder and those with passive-dependent or anxious personality disorder are at greater risk of becoming dependent on benzodiazepines than anxious patients without personality disturbance. Ashton (1989) describes two types of individuals who become dependent on benzodiazepines, those with a neurotic personality and those with a psychotic personality. According to Ashton, the former take benzodiazepines for protection and the latter take them for kicks. It is important to note that studies of personality characteristics of chronic benzodiazepine users have included only small, unrepresentative groups of benzodiazepine-dependent patients, and that the personality characteristics which have been identified may result from rather than precede the long-term use of these drugs.

A number of explanations have been put forward to account for the relationship between these demographic, social, and personality factors and long-term benzodiazepine use. For example, the high incidence of long-term tranquilliser use among women appears to have occurred for a number of reasons, ranging from the greater proportion of women than men who consult their doctor about emotional problems, to advertising campaigns which present tranquillisers as a solution to problems which result from the traditional female role (Curran & Golombok 1985). However, the underlying psychological mechanisms in the development of benzodiazepine dependence remain unclear. Psychological theories of addiction have tended to focus on dependence on opiates and on alcohol rather than on benzodiazepines, although there has been a shift in recent years towards more global explanations of addictive behaviour (Orford 1985).

Behaviour theorists argue that drugs are powerful primary reinforcers both because they produce pleasant effects and because they can remove aversive states (Goldberg & Stolerman 1986). According to this view, it would seem that the long-term use of benzodiazepines develops because these drugs have a pleasant sedating effect and because they relieve feelings of anxiety. Once physical dependence is established, benzodiazepines continue to act as powerful reinforcers by relieving the unpleasant withdrawal symptoms which develop when medication is stopped, and thus the long-term use of these drugs is maintained. Secondary reinforcement also appears to be important in chronic benzodiazepine use. Where situations occur in which drug-taking is reinforcing, for example where a benzodiazepine reduces anxiety in a stressful situation, the next time that a similar situation occurs the individual is more likely to take a tranquilliser.

Cognitive theorists suggest that an individual's expectations also play a part in drug taking (Marlatt & Donovan 1981; Marlatt 1987). It would seem, therefore, that whether or not a benzodiazepine is effective in reducing anxiety is determined, in part at least, by whether or not the individual expects anxiety to be reduced by medication and interprets the experience of medication in that way. According to this view, it would appear that the long-term use of benzodiazepines is maintained by cognitive appraisal of what is likely to happen as a result of medication or as a result of stopping medication. Although this theory has not been applied directly to benzodiazepine dependence, studies which have examined reasons for tranquilliser use indicate that such mechanisms may be operating. For example, in a survey of long-term psychotropic drug taking by Murray (1981), approximately three-quarters of current long-term users felt that the drugs helped them, and 87 per cent agreed with the statement 'I don't like taking these tablets but I could not manage without them'.

These psychological theories have important implications for the treatment of benzodiazepine dependence. For example, when stressful situations or unpleasant withdrawal symptoms have become cues for taking tranquillisers, it is important that patients learn alternative coping strategies. These strategies have arisen from both behavioural and cognitive approaches to the understanding of tranquilliser use and will be discussed later.

COGNITIVE EFFECTS OF LONG-TERM TRANQUILLISER USE

Psychologists have tended to focus on the effects of benzodiazepines on cognitive functioning, i.e. the effects on concentration, memory, and other cognitive tasks. Since the introduction of the benzodiazepines in the 1960s, a large number of controlled studies of non-patient subjects have provided clear evidence that, in the short term, normal therapeutic doses of these drugs impair cognitive functioning (McNair 1973; Wittenborn 1979; Hindmarch 1980;

Johnson & Chernik 1982). However, little is known about the cognitive effects of these drugs in the long term. Very few studies have examined the cognitive effects of these drugs on anxious patients, and those which have done so have followed up the patients for only a few weeks after beginning a course of medication. Indications that long-term medication might impair cognitive functioning came from a study by Petursson *et al.* (1983) of psychomotor performance during withdrawal from long-term benzodiazepine treatment. It was shown that patients who had taken benzodiazepines for over one year showed poor psychomotor test performance. However, these findings were inconclusive due to biases in sampling.

In an attempt to establish whether or not cognitive ability is impaired in long-term benzodiazepine users, and to determine the nature and extent of any deficit, a further study has been carried out by Golombok *et al.* (1988). Fifty patients currently taking benzodiazepines for at least one year, thirty-four who had stopped taking benzodiazepines, and a matched control group of subjects who had never taken benzodiazepines or who had taken these drugs in the past for less than one year were included in the study. Those currently taking benzodiazepines were obtained through the records of several general practitioners in the London area. The control subjects were recruited from voluntary organizations and employment agencies, and the subjects who had withdrawn from medication were obtained from both general practice and the outside agencies. Each subject was administered a battery of neuropsychological tests designed to measure a wide range of cognitive functions. These included tests of attention, memory, learning, psychomotor function, visual spatial perception and visual spatial organization, verbal fluency, and the ability to use abstract concepts. In addition, a test was administered to provide a measure of intellectual ability before the possible development of drug-related deterioration, and a measure of the subject's level of anxiety at the time of testing was also obtained. A global measure of benzodiazepine intake was calculated for each subject by multiplying the length of time for which the subject had taken a particular benzodiazepine with its dose for each benzodiazepine taken, and then summing these scores. As the subjects who had been prescribed benzodiazepines ranged from those who had taken a large dose for a long period of time to those who had a relatively low intake, the data were analysed by regression techniques which utilized the continuous nature of the degree of benzodiazepine intake.

In the first part of the analysis, patients currently taking benzodiazepines and subjects who had never taken these drugs or had done so in the past for less than one year and who were matched for age, further education, and premorbid IQ were included to look at the effects of chronic benzodiazepine use on cognitive functioning. It seems from the results that the long-term use of benzodiazepines is associated with cognitive impairment. Two areas of functioning appear to be affected. The first is visual-spatial ability. The second concerns attention or, more specifically, the ability to sustain attention on a repetitive task under time pressure. There was no evidence of impairment in global measures of intellectual functioning such as memory, verbal fluency, flexibility, and simple reaction time.

The tests which showed impaired performance are those which are generally affected by posterior rather than frontal cortical lesions. It was found that the patients function normally on tests which are indicative of frontal damage, which suggests that benzodiazepines have a specific effect on the posterior cortex. This raises the question of why these drugs show such a specific effect. The effects of benzodiazepines are generally believed to be mediated through benzodiazepine receptors in the central nervous system. Receptors allow communication to take place between cells and are highly selective in order to discriminate between various chemical signals. However, there is no evidence that either the number of benzodiazepine receptors or the strength with which a benzodiazepine drug binds to a benzodiazepine receptor is greater in the posterior cortex. Research on the mode of action of benzodiazepines may be at too early a stage to explain the specificity of their effects on cognitive functioning.

It is difficult to conclude whether or not the cognitive effects of the long-term use of benzodiazepines are different in nature to the effects of a single dose or a short course of these drugs. A particular problem is that the tests used in short-term studies fail to tap a wide range of cognitive abilities. The development and course of cognitive impairment is also uncertain because of the dearth of information between the first few weeks of medication and one year of continuous administration. Patients may become tolerant to the cognitive effects of these drugs before further impairment develops. Alternatively, cognitive ability might slowly deteriorate from the start. However, the degree of impairment does appear to be greater after chronic medication. In short-term studies it is usual for subjects to act as their own controls which increases the sensitivity to the effects of the drug. The 'between-subjects' design in the present investigation has an error term which is inflated by individual differences in performance, so that a greater drug effect is needed for significance to occur.

It is impossible to determine how long it is safe for a patient to continue to take benzodiazepines, or at what dose, before cognitive ability will begin to deteriorate. Nevertheless, it is clear from the inspection of these data that taking a low dose for a short time has little effect, while a high intake is almost certainly harmful. An example of medium intake would be six years of continuous medication at a dose towards the upper limit of the therapeutic range. The data are not precise enough to indicate a cut-off point. As with alcohol, the effect is cumulative – the higher the intake, the greater the risk.

It remains possible that cognitive impairment in chronic benzodiazepine users is not a direct consequence of these drugs but, instead, results from an intervening factor. In particular, it could be argued that patients with the highest benzodiazepine intake are also the most anxious, and that the anxiety for which the benzodiazepines are prescribed is responsible for their poor performance. However, the lack of relationship in this investigation between anxiety and test performance rules this out as an explanation for the findings reported. Neither can the results be attributed to the acute effects of benzodiazepines taken at the time of testing as the dose taken on that day was also shown to be unrelated to cognitive impairment. It is also important to point out that subjects at risk for brain damage for reasons other than benzodiazepine intake were not included in the sample. No subject with a history of excessive alcohol use, epilepsy, brain injury, psychotic illness, cerebrovascular accident, or the taking of monoamine oxidase inhibitors or major tranquillisers was included in the study. Pre-existing impairment cannot be excluded as a possible explanation but this is not likely in view of the significant correlation between impairment and benzodiazepine intake. Moreover, the subjects were matched for premorbid IQ using a measure of intellectual ability before the possible development of drug-related deterioration. It seems, therefore, most likely that cognitive impairment in long-term benzodiazepine users is caused by the drugs themselves rather than extraneous factors.

In the second part of the analysis, subjects who had withdrawn from long-term benzodiazepine medication were compared with patients who were still taking these drugs to examine whether stopping benzodiazepines is followed by a return to normal cognitive functioning. The patients still on medication were found to have a significantly higher benzodiazepine intake than those who had withdrawn. In order to balance the two groups for benzodiazepine intake, patients with a high intake who were still taking these drugs had to be excluded. Subsequently, no significant differences in cognitive functioning were found between the groups. A further comparison between those who had withdrawn from medication and subjects who had never taken benzodiazepines also failed to show differences in performance. So the findings of the comparison between subjects who had stopped taking benzodiazepines and those still on medication remain inconclusive. Those who were no longer taking these drugs had had a comparatively low intake of benzodiazepines and were, therefore, unlikely to have shown much impairment while on medication. In order to determine whether or not patients who do become impaired return to normal cognitive functioning when they withdraw, it would be necessary to investigate patients who had withdrawn from a high benzodiazepine intake. However, the fact that the sample in this study comprised only subjects with a low intake, suggests that few of those with a high intake manage to withdraw.

Cognitive functioning in long-term benzodiazepine users has also been investigated by Lucki *et al.* (1986). The performance on a battery of psychomotor and cognitive tasks of forty-three patients who had been taking benzodiazepines daily for an average of five years was compared with a control group of age-matched drug-free patients diagnosed with anxiety disorder. The authors reported that no significant differences were found between the groups for the Digit Symbol Substitution Test, the Symbol Copying Test, the Letter Cancellation Test, or a Verbal Recall Test. Only the Critical Flicker Fusion Threshold was significantly lower for chronic benzodiazepine users when compared with anxious controls. The authors concluded that their results did not support the idea that cognitive impairment is produced in patients by the regular long-term use of benzodiazepines. It is important to note, however, that the data analysis did not take account of the actual duration or dose of medication. In fact, the findings of Golombok *et al.* and Lucki *et al.* are not contradictory as they first appear as, in the former investigation, it was only those individuals who had taken a high dose for a long period of time who were found to be at risk.

PSYCHOLOGICAL TREATMENT OF LONG-TERM TRANQUILLISER USE

Psychological approaches to the management of long-term benzodiazepine users have emphasized tailoring behavioural and cognitive therapeutic techniques to the needs of dependent patients. Behavioural techniques are based on models which are derived from learning theory. According to this view, symptoms such as anxiety are considered to be learned, either as a result of classical conditioning where an association builds up between a particular stimulus and an anxiety response, or as a result of operant conditioning where it becomes rewarding for the patient to avoid situations in which he or she feels anxious. The aim of behaviour therapy is for the patient to 'unlearn' the anxiety response. The most common behaviour therapies for anxiety are the exposure therapies where the patient is exposed to the stimuli which produce anxiety until he or she becomes used to them and the anxiety response no longer occurs. Cognitive theorists hold the view that symptoms such as anxiety result from disturbances in thinking, and that people who are anxious misinterpret harmless events as threatening and overestimate the danger in any situation. Therapeutic techniques based on this approach are aimed at identifying and modifying the thoughts which appear to cause anxiety to help the patient develop a more realistic way of perceiving his or her environment.

The use of these techniques in the group treatment of benzodiazepine dependence is described in a study by Higgitt *et al.* (1987). Ten out-patients, four men and six women, aged between 32 and 65 years were included in the group. Of those, eight had been prescribed benzodiazepines as anxiolytics, one had been prescribed these drugs for anorexia and depression, and the remaining patient had no psychiatric diagnosis. The mean length of time on medication was twelve years and four patients were taking a daily dose which was above the normal therapeutic range. All but one patient had previously tried unsuccessfully to withdraw. All patients' levels of anxiety and depression as well as benzodiazepine withdrawal symptoms were assessed at the beginning of therapy and weekly until the end of treatment and patients kept a standardized daily diary of benzodiazepine consumption from the first meeting of the group onwards. The first ten sessions of the group were weekly, followed by a four-month period of fortnightly or three-weekly meetings, with a follow-up meeting after ten weeks. The group met for twenty sessions in all over a thirty-nine-week period.

The principal focus of treatment was a gradual reduction of drug intake at a rate determined by the intensity of that particular patient's withdrawal symptoms. This approach has been described in detail by Higgitt *et al.* (1985). A graded withdrawal schedule was designed individually for each patient, and the patients reported their ability to meet their targets to the therapists and the group. The schedule was reviewed at each group meeting in the light of the individual's withdrawal symptoms and external stressors. During the first week all patients were requested to keep to the dose they had been taking before joining the group to provide a baseline from which to monitor benzodiazepine reduction. They were also asked to fix their daily intake at a constant level, and to divide their daily dose into three or four equal doses to be taken at set times of the day. This was to break the habit of taking a pill in response to specific cues. The patients were also asked to monitor their subjective need for benzodiazepines at the times of pill taking to help in the planning of their withdrawal programme. Dose reduction began by asking patients to omit the daily dose which they felt they could most easily do without. As treatment progressed, further doses were reduced, beginning with the one which was needed least and ending with the one which was most difficult to give up. In many instances, each dose needed to be tackled in stages, cutting it down by half, a quarter, or even one-eighth before it could be entirely eliminated. Two of the patients were unable to keep to a fixed daily intake. They were advised to set a maximum dose to be taken each day until they felt ready to reduce to a lower daily limit. Throughout treatment, the importance of a gradual decrease in pill taking to minimize withdrawal symptoms was emphasized. It was suggested that patients should remain at each reduced intake for at least one week as withdrawal symptoms could take some time to develop. It was stressed that they might have to remain at some stages of withdrawal for several weeks before symptoms would disappear or would be at a tolerable level. It was also emphasized that gradual withdrawal gives an opportunity for alternative coping strategies for anxiety to be learned and practised to replace drug taking.

During the period of graded withdrawal, anxiety management training was instituted, tailored to the needs of both the group as a whole and individuals within the group, all of whom were at different stages of withdrawal. Faulty cognitions concerning benzodiazepine dependence were corrected during the initial phases of the intervention and the mechanisms of withdrawal symptoms were clarified. For example, it was explained that symptoms such as chest pain and palpitations resulted from anxiety rather than heart disease, and that it was not always the case that withdrawal symptoms increased as the daily dose of benzodiazepines was reduced. Relaxation techniques were taught and each patient was provided with a relaxation tape to use at home. Relaxation was suggested as an alternative to benzodiazepines throughout the withdrawal period. For those with marked agoraphobia, the principles of systematic desensitization were explained and recommended. This involved the patient in going outside into situations which caused mild anxiety and gradually building up to more anxiety-provoking ones. Various cognitive restructuring and problem-solving techniques were discussed with individual patients at different stages as the need arose. As the programme progressed, the sessions became less structured and a greater proportion of time was spent in general discussion.

By the end of treatment, three patients had withdrawn completely from benzodiazepines, and six of the remaining seven had reduced their medication to at least 50 per cent of their initial dose. At one year follow-up, seven patients were no longer on medication and two had reduced to at least one third of their initial dose. The remaining patient showed no reduction in intake. A particularly encouraging aspect of the results was the patients' success in maintaining their level of drug reduction following termination of treatment and in a number of cases a continuation in reduction of drug intake during the follow-up period. In general, withdrawal symptoms, anxiety, and depression improved alongside reduction in drug intake, and these improvements were maintained at three-month and one-year follow-up. However, many patients experienced clinical depression at some stage during withdrawal, and three patients became agoraphobic to the extent that they were completely housebound. The application of a variety of psychological therapeutic techniques appeared to be a beneficial part of treatment. It is important, however, that the use of these techniques should be flexible and tailored to the needs of each patient. In fact, the variation among group members in intensity and type of withdrawal symptoms would have made it impossible to apply a rigid programme.

Sanchez-Craig *et al.* (1987) have reported a study of individual cognitive behavioural treatment for benzodiazepine dependence. In a double-blind out-patient trial, forty-two long-term users of therapeutic doses of benzodiazepines were assigned either to gradual tapering of their daily active dose or to abrupt cessation of benzodiazepine intake by the substitution of placebo tablets for active benzodiazepines. After a two-week baseline period in which they took their benzodiazepines as usual, weekly one-hour sessions of cognitive behavioural treatment were provided for about five weeks. The emphasis of therapy was to set goals for reduction, to identify the circumstances of drug use, and to develop skills for coping with these circumstances without using tranquillisers. During the first session, basic information about what symptoms might be expected during withdrawal was presented. A goal for dosage reduction in the subsequent week was set in each session by mutual agreement. The patients were also introduced to cognitive coping techniques to help them deal with withdrawal symptoms and anxiety-provoking circumstances. For example, as alternatives to dealing with anxiety by using a drug, subjects were instructed to develop self-statements either to inhibit the tendency to turn immediately to the drug (i.e. 'stop and think before you take a tranquilliser') or to reappraise the meaning of anxiety (i.e. 'feeling anxious won't really harm me') or to remind themselves of their capacity to cope (i.e. 'I have been able to cope with similar situations without using my drug'). It was found that 62 per cent of the subjects were abstinent or improved by the end of treatment, 52 per cent of the subjects in the drug group and 74 per cent of subjects in the placebo group. At the one-year follow-up, 47 per cent and 39 per cent of subjects in the drug and placebo groups respectively were abstinent or improved (i.e. showed a reduction in plasma benzodiazepine level of at least 50 per cent). Although there were no differences in overall treatment outcome, those treated with placebo showed more prominent withdrawal symptoms but were significantly more successful in maintaining abstinence throughout the one-year follow-up period. The authors argued that it may be advantageous to expose patients who are dependent on relatively low doses of benzodiazepine to some withdrawal distress during treatment to provide a supervised learning opportunity. They suggest that the stronger the evidence that one can cope with stressful situations without resort to a tranquilliser, the more likely it is that drug use will be rejected as a coping device.

It seems from the two studies which have examined the efficacy of psychological treatments for benzodiazepine dependence that cognitive behavioural techniques are helpful for some patients at least. Whether or not the higher success rate at one-year follow-up in the study by Higgitt *et al.* results from a group approach to treatment, the greater number of sessions, or differences in the therapeutic techniques employed (e.g. relaxation training in addition to cognitive strategies) remains unknown in the absence of further research.

A follow-up study of patients treated for benzodiazepine dependence has also been carried out to evaluate the long-term efficacy of individual out-patient treatment, and to examine some demographic and clinical predictors of outcome (Golombok *et al*. 1987). All sixty-three new patients referred to the Psychopharmacology Unit of the Maudsley hospital in London between 1980 and 1985 who received treatment for benzodiazepine dependence were invited to take part in the study. Seventy per cent of the sample had been prescribed benzodiazepines for anxiety-related symptoms, 13 per cent for a physical illness, 6 per cent for insomnia, and 11 per cent for other problems. All had taken these drugs for at least two years (mean=10 years), and most had made at least one unsuccessful attempt at withdrawal before attending the Maudsley hospital. Over half of the patients had received previous psychiatric treatment either as out-patients (47 per cent) or as in-patients (18 per cent). All had been treated for benzodiazepine dependence as out-patients by gradually reducing drug intake according to the patients' withdrawal symptoms without the systematic introduction of additional anxiety management techniques.

Of the sixty-three patients contacted, forty-six (73 per cent) agreed to participate. Examination of the case notes of all sixty-three patients showed those who participated to be representative of the total sample in terms of age, sex, social class, length of benzodiazepine use, and previous psychiatric care. Approximately 50 per cent of those who did not take part had successfully withdrawn at the time of discharge compared with 76 per cent of the participants. This difference in outcome was not statistically significant. The forty-six subjects who agreed to participate were interviewed to obtain data on demographic characteristics, life circumstances at the time of withdrawal, drug history, experiences of withdrawal, and psychiatric history. The interviewer also administered measures of social support, psychiatric disturbance, and withdrawal symptoms. It was found that 54 per cent of patients had withdrawn from medication when followed up one to five years after treatment for benzodiazepine dependence. Patients were classified as having withdrawn from benzodiazepines if they had been abstinent from these drugs for at least one month before follow-up, and the mean length of time since stopping these drugs was nineteen months. General practitioners were asked for details of recent benzodiazepine prescriptions to verify the patients' accounts, and these were confirmed in all cases.

The patients experienced the usual pattern of withdrawal symptoms while reducing their benzodiazepine intake. After stopping medication the majority of the successful patients reported continuing anxiety-related symptoms, insomnia, and depression. Twelve had been prescribed antidepressants during the withdrawal period. Twenty-two per cent of the sample had relapsed after a period of abstinence of at least one month. In almost half of these cases, the reason for relapse was attributed to external stress. Half of the patients who relapsed proceeded to withdraw permanently from benzodiazepines at a later date.

The subjects were divided into two groups to examine factors associated with outcome. Group 1 had successfully withdrawn from benzodiazepines (N=25). Group 2 had failed to withdraw or had relapsed after stopping their medication (N=21). The most striking difference between the two groups of patients was that women were significantly more likely than men to succeed in withdrawing from benzodiazepines. Twenty-two of the thirty-two women had stopped their medication while only three of the fourteen men had achieved this goal. Although the successful and unsuccessful patients did not differ in the availability and adequacy of social support, the successful patients were less likely to have an intimate relationship. Perhaps surprisingly, previous benzodiazepine intake, dose and elimination half-life of benzodiazepine taken prior to withdrawal, psychiatric history, and experiences of withdrawal were not related to outcome.

The success rate of 54 per cent seems low compared with that found in other studies. However, no other investigation has monitored patients' progress for more than six months after treatment for benzodiazepine dependence. The follow-up period in the present investigation ranged from one to five years after treatment and averaged over one and a half years after withdrawal from medication for the successful patients. It seems, therefore, that not all patients who managed to withdraw from medication after treatment recover permanently from benzodiazepine dependence. In addition, most of the successful patients continue to experience anxiety-related symptoms after the withdrawal period, and many become so depressed as to warrant the prescription of antidepressants. Nevertheless, a long-term success rate of over 50 per cent is encouraging, and it is worth noting that half of the patients who relapsed proceeded to withdraw at a later date.

The higher rate of withdrawal among women contrasts with the widely held belief that women are less likely than men to be successful in withdrawing from medication. It is important to remember, however, that the patients who were included in this study had generally made several unsuccessful attempts at withdrawal before attending the psychopharmacology unit and over half had received previous psychiatric care. It is possible that for patients like these, who experience particular problems in withdrawing from medication, men have more difficulties than women.

Although the conclusion of this study that outcome is not associated with benzodiazepine intake, psychiatric history, or experiences of withdrawal must be limited, the sample size is large enough to indicate that the contribution of these variables is relatively small. This suggests that we should not feel discouraged from attempting to withdraw patients who have taken benzodiazepines at a high dose for long periods of time, or who have made previous unsuccessful attempts at withdrawal. Similarly, severity or type of withdrawal symptoms were not predictive of outcome. These data were obtained retrospectively, however, and there may have been differences in recall between the two groups.

In a study of the determinants of relapse in alcoholics, smokers, opiate addicts, compulsive gamblers, and uncontrolled eaters by Marlatt and Gordon (1980), it was concluded that relapse often occurs in response to stress. Benzodiazepine users are by nature particularly susceptible to the effects of stress and, therefore, to relapse. As a gradual withdrawal regimen alone is inadequate for long-term success for many patients, it seems that psychological adjuncts should also be included in treatment to provide patients with alternative coping strategies. In the study of the group treatment of benzodiazepine dependence (Higgitt *et al.* 1987) in which a variety of anxiety management techniques was introduced, the researchers found a higher success rate at one-year follow-up than in this follow-up study of patients who had been put on a gradual withdrawal programme alone. It seems that in order to achieve permanent withdrawal from benzodiazepines, it is important that patients not only gradually reduce their benzodiazepine intake, but also learn to cope with stressful situations in ways other than by medication.

CONCLUSION

In recent years there has been a move towards models of addictive behaviour which incorporate developmental and interactionist approaches to understanding the processes involved in drug dependence (Orford 1985; Marlatt & Baer 1988). These models emphasize that there are many determinants of dependence and that different factors operate at the different stages of initiation, maintenance of use, and withdrawal. For example, the pharmacological effects of the drug, such as anxiety reduction after benzodiazepine ingestion or unpleasant withdrawal symptoms after stopping medication, are clearly important in motivating people to become long-term users. However, factors such as the individual's expectation that the drug will reduce an unpleasant emotional state or make him or her more able to deal with stress have also been shown to be important. This multifaceted approach to the understanding of drug dependence has resulted in treatment packages which, rather than simply focusing on reducing medication, make use of a variety of behavioural and cognitive techniques to help individuals understand and cope with the psychological aspects of dependence. With respect to tranquillisers, psychologists have contributed to the understanding of long-term use by identifying psychological processes which may be involved, but it is only by applying this information to prevention and treatment that a significant and lasting contribution can be made.

ACKNOWLEDGEMENT

The studies described in the treatment section were carried out in collaboration with Dr Anna Higgitt.

REFERENCES

Ashton, H. (1989) 'Risk of dependence on benzodiazepine drugs: a major problem of long-term treatment', *British Medical Journal* 298: 103–4.

Cooperstock, R. (1976) 'Psychotropic drug use among women', *Canadian Medical Association Journal* 115: 760–3.

Cooperstock, R. (1978) 'Sex differences in psychotropic drug use', *Social Science and Medicine* 12B: 179–86.

Curran, V. & Golombok, S. (1985) *Bottling It Up*, London: Faber & Faber.

Goldberg, S. R. & Stolerman, I. P. (1986) *Behavioural Analysis of Drug Dependence*, New York: Academic Press.

Golombok, S., Higgitt, A., Fonagy, P., Dodds, S., Saper, J., & Lader, M. (1987) 'A follow-up study of patients treated for benzodiazepine dependence', *British Journal of Medical Psychology* 60: 141–9.

Golombok, S., Moodley, P., & Lader, M. (1988) 'Cognitive impairment in long-term benzodiazepine users', *Psychological Medicine* 18: 365–74.

Higgitt, A., Fonagy, P., & Lader, M. (1985) 'Clinical management of benzodiazepine dependence', *British Medical Journal* 291: 688–90.

Higgitt, A., Golombok, S., Fonagy, P., & Lader, M. (1987) 'Group treatment of benzodiazepine dependence', *British Journal of Addiction* 82: 517–32.

Hindmarch, I. (1980) 'Psychomotor function and psychoactive drugs', *British Journal of Clinical Pharmacology* 10: 189–209.

Johnson, L. C. & Chernik, D. A. (1982) 'Sedative-hypnotics and human performance', *Psychopharmacology* 76: 101–13.

Lucki, C., Rickels, K., & Geller, A. M. (1986) 'Chronic use of benzodiazepines and psychomotor and test performance', *Psychopharmacology* 88: 426–33.

McNair, D. M. (1973) 'Antianxiety drugs and human performance', *Archives of General Psychiatry* 29: 611–17.

Marlatt, G. (1987) 'Alcohol, the magic elixir: stress, expectancy, and the transformation of emotional states', in E. Gottheil, K. A. Druly, S. P. Pashko & S. P. Weinstein (eds) *Stress and Addiction*, New York: Brunner/Mazel.

Marlatt, G. A. & Baer, J. S. (1988) 'Addictive behaviours: etiology and treatment', *Annual Review of Psychology* 39: 223–52.

Marlatt, G. A. & Donovan, D. M. (1981) 'Alcoholism drug dependence: cognitive social learning factors in addictive behaviours', in W. E. Craighead, A. E. Kazdin & M. J. Mahoney (eds) *Behaviour Modification: Principles, Issues, Applications*, Boston: Houghton Mifflin.

Marlatt, G. & Gordon, J. (1980) 'Determinants of relapse: implications for the maintenance of behaviour change', in P. Davidson & S. Davidson (eds) *Behavioural Medicine: Changing Health Lifestyles*, New York: Brunner/Mazel.

Mellinger, G. D., Balter, M. B., & Uhlenhuth, E. H. (1984) 'Prevalence and correlates of long-term regular use of anxiolytics', *Journal of the American Medical Association* 251: 375–9.

Milby, J. B. (1981) *Addictive Behaviour and Its Treatment*, New York: Springer.

Murray, J. (1981) 'Long-term psychotropic drug taking and the process of withdrawal', *Psychological Medicine* 11: 853–8.

Orford, J. (1985) *Excessive Appetites: A Psychological View of Addictions*, Chichester: Wiley.

Petursson, H., Gudjonsson, G. H., & Lader, M. (1983) 'Psychometric performance during withdrawal from long-term benzodiazepine treatment', *Psychopharmacology* 81: 345–9.

Sanchez-Craig, M., Cappell, H., Busto, U., & Kay, G. (1987) 'Cognitive-behavioural treatment for benzodiazepine dependence: a comparison of gradual versus abrupt cessation of drug intake', *British Journal of Addiction* 82: 1317–27.

Tyrer, P. (1989) 'Risks of dependence on benzodiazepine drugs: the importance of patient selection', *British Medical Journal* 298: 102–5.

Williams, P. (1983) 'Factors influencing the duration of treatment with psychotropic drugs in general practice: a survival analysis approach', *Psychological Medicine* 13: 623–33.

Wittenborn, J. R. (1979) 'Effects of benzodiazepines on psychomotor performance', *British Journal of Clinical Pharmacology* 7: 61–7.

2 Personal troubles and public issues: the sociology of long-term tranquilliser use

Jonathan Gabe

The notion that benzodiazepine tranquilliser use and dependence is at heart a medical problem is still popular in medical circles. Such a view reflects the continuing influence of the biomedical model among clinicians. The model assumes that existential distress is best conceived of as the symptom of a disease (Cooperstock & Lennard 1979) which can be fully accounted for by 'deviation from the norm of measurable biological variables' (Engel 1977). From this standpoint, restoring the patient to 'normal' represents a medical problem requiring a medical solution.

From a sociological point of view, however, this stance is excessively narrow because it ignores the fact that disease is only one component of ill-health (Field 1976). The experience of illness, which depends on the social response to disease, is also important. With regard to long-term tranquilliser use this means that the experience of taking these drugs and the social consequences of doing so need to be considered if the phenomenon is to be understood satisfactorily. It is also the case that the medical model ignores the crucial role that social, cultural, and economic factors play in the generation of distress and hence in long-term tranquilliser use. Moreover, it is overly individualistic in orientation (Doyal 1979; Stacey 1988), with the reasons for such drug use and the responsibility for stopping being seen as residing largely within the individual.

There would therefore appear to be a need for a model which emphasizes the role of the social in long-term tranquilliser use – a need which sociologists have started to meet in recent years. To illustrate their contribution in this area I intend to concentrate on four issues: the reasons for long-term tranquilliser use among women; the social meaning of such use for patients and their doctors; the history of long-term tranquilliser use as a social problem;

and the extent to which this drug use functions as a form of social control. The first two of these issues are concerned with what the American sociologist C. Wright Mills (1959) has called the 'personal troubles of milieu': that is troubles concerning an individual's self and those limited areas of social life of which he or she is directly and personally aware. The latter two have to do with what Mills called 'public issues of social structure': things which transcend the individual's local environment and the range of his or her inner life and are seen by the public as threatening some cherished value.

The treatment of these issues also represents an example of what social theorists like Giddens (1986) have called a critical sociology: that is one that sees its task as contributing to a critique of the existing form of society and is concerned about the practical consequences of analysis for those whose conduct forms its object of study.

REASONS FOR LONG-TERM TRANQUILLISER USE

To date surprisingly little work has been undertaken by sociologists in this area and what there is has been concerned only with explaining current use. However, the results of this work may also help us understand long-term use.

From a sociological standpoint one of the most pertinent questions to ask is 'why are women twice as likely, on average, to receive a benzodiazepine prescription as men?' One of the first sociologists to address this was the late Ruth Cooperstock (1971) who developed an explanatory model based on sex role theory. She hypothesized that women in contemporary western societies take more tranquillisers than men because: 1) they are permitted greater freedom to explore their feelings than men and are hence more likely to recognize emotional problems in themselves; 2) they feel freer than men to bring their perceived emotional problems to the attention of a doctor; 3) doctors, especially male doctors, expect women patients to be more emotionally expressive than men. They are therefore more likely to encourage such expressiveness among women patients and to prescribe tranquillisers.

Cooperstock's propositions were not tested empirically until the work of Mant *et al.* (1983) and Cafferata *et al.* (1983). Mant and her colleagues surveyed 1300 adult patients attending fifteen randomly selected male general practitioners in Sydney, Australia, during a one-week period. They also collected information from the doctors on each of the patients in the sample.

They found clear support for a *consulting* hypothesis – i.e. it is more socially acceptable for women than men to go to the doctor – and limited support for the *stereotyping* hypothesis, in that the doctors were much less likely to detect psychological ill-health among men. The findings did not support Cooperstock's *reporting* hypothesis, i.e. that it is more socially acceptable for women to admit to having symptoms, especially of emotional distress.

Cafferata and her colleagues (1983) broadened the debate by testing empirically not only the sex role theory but also *social support* and *social stress* theories. They conducted a secondary analysis of data on family circumstances and psychotropic drug use of adults in 11,000 households in the United States.

Evidence was found to support all three theories. For example, they reported that women in traditional families (in which the male is in paid work and the female fulfils the housewife role) were more likely than their spouses to be taking minor tranquillisers, suggesting that the traditional female role leads to more illness. They also found that women in non-intact families and those caring for a spouse in poor health were more likely to be using tranquillisers. This, they concluded, lent credence to social support and stress theories, which suggest that women may be more sensitive than men to the effects of less supportive or more stressful family circumstances.

In sum, the studies reviewed here suggest that the tendency for women to be given tranquilliser prescriptions more often than men can only be partly explained in terms of sex role theory, with its propositions about gender differences in consulting behaviour and doctor stereotyping. The recipients' structural position in the household and the amount of social support and social stress experienced by those in this position also needs to be considered.

THE SOCIAL MEANING OF TRANQUILLISER USE

A few sociologists have also recently started to consider the social meanings which tranquillisers have for patients and their doctors. Meaning, in this context, refers to the interpretation a person gives to an object or event in his or her life. Such meanings arise out of interaction with others and are subject to development and change over time (Blumer 1969). By focusing on the meaning of long-term tranquilliser use attention is drawn to the processual nature of drug usage. This in turn provides a starting point for understanding *how* the association between long-term benzodiazepine use and particular causal variables comes about.

To illustrate this approach I shall report some findings from a study of tranquilliser users and their doctors undertaken by Gabe and his colleagues (Gabe & Lipshitz-Phillips 1984; Gabe & Thorogood 1986) and a study of tranquilliser users undertaken by Cooperstock and Lennard (1979). Both studies represent a contribution to the kind of critical sociology discussed earlier. Thus patients were treated during the analyses not as members of a single homogeneous population, but as belonging to different social groupings whose life chances are structured unequally in terms of wealth, power, and privilege.

The study by Gabe and colleagues involved in-depth, semi-structured interviews with eighty-seven patients and fourteen general practitioners from two practices in London, England. The patients were female, between 40 and 60 years of age, and two-thirds were working class. Thirty-nine were long-term users who had taken benzodiazepines consistently over a number of years, thirteen had used the drug for a couple of weeks at a time and for a two-year period at most, and the remainder had not used it at all over the previous decade. Of the doctors the majority were male and their average age was 35.

Cooperstock and Lennard's study was based on group discussions with sixty-eight tranquilliser users in Toronto, Canada, who had answered a newspaper advertisement inviting them to discuss the consequences of their tranquilliser use. The majority of this sample were also middle aged (the mean age was 46) but they were mainly middle class, unlike the London sample, and almost a quarter were male. Nearly all had used benzodiazepines for over a year and two-thirds had used them for longer than four years.

Given the constraint of space I shall concentrate on three aspects of these studies: the meaning of tranquillisers to long-term users and their doctors, the relationship between such drug usage and the availability of other resources for managing everyday life, and the social consequences of taking these drugs on a long-term basis.

The meaning of tranquillisers was addressed by Gabe and Lipshitz-Phillips (1984). They found that when the long-term users in their sample were asked what they felt about taking benzodiazepines a range of opinions were expressed. Some stated they were concerned about the danger of becoming dependent on these drugs and felt that they might be harming their body or mind by ingesting such unnatural substances. Others said they felt tranquillisers were helpful in that they offered them 'peace of mind', and yet others expressed both views. Overall the majority of long-term users seemed to feel ambivalent about their drugs, reflecting the fact that taking them crosses the boundaries of warrantable behaviour (treatment for illness) with moral culpability (not 'coping' and being reliant on the 'crutches' of a drug) (Gabe & Bury 1988).

It is noteworthy that these users also expressed a range of views about what using these drugs meant to them. Some seemed to see benzodiazepines as a 'life-line': that is something which they felt they needed to take continuously, and thus depended on, simply to keep going in the face of unresolved problems. Others appeared to view the drug as a 'standby' to be kept in reserve and used occasionally to meet some short-lived crisis, and yet others talked as if they had conceived their drug usage in both these senses at some point in time. Three-quarters of the users, however, seemed to look upon their drug taking in only *one* way, with slightly more referring to them as a life-line than as a standby.

When Gabe and Lipshitz-Phillips related the long-term users' accounts of the meaning of their drug-taking behaviour to their feelings about these drugs they found that those who talked about them only as a life-line were far more likely to express mixed feelings, whereas those referring to them as a standby were more likely to express consistently negative feelings about the drugs. Thus, using benzodiazepines as a life-line was directly linked with feelings of ambivalence.

Not surprisingly, they found that those who talked of benzodiazepines as a life-line were markedly less likely than other patients to have stopped taking them, recently or in the past. In all, half the users indicated that they had stopped taking the drug and most of these claimed to have done so on their own initiative. They said they had been motivated to stop either because they feared they were becoming over-reliant on them or because they were worried by the drug's physical side effects, or more positively because they no longer needed them.

Overall, then, many of the long-term users seemed to be aware of the dangers of dependence on the drugs and by extension on the doctor and, while often finding them helpful, had not infrequently tried at some stage to stop taking them.

The doctors who were interviewed also referred to the danger of dependence which, as they emphasized, ran counter to their long-term goal of promoting patient autonomy. All prescribed benzodiazepines in varying degrees but almost half of them had such doubts about it that they said they preferred not to prescribe. The remainder expressed mixed feelings and said that, while they felt the drugs had some value in the acute stage of a crisis, there was a danger of patients becoming reliant on them and treating them as 'magic pills'.

Whatever their reported prescribing patterns or their feelings about the drug all the doctors also emphasized that they offered alternatives to tranquillisers and that these at times met their patients' needs. Foremost among these alternatives were the doctors themselves and the time and support they provided, and leisure activities like jogging and yoga.

This research therefore suggests that long-term users are not simply passive recipients of what doctors prescribe, as is commonly supposed, but active participants in the process, aware of the dangers of relying on benzodiazepines and trying themselves to alter their behaviour. Similarly, the doctors, in this study at least, were not mindlessly prescribing these drugs in response to requests from patients but were actively assessing the risks and benefits and offering their patients alternatives to tranquillisers. While dependence is clearly an important issue, this study suggests that the argument has been overstated. For it seems that it is possible to take and prescribe benzodiazepines over a long period without necessarily experiencing or creating total dependence.

The finding that patients feel ambivalent about taking tranquillisers also has practical implications. Given that long-term use of benzodiazepines seems to depend on successfully splitting feelings of need from fears of dependence, general practitioners, clinical psychologists, and others trying to wean patients off these drugs may be more successful if they try and mobilize the latter feelings when discussing these patients' drug use with them (Gabe & Lipshitz-Phillips 1982).

The *second* issue regarding the meaning of long-term tranquilliser use that I want to consider concerns the way in which this drug use is related to the availability of other resources for managing everyday life. According to Gabe and Thorogood (1986) who considered this question, such resources are unequally distributed on the basis of social group membership and can variously be experienced as enabling and/or constraining. In what follows I shall be concerned only with the resources available to the working-class women in their study – representing two-thirds of the total sample. When Gabe and Thorogood analysed these women's comments about the resources other than tranquillisers that were available to help them manage their lives, they found that those who were long-term users had access to fewer resources than other women in the study. Moreover, those resources that were available to them were rarely experienced in such a way as to enable them to manage their lives without recourse to tranquillisers.

Three resources in particular seemed to constrain the long-term users to maintain their pattern of drug use – paid work, children and partners, and leisure. Regarding paid work, Gabe and Thorogood found that the long-term users were not only less likely to have a full-time job than other women but that those who were so employed were more likely to express mixed feelings about their situation. It would thus seem that while the absence of paid work may deprive the long-term users of a resource which might make their lives easier, thereby reducing the need for tranquillisers, those users with access to this resource did not experience it in a sufficiently positive way to enable them to change the nature of their drug use.

Gabe and Thorogood also found that long-term users were more likely to be divorced and not to have children living at home. Moreover, if these tranquilliser users were living with partners and/or their children they were less likely than the other women to find these kin supportive. It would thus appear that long-term users either lack access to potentially supportive social resources or find that those that are available are unsupportive and a poor substitute for tranquillisers. In such circumstances the existing pattern of drug use is likely to be maintained.

This study also revealed that long-term users were markedly more likely than other women to state either that they lacked all opportunities for leisure or that they had few leisure options open to them. As this resource was experienced as enabling and as a relaxant, these long-term users' limited access to it would seem to place them at a considerable disadvantage and further helps to explain why they continued to use tranquillisers to manage their daily lives. It also raises doubts about the usefulness of GPs advising women patients who are long-term users to try activities like jogging or yoga in place of tranquillisers.

Overall, then, it appears that three resources – paid work, children and partners, and leisure – had a particularly important influence upon the long-term users' drug-taking behaviour. These women's access to and relationship with these resources combined with their views about tranquillisers to maintain their existing pattern of drug use.

In addition Gabe and Thorogood discovered a link between long-term benzodiazepine use and another psychotropic resource – cigarettes. They found that these users were more likely than other women both to smoke cigarettes and to describe their experience as enabling. Long-term users' relationship with cigarettes is, it would seem, in part at least a consequence of their access to and negative experience of the other resources that have been mentioned. In the absence of such resources these women had turned to cigarettes to bolster the apparently insufficiently relaxing powers of tranquillisers and, like the women smokers studied by Graham (1987), enhance their sense of well-being by creating time for themselves.

The *third* and final issue relating to the meaning of tranquillisers concerns the social consequences of taking these drugs on a long-term basis. Cooperstock and Lennard (1979) addressed this issue and found some interesting differences between the female and male participants in their discussion groups. For the women users the drug was most often seen as 'permitting' them to maintain themselves in the traditional female role of wife, mother, and houseworker. Frequently they indicated that they resented being restricted to this caring and nurturing role but said that they saw no alternative. Others described their drug use as enabling them to cope with unresolved conflicts, often concerning the relationship with their spouse or children, while a few talked about taking tranquillisers as a learned habitual mode of reacting to stressful 'life events'.

For the male users, on the other hand, these drugs were seen solely as a means of maintaining their occupational role. They talked about using benzodiazepines like Valium to control somatic symptoms relating to the competitive nature of their jobs and the responsibilities that went with their position. For a number there was little prospect of changing their job status so tranquillisers were seen as the only way of alleviating their sometimes incapacitating symptoms.

In sum Cooperstock and Lennard found that long-term use was best understood as a means of maintaining gendered social roles. While women used tranquillisers to enable them to endure their role within the home, men used the drug to sustain themselves in their occupational role.

THE HISTORY OF LONG-TERM TRANQUILLISER USE AS A SOCIAL PROBLEM

Since the early 1970s a number of sociologists have considered tranquilliser use from the standpoint of it being a public issue as well as a personal trouble (Lennard *et al.* 1971; Muller 1972; Jefferys 1973). To illustrate the contribution that sociology can make in this area I shall consider first some research by Gabe and Bury (1988) concerning the extent to which long-term tranquilliser use and dependence has come to be seen as a social problem in Britain. This research identified *three* stages a problem must go through: 1) emergence – for a problem to emerge certain objective conditions need to be met; 2) legitimation and mobilization of public opinion – the problem needs to be legitimated by the media and public opinion orchestrated; 3) recognition by the state – the state needs to underwrite any response it makes with a substantial political commitment and financial outlay. It should be pointed out here that they mean by the state not just the government but also institutions like the civil service, the judiciary, and the police. Also, they do not assume that the movement between stages is a straightforward and linear process. On the contrary, they see it as contingent and hence highly problematic.

Starting with *emergence* they suggested that long-term tranquilliser use has emerged as a problem for two reasons. First, objective evidence has been accumulated about the real harm and distress caused by long-term use at therapeutic dose and its incidence. Thus they noted that since the early 1980s a growing number of studies have found that patients agreeing to or requesting withdrawal from long-term benzodiazepine use at therapeutic dose have experienced symptoms of physical dependence (such as intolerance of noise and light, bad headaches, and a dry mouth) on withdrawal and that these symptoms could last a year or more. Furthermore, they reported that those studies which had used representative samples and control groups found that between 27 per cent and 45 per cent of long-term users were dependent on their drugs.

Second, they argued that long-term use has emerged as a problem because scientific experts and representatives of mental health pressure groups have claimed in public that benzodiazepines were a) being overused and misused and b) had the potential to cause physical dependence at normal therapeutic dose. Claims about overuse and misuse in Britain were said to have been made in the 1970s in response to the growth in tranquilliser prescriptions. By the early 1980s these were seen as having been superseded by claims about benzodiazepines' dependence potential and the existence of a 'withdrawal syndrome' in line with current clinical and epidemiological research.

According to Gabe and Bury the next stage in the process has involved the media. They argued, on the basis of an analysis of British television and radio programmes, that the media have played a major part in *legitimating* the concept of tranquilliser dependence as a social problem and *mobilizing* public opinion around the issue. For example, they noted that *That's Life*, the popular television consumer programme with an audience of around 10 million people at peak viewing time on Sunday evenings, considered the subject on at least four occasions between 1983 and 1985. An analysis of the transcripts of these programmes revealed that the programmes offered a platform for the competing claims of medical experts and pressure group representatives about the prevalence of tranquilliser dependence, with the estimate escalating from programme to programme. In the first programme 5 million people were said to be taking one form of tranquilliser or another and a quarter of a million were said to be unable to get off them. In a later programme, however, 10 million people were said to have taken tranquillisers and 50 per cent of current users were considered to be unable to come off them. This led Gabe and Bury to suggest that, as far as the media were concerned, the bigger the estimates the more dramatic the problem and the more newsworthy the coverage. The result, however, was that benzodiazepine dependence was portrayed as being of epidemic proportions.

They also found that *That's Life*, in common with other programmes, presented a particular image of long-term tranquilliser users as people who had been 'completely taken over' by the drug. Individual users, usually women, were portrayed as victims of a menacing force over which they had little or no control. Such imagery provided little chance for the variable nature of benzodiazepine use to come across, alongside issues of dependence. For instance, no mention was made of tranquillisers used only as sleeping pills, or of their intermittent or sporadic use in managing personal crises.

Besides providing a terrain for claim-making activity it was argued that the media also played an essential role in *mobilizing public opinion*, as the postbag to *That's Life* following their programmes on tranquillisers demonstrated. Two reasons were suggested why programmes like this 'worked' with the public. First was the ambivalent attitudes of many tranquilliser users which were discussed earlier. Such ambivalence created a receptiveness to the issue among specific publics, especially middle-aged women, and even 'demanded' that the media should attend to the problem. Second was the revival of concern about illegal drug use. The climate in Britain in recent years has been one of extreme concern if not outright panic over the use of illegal drugs, especially among the young, with politicians being pressed to state what they intended to do to combat 'this greatest menace in peace time' (Home Affairs Committee 1985). This greater sensitivity to the deleterious effects of illicit drug use was seen as informing responses to licit drug taking, even in the face of limited evidence of dependence.

Finally, Gabe and Bury argued that the extent to which long-term tranquilliser use has been seen as a social problem has been determined by the *response of the state*. The evidence reviewed indicated that the British state has been equivocal. While it has made several statutory changes, committed certain monies to support voluntary organizations providing services for those on tranquillisers, and issued advice to all doctors about the dependence potential of benzodiazepines, an analysis of the motives behind these actions suggested that it has not yet embraced long-term tranquilliser use as a full-blown social problem. For example, its decision in 1984 to introduce the 'limited list' was arguably motivated more by the need to reduce the NHS drugs bill in line with general cuts in welfare spending, rather than as a way of tackling long-term tranquilliser use. Likewise, drafting legislation in 1985 to bring benzodiazepines under the Misuse of Drugs Act 1971 and make them controlled drugs seemed to be motivated primarily by the need to ratify the United Nations Convention on Psychotropic Substances of which it was a signatory (ISDD 1986). In 1984 the UN had voted to accept the World Health Organisation's recommendation to control thirty-three benzodiazepines under the Psychotropic Convention. To implement this convention Britain had to duplicate the UN's decision in its domestic legislation. If the state had been more concerned about benzodiazepines, they argued, it would surely have put them in a schedule that imposed more than minimal controls.

Gabe and Bury suggested that the state's reluctance to accept tranquillisers wholeheartedly as a social problem may in part be because these drugs have not been taken in the main by social groups like working-class youth who are seen as a threat to law and order, but by otherwise respectable middle-aged women (and to a lesser extent men). They noted that it may also reflect a reluctance to challenge the professional autonomy of doctors. Whatever the reason, it would seem that long-term use remains relatively low on the policy agenda despite the public debate that has occurred on this topic in Britain.

TRANQUILLISERS AS SOCIAL CONTROL

The second public issue I want to consider is concerned with tranquillisers as a means of social control. This concept, which broadly refers to the ways in which social order and stability are maintained, was first linked with the prescribing and use of these drugs by Waldron (1977) and Conrad (1979). It was Koumjian (1981), however, who undertook the most broad-ranging analysis of this issue. For him, tranquillisers functioned as a means of social control primarily because they involved the medicalization of everyday life. He argued that the prescription and use of these drugs depended on a redefinition of social problems as medical problems and resulted in certain specific social effects. In support of this proposition he noted the increased number of people going to the doctor with social problems such as loneliness or marital discord who were treated simply for symptoms of anxiety and prescribed Valium. In so doing doctors were said to have encouraged their patients to deny or ignore the social concomitants of their distress, thereby helping to minimize pressure for social change. He noted too that benzodiazepines were prescribed more frequently to older people and to women and, on a long-term basis, to members of lower socio-economic groups.

In addition, although not remarked on by Koumjian, it could be argued that the attitudes and behaviour of doctors prescribing tranquillisers have enhanced social control in that they have reinforced existing hierarchical social relations. For example, it may be that doctors have suggested more often to female and working-class patients than to male and middle-class patients that their symptoms were a consequence of *their* failure to look after themselves adequately.

Besides identifying the mechanisms of social control it is also possible to identify certain factors which have promoted the use of benzodiazepines in social control. For Koumjian two in particular were deemed to be important: drug company promotion and the conditions of modern medical practice. He noted that the pharmaceutical industry spent a significant amount of its revenue from the sales of minor tranquillisers on promotion through 'detail' men and women and advertising in journals and that much of this promotional activity encouraged doctors to prescribe tranquillisers for social problems. Such money appeared to be well spent, he suggested, as many doctors in the study he quoted reported that their first source of drug information was the drug company sales representative or company house mail and periodicals. As for the conditions of modern medical practice, he argued that lack of time to explore a patient's problem with them fully and a lack of training in the social context of medicine often played a major part in influencing the doctor's decision to prescribe.

While this social control model has been useful in that it has brought into relief the influence of structural factors on tranquilliser prescribing and use, a critical sociology also needs to consider to what extent such a model is supported empirically.

Gabe and Lipshitz-Phillips (1984) explored this issue with interview data from the study of patients and doctors referred to earlier. They found little support for tranquillisers' involvement in the medicalization of everyday life in that there was little to indicate that the prescribing and use of these drugs necessarily involved the individualization of social problems. For example, the majority of doctors operated with a multicausal rather than monocausal model when explaining their patients' symptoms and seemed unlikely to impose individualized explanations on a patient if they felt that interpersonal factors were relevant to his or her predicament. The patients, on the other hand, were rather more likely both to perceive a single cause for their symptoms and to suggest physical and psychosomatic factors as their cause. This was, however, less the case with long-term users than with other patients.

Turning to the second mechanism of social control, the legitimation of existing gender and class relations, the evidence here was more equivocal. As regards gender, there were grounds for suggesting that both doctors and patients operated with negative stereotypes such as perceiving women as psychologically or physiologically more fragile than men and as limited by their reproductive function. They employed these stereotypes to explain why women received and used more benzodiazepines than men. The proponents of the social control argument would contend that to a considerable extent it is the pattern of differential prescribing which reinforces such negative stereotypes.

At the same time there was much in their data which would appear to contradict the social control thesis. Thus, nearly all the doctors maintained they they did not respond to their patients in terms of preconceived ideas about gender differences in illness or psychological make-up. Instead they pointed out that more women than men experiencing anxiety symptoms came to the surgery: consequently they prescribed more benzodiazepines to women. It could be argued, therefore, that it was the women patients who were acting in terms of negative gender stereotypes independently of their doctors.

Furthermore, even if the women patients showed signs of operating in terms of negative gender stereotypes there was no evidence to suggest their experience of the consultation reproduced or enhanced these stereotypes. Although a number of long-term users made a link between gender inequalities and benzodiazepine use in general they seldom made such a link as far as they themselves were concerned.

As for the data on class this too could be interpreted in more than one way. For example, the fact that the doctors said that they were prescribing more to working-class patients and justified doing so on the grounds that such patients only wanted pills or were in greater need could be taken to mean that, whether conscious of it or not, they were operating with a notion of the working class as incapable of resolving their social problems on their own. This could be interpreted as evidence of negative stereotyping which would reinforce social control.

At the same time Gabe and Lipshitz-Phillips' data did not suggest that the doctors held a view of working-class patients as inferior to others. A significant number indicated that, irrespective of social class, they talked to their patients and tried to encourage them to reduce the number of benzodiazepines taken. It could be argued, therefore, that the doctors' acknowledgement of the fact that they prescribed more frequently to working- than to middle-class patients reflected a recognition of the social origins of the suffering of working-class patients and the need to try and alleviate this suffering.

Finally, to what extent did the data from this study support Koumjian's contention that drug company promotion and the conditions of modern medical practice have encouraged the use of benzodiazepines as a form of social control? Again the picture is mixed. For example, most of the doctors in the study maintained that they were not influenced by the drug companies, either by their literature or by personal visits from their representatives. Indeed, nearly half said they had a policy of not seeing representatives of drug companies at all. At the same time, it could be argued that these responses simply illustrated an attempt by the doctors to project themselves as independent, judicious prescribers not open to the influence of the drug companies. Gabe and Lipshitz-Phillips however felt it was unlikely that they were trying to project themselves in this way as their remarks were consistent with their attitudes about benzodiazepine prescribing.

As for the impact of organizational factors on prescribing, this was recognized as being significant, although by only a minority of doctors. Just over a third said they felt that running behind time, a full waiting-room, and administrative interruptions combined to increase the likelihood that they would take the 'easy option': that is to prescribe tranquillisers rather than try and reach agreement with the patient about an alternative course of action. However, the other doctors and almost all the patients who were long-term benzodiazepine users did not mention the effects of organizational factors on the consultation.

In sum, it would seem that the contention that tranquillisers represent a form of social control received only limited empirical support from Gabe and Lipshitz-Phillips' study. While there was little to suggest that the prescribing of these drugs medicalized everyday life there was some, albeit equivocal, support for the proposition that it legitimated gender and class relations. There was, however, only limited evidence that factors such as drug company promotion and the conditions of modern medical practice promoted benzodiazepines as a form of social control. This suggests that, while the concept of social control has made a valuable contribution to understanding social action and the impact of structural factors on the doctor-patient relationship, its application to tranquillisers has been too mechanistic and has resulted in overgeneralizations. While the prescribing of these drugs may result in social control, this is not necessarily the case and should not be assumed in advance.

CONCLUSION

This chapter has focused on the contribution which sociologists have made to understanding four aspects of long-term tranquilliser use – the reasons for such drug use among women, the social meanings attached to their use by patients and their doctors, the history of these drugs as a social problem, and the extent to which prescribing them functions as a form of social control. These topics have been selected for consideration in order to try and demonstrate the scope of sociology as critique for enhancing our understanding of both 'personal troubles of milieu' and 'public issues of social structure'. The evidence presented would seem to confirm that long-term benzodiazepine use cannot be seen simply as a medical problem but needs to be placed within a social, cultural, political, and economic context. Only then will the issues currently facing these drug users and those trying to wean them off such drugs be adequately comprehended.

ACKNOWLEDGEMENTS

I should like to thank Mike Bury and Paul Williams for their comments on an earlier draft of this chapter.

REFERENCES

Blumer, H. (1969) *Symbolic Interactionism*, Englewood Cliffs, NJ: Prentice-Hall.

Cafferata, G., Kasper, J., & Bernstein, A. (1983) 'Family roles, structure and stressors in relation to sex differences in obtaining psychotropic drugs', *Journal of Health and Social Behaviour* 24: 132–43.

Conrad, P. (1979) 'Types of medical social control', *Sociology of Health and Illness* 1(1): 1–11.

Cooperstock, R. (1971) 'Sex differences in the use of mood-modifying drugs: an explanatory model', *Journal of Health and Social Behaviour* 12: 238–44.

Cooperstock, R. & Lennard, H. (1979) 'Some social meanings of tranquilliser use', *Sociology of Health and Illness* 1(3): 331–47.

Doyal, L. (1979) *The Political Economy of Health*, London: Pluto Press.

Engel, G. (1977) 'The need for a new medical model: a challenge for biomedicine', *Science* 196: 129–35.

Field, D. (1976) 'The social definition of illness', in D. Tuckett (ed.) *An Introduction to Medical Sociology*, London: Tavistock.

Gabe, J. & Bury, M. (1988) 'Tranquillisers as a social problem', *Sociological Review* 36(2): 320–52.

Gabe, J. & Lipshitz-Phillips, S. (1982) 'Evil necessity? The meaning of benzodiazepine use for women patients from one general practice', *Sociology of Health and Illness* 4(2): 201–9.

Gabe, J. & Lipshitz-Phillips, S. (1984) 'Tranquillisers as social control?' *Sociological Review* 32(3): 524–46.

Gabe, J. & Thorogood, N. (1986) 'Prescribed drug use and the management of everyday life: the experiences of black and white working class women', *Sociological Review* 34(4): 737–72.

Giddens, A. (1986) *Sociology – A Brief But Critical Introduction*, 2nd edition, Basingstoke: Macmillan Education.

Graham, H. (1987) 'Women's smoking and family health', *Social Science and Medicine* 25(1): 47–56.

Home Affairs Committee (1985) *Interim Report on Drug Misuse*, London: HMSO.

ISSD (Institute for the Study of Drug Dependence) (1986) 'Tranquillisers controlled but possession illegal', *Druglink*, May/June: 5.

Jefferys, M. (1973) 'Medicine takers', *Journal of Royal College of General Practitioners* 23(Suppl. 2): 9–11.

Koumjian, K. (1981) 'The use of Valium as a form of social control', *Social Science and Medicine* 15E(3): 245–9.

Lennard, H. L., Epstein, L. J., Bernstein, A., & Ransom, D. C. (1971) *Mystification and Drug Misuse*, New York: Harper & Row.

Mant, A., Broom, D., & Duncan-Jones, P. (1983) 'The path to prescription: sex differences in psychotropic drug prescribing for general practice patients', *Social Psychiatry* 18: 185–92.

Mills, C. W. (1959) *The Sociological Imagination*, Oxford: Oxford University Press.

Muller, C. (1972) 'The overmedicated society: forces in the marketplace for medical care', *Science* 176(4034): 488–9.

Stacey, M. (1988) *The Sociology of Health and Healing*, London: Unwin Hyman.

Waldron, I. (1977) 'Increased prescribing of Valium, Librium and other drugs – an example of economic and social factors in the practice of medicine', *International Journal of Health Services* 7(1): 37–62.

3 The culture of long-term tranquilliser users

Michael Montagne

Nervous disorders, such as anxiety, are culturally defined in a number of different ways, and, thus, a variety of reasons exist for seeking care and for treating these conditions. Anxiety and related nervous conditions are a culturally interpreted set of symptoms, not a culture-bound illness (Low 1985). In Guatemala, nerves are an expression of anger; in Costa Rica, they are suggestive of family problems and abandonment; in Appalachia (US), they are a symptom of an impoverished lifestyle and cultural deprivation; and in Newfoundland, they are a sign of worry and fear in the maintenance of cultural roles (Low 1985). While there are commonalities in symptom states, there are much greater differences in the interpretation and meaning of these states, their presumed aetiology, and their resolution. Nerves are often attributed to tragedy, misfortune, or difficulties in life, and there is a rich array of cultural meanings reflected in the term 'nerves' (Nations *et al.* 1988).

Anxiety, with the presence of specific physical symptoms, can range from an unhealthy response to a stressful event or situation, to an inability to respond to an unresolved personal or social problem, to a vague sense of being dissatisfied with one's life. Which condition, situation, or experience then is anxiety provoking to the extent that medical help is needed, and which one does not necessitate such assistance? And in which medical case is the use of a chemical substance appropriate, and in which one should non-drug therapies be used? Is long-term tranquilliser use the result of a perceived social or psychological need, a chronic anxiety state, a dependency state, or an artefact of cultural hegemony and the social order? In this chapter, long-term tranquilliser use is examined from an anthropological perspective, with the goal of describing the culture of those involved in the giving and taking of these drugs.

DRUG TAKING FROM AN ANTHROPOLOGICAL PERSPECTIVE

There are a number of theoretical orientations in anthropology, but, excluding biophysical anthropology and archaeology, there are arguably two main conceptual approaches (Kaplan & Manners 1972). These two approaches reflect differences in the focus of inquiry. The structural approach emphasizes the *nature* of cultural phenomena, focusing on form and function (Lévi-Strauss 1963; Radcliffe-Brown 1952). The nature of social systems or structured sets of relations, and the ways in which their different parts exist and interrelate with one another through functional activities, are of greatest interest. The symbolic approach emphasizes the *meaning* of cultural phenomena, focusing on language and the use of symbols in social interactions (Geertz 1973). The system of symbols that give people an orientation to life and an ability to interpret and understand everyday reality is of greatest interest. A symbol is any object, act, or event that serves as a vehicle for the conception of reality and the attribution of meaning. In both approaches, however, the primary goals are to describe a specific culture in terms of its functioning, continual maintenance, and its ability to adapt to change, and to determine its influence on the beliefs and behaviours of its individual members.

The term 'culture' has been defined in myriad ways. Culture may be viewed as the objects, collective structures, meanings, and mechanisms that have become institutionalized to the point where they can define or influence traditional behaviour at a societal level. Other viewpoints consider culture to be something that is acquired by an individual member of a society, and it consists of a constellation of knowledge, beliefs, customs, laws, behaviours, morals, and other abilities. The symbolists would also state that culture is the historical transmission of meaning, through symbols, which provides and reinforces a world-view for people. There are also differences in research methodology and the ultimate description of a culture that is derived from an anthropological inquiry. One method is to take an insider's perspective (classically termed the emic approach) by describing the culture in terms of its members' conceptual categories. Another method takes an outsider's perspective (termed the etic approach) by describing the culture in terms of the investigator's (i.e. anthropologist's) conceptual categories. Each method has its strengths and weaknesses (Pelto & Pelto 1978).

Anthropological studies of psychoactive drug use can improve our understanding of the social norms and cultural beliefs that influence tranquilliser use. A great deal of work has been done on the cross-cultural aspects of alcohol use. In many cultures, alcohol is used in ritualized ways to help deal with persistent dangers and other societal problems, but social sanctions and controls are usually in place so that alcohol use does not become problematic (McCarthy 1959). Some cross-cultural research on alcohol has concluded that the primary function of alcoholic beverages in most societies is to reduce anxiety and stress resulting from cultural changes and deprivation (Everett *et al.* 1976). There is also a shifting phenomenon, so that if something valuable as a calmative is removed from the culture, something else will take its place, since the need still remains. A great deal of tranquilliser use may be due to the influence of increased societal stress, especially the special stressors of industrial societies, and thus the need for a substance with calmative effects.

Metaphors for alcohol and its use are important in culturally defining certain patterns of use in some situations as social problems, thus making them open to societal control, such as the case with drinking-driving. In this example, partial, qualified, and fragile knowledge is continually transformed into certain and consistent fact. This allows for the creation of technical and moral realities that are given form and meaning through culturally shared facts and beliefs, which can then be invoked to control behaviour (Gusfield 1981). Cultural factors also appear to be related to sobriety and drunkenness through different aspects of cultural organization, societal stability, and cultural beliefs about alcohol and drinking customs (MacAndrew & Edgerton 1969; Pittman & Snyder 1962).

Cross-cultural studies of other psychoactive substances have also shown the importance of rituals and social sanctions. Drug use, effects, and problems can vary greatly from culture to culture, as in the case of cannabis (DeRios 1976; Rubin 1975). Rituals can control drug use and limit or prevent problems (DeRios & Smith 1977a; 1977b). Rituals, which are stylized and prescribed behaviours surrounding the use of a drug, and sanctions, which are norms regarding whether or not a particular drug should be used, help to: define and approve controlled drug use and to limit or prevent uncontrolled drug use, limit use to specific physical and social settings that are more conducive to a positive experience or result, incorporate specific principles of use (e.g. small amounts, on special occasions), identify potential untoward effects and prescribe relevant precautions to be taken, and assist the drug users in interpreting and giving meaning to the drug experience (Du Toit 1977; Zinberg 1984; Zinberg & Harding 1982). The cultural belief system gives meaning and description to a drug-taking experience, and a lack of cultural controls can lead to difficulties in interpreting, and thus benefiting from, the experience, which can become negative (Wallace 1959).

In some cultures, drug cults have arisen in response to acculturative pressures. In most cases, cultures control drug use, and thus limit problems, by ritual rather than by legal means. Certain types of psychoactive drug use are not employed to reduce anxiety, the symptom state, but rather to give an understanding of and power over its cause (e.g. personal, social, spiritual), or to redefine it in a way that makes it culturally manageable. The use of drugs in this manner is almost always in a cultural context, with a ritual of use and a specific, culturally valued reason for use. Thus, use or misuse becomes a cultural, not a biomedical, phenomenon by definition (DeRios & Smith 1977a; 1977b). Culture is also important in the prevention and treatment of drug use problems (Edwards & Arif 1980; Strug *et al.* 1986).

IMAGES AND METAPHORS OF TRANQUILLISERS AND TRANQUILLISER USE

Metaphors are used by both the patient and health professionals, often with different connotations, to describe a drug's effects and to communicate about issues of identity and change involved in the giving and taking of psychotherapeutic medications. Metaphors are, in reality, ascriptions, but they are often used as descriptions as well (Szasz 1974). A number of patient-derived metaphors, with both positive and negative connotations, were identified in one interesting study (Rhodes 1984). The use of psychotropic medications was viewed as influencing the patient's mind and thoughts by releasing or blocking them, by straightening or distorting them, and by mobilizing or immobilizing them. This study also found that the professional staff used some of the same metaphors as the patients, but, in addition, other metaphors were used only by the health professionals. They primarily viewed the effects of tranquillisers as a filtering phenomenon, which led to the clearing of the patient's mind. The drugs themselves were viewed negatively in some circumstances by the professional staff, as band-aids or as crutches. The use of similar and different metaphors by patients and professionals reflects their somewhat separate, but very much related cultures.

Metaphors are also important to long-term users of psychotropic drugs in describing the meanings that their drugs have for them, their modes of use, and the effects that they experience (Montagne 1988a). Drugs are viewed as props, helpers, security, and even as a 'person' (e.g. a missing mate or friend). Helman (1981) discovered that three main images or metaphors existed in the group of patients he studied: psychotropic drugs were food, basic to one's existence and necessary for social and psychological survival; fuel, helping the patient adjust their personality and functioning to conform with familial and societal expectations; or tonics, restoratives for temporary amelioration of episodic symptom states. Those patients who viewed their drugs as tonics expressed maximum control over their drug use, tended to self-medicate as needed, and even held relatively anti-drug views in general. Those who viewed their drugs as food expressed little control over their drug taking.

The ritual of interacting with a physician and receiving a prescription is imbued with symbolism and metaphors. The process of diagnosing and prescribing consists of three interacting levels of symbolic exchange: the act of ingestion; enhancement by the illness, especially in the presence of symptoms; and the investiture of this symbolism by the physician's act of drug giving (Pellegrino 1976). The act of taking a drug fulfils an ingrained habit: the need to take something when confronted with illness. The culturally based interpretation of symptom states and responses to such states provides for additional symbols that attach meaning to, and thus understanding of, the illness experience. And the healer's act of prescribing a drug enhances and solidifies the interaction, reinforces the healer's power to cure, and provides the patient with a sense of satisfaction and resolution to the problem. In the specific case of long-term tranquilliser use, it is likely that as the pharmacological element in the drug's effects declines (i.e. less activity physiologically or behaviourally due to tolerance or some other biological phenomenon), the symbolic element becomes more important in bringing about and shaping the profile of effects that are experienced by the user (Becker 1967; Lin & Poland 1986).

Metaphorical notions of drugs, their effects, and their use exist with regard to tranquillisers. Within two years of its introduction, meprobamate was all the rage, more of a cultural phenomenon than a significant medical advance. It was called 'penicillin for the blues'; an appropriate metaphor since the antibiotics, the exemplars of the 'magic bullet' concept of pharmacotherapy, were still a wonder to the general public. Relaxing was called 'miltowning', and mixing meprobamate with a Bloody Mary was referred to as a Miltown Cocktail (Pekkanen 1973). The drug's name became ubiquitous in societal discourse. It was the topic of conversation at coffee klatches and garden club parties in expanding suburbia. The benzodiazepines have become a mass cultural phenomenon too, even more so than meprobamate. The appearance of these drugs in both serious and humorous circumstances in films, literature, and other media only reinforced their popularity. Negative attitudes towards benzodiazepines, on the part of health professionals and society, increased however throughout the 1970s (Woods *et al.* 1987). By the 1980s, many health advocacy groups, governmental agencies, and even the popular literature more often portrayed benzodiazepines as dangerous and enslaving drugs.

It has been suggested by Gabe and Thorogood (1986) that tranquillisers are viewed by patients as a resource, like paid work, social support, leisure, housing, cigarettes, and religion, which is available to a person in managing everyday life activities and in assisting decision-making processes. In their study, the meaning of tranquillisers as a resource was similar for both Afro-Caribbean and white women, being seen as both enabling and constraining. It was the meaning and availability of other resources which was instrumental in dictating whether or not use would continue over some period of time. In another study, all women users were found to have anti-drug beliefs, thus indicating that they may view their drugs as an evil necessity (Gabe & Lipshitz-Phillips 1982). This is a significant finding, since the anti-drug cultural mind-set did not completely prevent them from using tranquillisers, possibly because they viewed favourably their relationships with their physicians. Use seemed to depend then on a successful balancing of, or choosing between, a perceived need for the drug's effects and a fear of moral weakness or chemical dependence as a result of use. Additional metaphors include the images that tranquillisers are a life-line, to help in facing unresolved problems, or a standby, ready to use in a crisis situation (Gabe & Lipshitz-Phillips 1984).

It is important to note that the metaphors uncovered in some of these studies and similar social inquiries are labelled and defined by the researchers, based upon the patients' descriptions. Thus, the metaphors that exist for describing and understanding, and for giving meaning to, the tranquilliser experience can be generated by different sources (see Table 3.1 for a listing of images and metaphors of tranquillisers and tranquilliser use that have been identified in medical and social research, the media, and societal discourse). Since the intended meaning and the reasons for the creation of these metaphors can vary, it is very important to note if the source is the patient, the healer (or health professional), the pharmaceutical manufacturer and promoter, the social researcher (in this case, the anthropological investigator of drug taking), or media commentators, such as journalists. In many instances, it is difficult to know the original source of a metaphor, or there is the problem of a complex intertwining of a metaphor among different sources.

Table 3.1 Images and metaphors of tranquillisers and tranquilliser use

Tranquillisers as [is]	*Tranquilliser use as [is]*
magic bullet/placebo	vacation/break/escape
tool/vehicle/computer program	artificial paradise
passport/ticket	moral weakness
pacifier/consoler/comforter	normal daily event (afternoon tea)
helper/missing mate/friend	military mobilization
enslaver/straitjacket	Turkish bath/relaxing setting
crutch/prop/support/band-aid	social image
lock/vice/prison	social control
life-line/life enhancer	fog/barrier/imprisonment
standby/security	evil necessity
resource	plague/scourge
food	zombification
fuel	
tonic	
hero/army/police	
other drugs	

There is an interesting variety of images and metaphors for tranquillisers and their use, which represent cultural beliefs about anxiety and nervousness and the treatment of such conditions. These metaphors have been generated by a number of different individuals and groups involved in issues surrounding the development and use of tranquillisers (Chapman 1979; Hughes & Brewin 1979; Lennard 1971; Montagne 1988a; Morgan 1983; Rhodes 1984; Smith 1985). Tranquillisers have been viewed as passports or tickets to tranquillity or normality, as the army or police who battle the intruder (i.e. anxiety), as enslavers or chemical straitjackets and even as other drugs (e.g. aspirin for the soul, mental laxatives, psychotropic vitamins, and 'weak' alcohol). Tranquilliser use has been thought of as a chemical vacation or break from work or other tasks, as a Turkish bath or some other relaxing setting (or even as an artificial paradise), and as a barrier to thinking or an imprisonment of the mind. And in the late 1970s and early 1980s, when denunciations of tranquillisers became commonplace a strong cultural image emerged that these substances were a plague or scourge on society.

The presence and influence of metaphors in the use of tranquillisers are quite extensive. Metaphorical thinking in tranquilliser use becomes most apparent and significant when the metaphors are applied in everyday interactions, and specific meanings are attributed to them. The essence of these metaphors is in understanding and experiencing the use and effects of tranquillisers in terms of a related concept or entity that is more concretely and clearly delineated in a person's world-view. When these metaphors, and their meanings, become fundamental to a patient, the analogue, indicated by 'as', evolves into the related concept. The metaphor ceases to be an analogy, and, instead, it becomes the related concept or entity, as signified by the semantic and conceptual transformation from 'as' to 'is' (see Table 3.1). As a result, these metaphors can structure patients' and health professionals' knowledge, experiences, and behaviours, and they are instrumental in the construction of social realities and cultural beliefs. These metaphors influence cultural beliefs and perceptions to such a degree that societal change is, or can be, brought about by the prevailing metaphorical structure. This, in turn, may influence the organization and provision of health care for patients with 'nervous' conditions, and, ultimately, the effectiveness of these drugs for individual patients.

CHEMICAL COMFORTERS OR CRUTCHES? SYMBOLIC ASPECTS OF TRANQUILLISER USE

A soft-spoken woman in her twenties is prescribed Valium by her therapist to help her get over her shyness. Valium helps her to become more assertive and less bothered by tension and anxiety. She views her medicine as a *magic pill* (Hughes & Brewin 1979). Many tranquilliser users, especially women, seem to ascribe a mystique to their favourite drug, which encompasses beliefs about the drug's potency and ritual of use (Prather 1979). Symptoms of anxiety or nervousness are usually clear to the person, but difficult to describe or explain to others. Knowledge of the tranquilliser's accessibility can become as important as the effects resulting from actual use. Dosage adjustments are often based on symptom states *and* value systems; there is a need to take the drug due to symptoms, but only one-half of the normal therapeutic dose is taken, so as not to appear bad or morally weak (Prather 1979). These beliefs in the efficacy of tranquillisers are very strong in regular users, and some of these beliefs are given to the patients by their physicians.

There is a strong cultural belief, in some western societies, that the use of tranquillisers is a moral problem, reflecting a passive mode of living with many tranquillising aspects (e.g. television). As one philosopher put it in the early 1970s:

> We have abandoned our old-fashioned values. We have given up our old gods. This nation [the US] has turned to tranquilizers almost as a way of life because people want things to come easily, they no longer want to work hard, to suffer any pain, to feel any stress or anxiety. . . . People who take these drugs are lazy, they do not want to take the trouble to find their own center. They are afraid to define their own existence, they let a pill do it for them. That's living.
>
> (Hughes & Brewin 1979: 23)

In the early 1970s, Americans in all social, racial, and economic groups held very conservative attitudes towards tranquillisers and their use (Manheimer *et al*. 1973). These attitudes were strongest among the very poor and least educated. Tranquillisers were seen as temporary palliatives that cured nothing, and use was viewed as a sign of moral weakness. In a sense, the results of this study confirmed Klerman's (1970; 1974) notion that pharmacological Calvinism condoned and sanctioned certain types of drug taking (e.g. tranquilliser use only for specific therapeutic purposes under direct professional supervision), yet condemned and forbade other types of drug taking (e.g. any other pattern of tranquilliser use for any other reason, especially if self-directed), even though it involved the same drug. This value foundation represents the dominant cultural belief system in most western societies, and the pharmacological version is based upon the conviction that if a drug makes you feel good, it must be morally bad or wrong to use it.

Critical and professional reviews of the benzodiazepine 'problem' have focused on the manufacturers, and to some extent physicians (Waldron 1977). The pharmaceutical industry, motivated by profit, has been viewed as providing biased information, medicalizing personal and social problems (thus creating indications for use that were unreasonable or later found to be untrue), overpromoting and advertising in a misleading manner, and encouraging the development and use of molecular variants (i.e. me-too drugs). These activities acculturated tranquilliser use and created expectations in many patients that tranquillisers can provide social support, and in many physicians that these drugs can provide technological cures for their patients' problems (Seidenberg 1976).

Advocacy groups and the media jumped quickly on the bandwagon. The Public Citizen Health Research Group (1982) published a number of articles and books which described the dangers of using these drugs without much of an accompanying view of their benefits: 'The truth is that *anyone* can get hooked, even at recommended dosages' (Public Citizen Health Research Group 1982: back cover). Valium and its chemical cousins were viewed as a form of chemical coping, for social and emotional problems of life. The blame was placed on the pharmaceutical manufacturers and their desire for profits and on physicians for wanting to 'push' these drugs on consumers. Lurid journalistic accounts (Hughes & Brewin 1979) and personal testimonies of tranquilliser use problems (Gordon 1979; Holden 1982) focused on the tranquillisers as the exemplar of the American 'pill-popping' way of life. In these accounts, the emphasis was on the drug, as an object, and on its manufacturer, and not on the consumers' drug-taking behaviours. In reality, the use of tranquillisers presented another opportunity for certain groups to attack a perceived overuse of drugs in society.

More recent analyses of the benzodiazepine phenomenon have shown that many objections to these drugs were unfounded, or they represented moral judgements and political motives disguised as medical concerns (Kilwein 1983; Smith 1985). Societal values and perceptions are very important in a drug's acceptance or rejection by health professionals and patients. With tranquillisers, there appears to be significant conflict between the cultural metaphor of health care and the pharmaceutical industry, and the metaphor expressed in western society's cultural media and public discourse (Morgan 1983). The professional metaphor emphasizes the biomedical disease model of anxiety and stress, thus justifying use of these drugs. The societal metaphor condemns tranquilliser use as a sign of moral weakness leading to moral and physical decay.

The cultural beliefs, value systems, and symbolic images regarding tranquillisers and their use can greatly influence decision-making on the part of both physician and patient (Melville 1980). In the biomedical researcher's and clinician's minds, there is the vision of anxiety in which the sympathetic nervous system is pulsating with neurochemicals. And of course, the best route to treatment is to suppress the physiological activity of these endogenous substances. The answer lies in pharmaceutical technology. A good deal of tranquilliser prescribing is done by general practitioners, or others without specific training in pharmacotherapeutics, and, thus, they do not have a well developed 'culture' of what constitutes optimal prescribing behaviour. They do not have a strong cultural sense to direct them. Those physicians with specialty training, on the other hand, may have been acculturated into the biological model of the brain. For instance, one prominent professional metaphor for tranquillisers views them as tools to fine-tune the body-machine or as a computer program to correct an error in the computer's (i.e. brain's) functioning (Chapman 1979).

HEALTH CARE OR SOCIAL CONTROL? STRUCTURAL ASPECTS OF TRANQUILLISER USE

It appears that, in general, most drugs pass through three stages of acceptance in western societies (Smith 1985). A newly introduced drug entity is usually overvalued, and soon it is overused in inappropriate ways. As problems arise from misuse, the drug becomes undervalued and often condemned. A balance is eventually achieved as the advantages and disadvantages are weighed in determining the therapeutic worth and rational use of the drug. It has been shown that the minor tranquillisers go through similar stages of acceptance (Cohen 1983):

1) euphoric ignorance – the new drug outperforms the older drug products, and long-term problems are not yet apparent;
2) paranoid uncertainty – disappointment and disillusionment set in as the drug turns out to be less safe than originally imagined (e.g. adverse reactions or drug use problems are reported with increasing frequency);
3) judicious evaluation – the benefits and value of using the drug become clearer, and it is used in a proper or more appropriate manner.

These three phases of professional and public response have been noted for the acceptance of all types of tranquillisers: bromides, sedative-hypnotics, meprobamate, and the benzodiazepines (Cohen 1983). It appears that most of the benzodiazepine tranquillisers are currently in the second stage of acceptance.

It may be that western medicine's strength of intense technological development and use of drugs is also its major weakness. Has medicine, and health care in general, become too reliant on the primary, or even universal, use of technology (which, in the majority of cases, means therapeutic interventions with chemical substances) to solve problems? Melville and Johnson (1982) have described the ideal drug product, from the manufacturer's perspective. Such a drug would be inexpensive to make, protected by world-wide patent, suitable for world-wide promotion, create a mild psychological dependence in its users, give the appearance of answering some expressed medical need, and be free of unmanageable side effects. Do tranquillisers, of any chemical type, fulfil these criteria? The media and government agencies, in the late 1970s, thought that this might be the case. One US Congressional hearing on benzodiazepine misuse opened with the following statement: 'Our message to the American people is clear: if you require a daily dose of Valium to get through each day, you are hooked and you should seek help' (US Senate 1979: 1). One psychiatrist at those hearings testified that Valium works *too well*. The second stage of paranoid uncertainty and condemnation, regarding acceptance of benzodiazepines, was in high gear.

One focal point of concern involved drug promotion activities, which have been important in the use of tranquillisers, especially the benzodiazepines. Promotional statements emphasized stress and tension, but these conditions were not well defined (US House of Representatives 1979; US Senate 1979; Waldron 1977). Even today, there is a general notion in many circles that tranquilliser advertising is misleading or inappropriate. An analysis of ads in a major medical journal over a fourteen-year period showed, however, that the promotion of benzodiazepines for personal problems disappeared after 1973 and is no longer a significant appeal (Gray & Smith 1983). These criticisms of drug promotion, media and journalistic accounts of drug use problems, and professional denunciations are important in affecting and shaping patients' attitudes and societal perceptions about drugs. In addition, subcultural social support networks are involved educationally and politically to alert tranquilliser users to the dangers and problems related to use ('Doctor Caligari' 1978).

There is also the issue of tranquilliser prescribing and use as a form of medicalization (Lennard & Cooperstock 1980). Due to the dominance of biological reductionism in medicine, wherein problematic human behaviour is described solely or ultimately in biological or biochemical terms, personal or social problems are redefined and relabelled as medical conditions. In most western societies health is a supreme value, and the physician is the universal healer. Yet the 'disease' that they are treating is ill-defined, and this may lead to uncertainty and frustration on the part of the physician. The prescribing of tranquillisers represents a solution to the problem of not being able to define and diagnose the disease clearly, in biological terms, and thus not knowing the corresponding treatment, and the problem of feeling uncertain about how to portray expertise to the patient. The lack of quality information about the drugs can further confuse the process of adequately diagnosing and treating the problem (Cooperstock 1974; Lennard 1971; Lennard *et al.* 1970; Waldron 1977). Most information about a drug is available primarily through promotional material provided by the pharmaceutical company, which under a capitalist value foundation has a profit motive. Some drug ads promise to solve problems of health and life in mythical ways. The imagery in some ad campaigns may reproduce an ideology conducive to the social order, the physician's ability to be diagnostically and therapeutically omniscient (Chapman 1979; Goldman & Montagne 1986).

The process of medicalization is also important in the way that it 'mystifies' the diagnosis and treatment of anxiety and related disorders (Lennard *et al.* 1970). The specificity of drug action, based on the 'magic bullet' concept, suggests to health professionals and patients that specific drugs alter specific emotional states and influence specific psychosocial processes. While some might refer to the primary 'effects' of benzodiazepines as being placebogenic in nature, from the user's perspective, especially if impaired socially or psychologically, those 'effects' are real. It should also be realized that many patients can discriminate between biological and behavioural disorders (Shaffer 1987). In this type of situation, the latent functions of drug prescribing and use can dominate, and, instead of managing the illness and reducing symptom states, these other functions come to the fore, including: enhancement of the symbolic power of technology and of the physician's ability to heal, legitimation of long-term illnesses without a cure, closure on the patient–physician interaction, and fulfilment by the physician of the contract or covenant with the patient (Smith 1980). Medicine, then, becomes a moral arbiter, assuming or dictating moral authority in the personal and social areas of life, and the health care system becomes the safety net for the failures of the social services and welfare systems.

The issue of tranquilliser use as social control has also been studied by some investigators (Koumjian 1981; Gabe & Lipshitz-

Phillips 1984). The redefining or relabelling of personal and social problems as medical conditions may legitimize and reinforce existing social relations. Instead of attempting interpersonal or structural changes to reduce the source of stress and anxiety, tranquillisers are prescribed for symptomatic relief. The use of tranquilliser prescribing as a means of social control can generate and maintain the physician's image of power, make patients dependent upon physicians and the health care delivery system, and control or oppress patients by gender or social class.

The diagnosis and treatment of anxiety and nervous disorders has also been greatly influenced by gender ideologies (Cayleff 1988). This influence seems to occur historically and cross-culturally, even with changes in the descriptors and metaphors used to characterize disease aetiologies and symptom states. The common feature of both past and cross-cultural explanations of these types of ailments is the gender of the patients and the behavioural symptoms they exhibit. This, in turn, influences the medical management of these behaviours and societal perceptions of the causes of such conditions. Some have argued that this is represented in the nature of ads and promotional activities for tranquillisers, through which cultural stereotypes are created and engendered (Prather & Fidell 1975). Female patients are viewed as emotional, irrational, and complaining, while male patients are viewed as unemotional, rational, and stoic. And, as a result, will each gender bring their behaviours as patients into greater congruence with the cultural expectations? Some researchers have shown that tranquillisers are used by women for role strain, in attempting to fit into traditional roles, and by men, when conflicts regarding work performance occur (Cooperstock & Lennard 1979).

UNDERSTANDING THE NATURE AND MEANING OF LONG-TERM TRANQUILLISER USE

Culture can impose specific epistemologies and value foundations on knowledge and behaviour. For instance, there are different models of madness (e.g. medical, moral, social, psychoanalytic, and psychedelic), each with its own aetiology of illness, methods of diagnosis, and approaches to treatment (Siegler & Osmond 1974). And in research on and treatment of chemical dependencies, the 'disease' model has become the symbolic substitute for the moral turpitude model, which it replaced (Shaffer 1987). There are also different value foundations which direct drug taking (Veatch 1974;

1977). There is, for example, a therapeutic ethic in western societies, which is a goal-oriented approach to achieving a state of harmony or equilibrium. Tranquilliser use, from the perspective of this ethic, attempts to produce happiness, contentment, accommodation, or adjustment. Other value foundations (e.g. the Wisdom of Nature or the Protestant/Puritan ethic) would oppose the use of tranquillisers, however, but for different reasons. While pharmacological Calvinism may be a dominant belief system, there are certainly valid indications for tranquilliser use; though again, this may be due more to cultural conditioning than to any specific diagnostic criteria in psychiatry (Rosenblatt & Dodson 1981). These value foundations are instrumental in both subcultural and societal reactions to drug use, and they can result in a direct conflict of interest, moral indignation, or presumed humanitarian behaviour (i.e. seeking to change the behaviour of a few to benefit the social whole) (Young 1971).

It appears that benzodiazepines are prescribed for three types of patients: those who present with an immediate problem that is transient in nature, those who are experiencing 'problems of living' and are exhibiting more serious and intense symptom states, and those with acute or chronic somatic diseases who need the tranquilliser to help in dealing with the anxiety and stress of their debilitating illness (Lennard & Cooperstock 1980). In which case does the potential for long-term use exist? One of the most important reasons appears to involve repeat, or refill, prescriptions. In a late 1960s study of long-term repeat prescriptions, a sizeable proportion consisted of those for barbiturates and tranquillisers (Balint *et al.* 1970). Other researchers have noted that psychotropic drugs, especially tranquillisers, represent a good proportion of repeat prescriptions, and that it's a function more of the physician's attitudes than of the patient's condition, for which the physician lacks an appropriate amount of quality information or knowledge (Melville 1980). In addition, repeat prescriptions are viewed by some patients as a sign of their physicians' approval to continue use (Murray 1981).

Some long-term users might not be regular, daily users, but more intermittent users, basing use on a specific situation or circumstance (Caplan *et al.* 1985; Williams 1983; Williams *et al.* 1982). For many patients, Valium is taken in anticipation of anxiety, instead of due to its actual occurrence (Caplan *et al.* 1985). For some patients, their physicians' prescribing behaviours might lead to long-term use. And for a small proportion of patients, long-term use represents significant symptom states, resulting from a psychological condition (e.g. anxiety, depression, or whatever) that has not been adequately managed or from a state of chemical dependency. Many users of drugs engage in a self-assessment of efficacy, the results of which have a profound impact on decisions to continue or to cease use (Arluke 1980). Many users also self-adjust their tranquilliser dose based upon the effects they are experiencing (Lennard & Cooperstock 1980). These decisions and behaviours are, for the most part, directed by a personal perception of the value and function of tranquillisers and their effects. These perceptions are grounded in the cultural belief system that gives meaning to the use of these drugs. The degree or type of tranquilliser use may vary then from culture to culture, or as the same culture defines or redefines the nature and meaning of the drug-taking experience (Montagne 1988a).

With the advent of the 1990s, technological developments and societal changes appear to be accelerating, especially in many developing countries, due to the dominant influence of western societies. Yet many countries are experiencing civil wars and terrorist activities by insurgency groups, and cultural transformations due to 'westernizing' activities. A number of studies have focused on acculturation, urbanization, and industrialization, and they have shown that social change, and perhaps an inability to adapt to such, can have significant disruptive effects on a culture (Kiev 1964). Significant social change may limit or prevent the secure pursuit of familiar life goals, reduce the importance of older values and rituals, and it can imply confusion or difficulty in the understanding and acceptance of the newer values and rituals. To the extent that individuals, communities, or whole societies can adopt, or adapt to, these changes, different degrees of psychopathology can be experienced, many of the severe forms requiring an intervention by an accepted healer. But in most instances, traditional forms of healing are viewed as a poor choice or lesser alternative, since western technology has given the tranquillisers to the world (Busnello 1980; Woods *et al.* 1987).

Recall that meprobamate and the benzodiazepines, when originally introduced into western societies, were viewed as drugs for the 'jitters of civilization'. Tranquilliser use and misuse have been increasing in many developing countries, especially in African and Middle Eastern societies (Edwards & Arif 1980). Western pharmaceuticals, especially psychotherapeutic agents, are readily available in developing countries in open markets and from travelling salesmen (Bledsoe & Goubaud 1985). These medicines are highly prized, and they are also very profitable items for sale or barter. In essence, given the pressures of cultural change and a lack of resources, pharmaceuticals are the least expensive, most accessible, and easiest to use form of health care technology that can be provided. In addition, they are viewed as pure and potent, all but assuring their efficacy in the minds of the indigenous population (WHO 1981). Can something be done to limit or prevent a similar phenomenon with tranquilliser use as has occurred in western societies? It is perhaps, as Huxley (1954: 64) has noted, that 'the need for frequent chemical vacations from intolerable selfhood and repulsive surroundings will undoubtedly remain'.

Cultural beliefs and structures help define and guide a society's authorized or approved uses of a particular drug, as well as the channels of distribution for use. These channels of distribution and the uses of drugs may be specified by a codified law or other decree, and are known as formal social controls, or they may be suggested by custom or practice, and are known as informal social controls. These controls can vary across cultures and within cultures, and at different periods in time. Traditional beliefs about disease and treatment (e.g. the classic 'hot' and 'cold' classification of illness) are used by many cultures in developing countries to reinterpret the function of many western medicines that are made available to them (Bledsoe & Goubaud 1985). Value is placed on a particular drug, and use is approved through social sanctions (for whom and why), and directed through rituals (when, where, and how to use), and this is based primarily upon the nature of the cultural organization (e.g. kinship groups, political integration and hierarchy) and its belief systems.

There really is no consensus within the medical community, and certainly not in most societies, on how to treat social and emotional ills. And no society or culture has developed well-defined rituals and social sanctions to direct and control the prescribing and use of tranquillisers (Zinberg 1984; Zinberg & Harding 1982). There appears to be a cultural lag in most societies, in which technology advances well ahead of that society's ability to adapt to and appropriately use the advance (Smith 1985), and also a value lag with technology evolving more rapidly than the development or use of value foundations to help deal with these changes (Montagne 1988b). Our ability in the future to limit or prevent inappropriate long-term tranquilliser use will depend upon the development and employment of these types of social sanctions and rituals.

REFERENCES

Arluke, A. (1980) 'Judging drugs: patients' conceptions of therapeutic efficacy in the treatment of arthritis', *Human Organization* 39: 84–8.

Balint, M., Hunt, J., Joyce, D., Marinker, M., & Woodcock, J. (1970) *Treatment or Diagnosis: A Study of Repeat Prescriptions in General Practice*, London: Tavistock.

Becker, H. S. (1967) 'History, culture, and subjective experience: an explanation for the social bases of drug-induced experiences', *Journal of Health and Social Behaviour* 8: 163–86.

Bledsoe, C. H. & Goubaud, M. F. (1985) 'The reinterpretation of Western pharmaceuticals among the Mende of Sierra Leone', *Social Science and Medicine* 21: 275–82.

Busnello, E. D. (1980) 'Psychosocial aspects of mental health care in developing countries – the role of the benzodiazepines', in R. G. Priest, U. V. Filho, R. Amrein, & M. Skreta (eds) *Benzodiazepines: Today and Tomorrow*, Baltimore, MD: University Park Press.

Caplan, R. D., Andrews, F. M., Conway, T. L., Abbey, A., Abramis, D. J., & French, J. R. P. (1985) 'Social effects of diazepam use: a longitudinal field study', *Social Science and Medicine* 21: 887–98.

Cayleff, S. E. (1988) 'Prisoners of their own feebleness: women, nerves and Western medicine – a historical overview', *Social Science and Medicine* 26: 1199–208.

Chapman, S. (1979) 'Advertising and psychotropic drugs: the place of myth in ideological reproduction', *Social Science and Medicine* 13A: 751–64.

Cohen, S. (1983) 'Current attitudes about the benzodiazepines: trial by media', *Journal of Psychoactive Drugs* 15: 109–13.

Cooperstock, R. (ed.) (1974) *Social Aspects of the Medical Use of Psychotropic Drugs*, Toronto: Addiction Research Foundation.

Cooperstock, R. & Lennard, H. L. (1979) 'Some social meanings of tranquilizer use', *Sociology of Health and Illness* 1: 331–47.

DeRios, M. D. (1976) *The Wilderness of Mind: Sacred Plants in Cross-Cultural Perspective*, Beverly Hills, CA: Sage Publications.

DeRios, M. D. & Smith, D. E. (1977a) 'The function of drug rituals in human society: continuities and changes', *Journal of Psychedelic Drugs* 9: 269–75.

DeRios, M. D. & Smith, D. E. (1977b) 'Drug use and abuse in cross-cultural perspective', *Human Organization* 36: 14–21.

'Doctor Caligari' (1978) *Psychiatric Drugs*, revised edition, San Francisco: Network Against Psychiatric Assault.

Du Toit, B. M. (ed.) (1977) *Drugs, Rituals and Altered States of Consciousness*, Rotterdam: A. A. Balkema.

Edwards, G. & Arif, A. (1980) *Drug Problems in the Sociocultural Context: A Basis for Policies and Programme Planning*, Public Health Paper No. 73, Geneva: World Health Organisation.

Everett, M. W., Waddell, J. O., & Heath, D. B. (eds) (1976) *Cross-Cultural Approaches to the Study of Alcohol*, The Hague: Mouton.

Gabe, J. & Lipshitz-Phillips, S. (1982) 'Evil necessity? The meaning of benzodiazepine use for women patients from one general practice', *Sociology of Health and Illness* 4: 201–9.

Gabe, J. & Lipshitz-Phillips, S. (1984) 'Tranquillisers as social control?' *Sociological Review* 32: 524–46.
Gabe, J. & Thorogood, N. (1986) 'Tranquillisers as a resource', in J. Gabe & P. Williams (eds) *Tranquillisers: Social, Psychological and Clinical Perspectives*, London: Tavistock.
Gabe, J. & Williams, P. (eds) (1986) *Tranquillisers: Social, Psychological and Clinical Perspectives*, London: Tavistock.
Geertz, C. (1973) *The Interpretation of Cultures*, New York: Basic Books.
Goldman, R. & Montagne, M. (1986) 'Marketing mind mechanics: decoding antidepressant drug advertising', *Social Science and Medicine* 22: 1047–58.
Gordon, B. (1979) *I'm Dancing As Fast As I Can*, New York: Harper & Row.
Gray, R. & Smith, M. C. (1983) 'Is criticism of tranquilizer advertising justified?', *Medical Marketing and Media* 18: 50–9.
Gusfield, J. R. (1981) *The Culture of Public Problems: Drinking-Driving and the Symbolic Order*, Chicago: University of Chicago Press.
Helman, C. G. (1981) '"Tonic", "fuel", and "food": social and symbolic aspects of the long-term use of psychotropic drugs', *Social Science and Medicine* 15B: 521–33.
Holden, A. (1982) *Prince Valium*, New York: Stein & Day.
Hughes, R. & Brewin, R. (1979) *The Tranquilizing of America: Pill Popping and the American Way of Life*, New York: Harcourt Brace Jovanovich.
Huxley, A. (1954) *The Doors of Perception*, New York: Harper & Row.
Kaplan, D. & Manners, R. A. (1972) *Culture Theory*, Englewood Cliffs, NJ: Prentice-Hall.
Kiev, A. (ed.) (1964) *Magic, Faith, and Healing*, New York: The Free Press.
Kilwein, J. H. (1983) 'Valium and values', *American Pharmacy* NS23: 51–7.
Klerman, G. (1970) 'Drugs and social values', *International Journal of the Addictions* 5: 313–19.
Klerman, G. L. (1974) 'Psychotropic drugs as therapeutic agents', *Hastings Center Studies* 2: 81–93.
Koumjian, K. (1981) 'The use of Valium as a form of social control', *Social Science and Medicine* 15E: 245–9.
Lennard, H. L. (1971) *Mystification and Drug Misuse*, San Francisco: Jossey-Bass.
Lennard, H. L. & Cooperstock, R. (1980) 'The social context and functions of tranquilliser prescribing', in R. Mapes (ed.) *Prescribing Practice and Drug Usage*, London: Croom Helm.
Lennard, H. L., Bernstein, A., Epstein, L. J., & Ransom, D. C. (1970) 'Hazards implicit in prescribing psychoactive drugs', *Science* 169: 438–41.
Lévi-Strauss, C. (1963) *Structural Anthropology*, New York: Basic Books.
Lin, K. M. & Poland, R. E. (1986) 'Ethnicity and psychopharmacology', *Culture, Medicine and Psychiatry* 10: 151–65.
Low, S. M. (1985) 'Culturally interpreted symbols or culture-bound syndromes: a cross-cultural review of nerves', *Social Science and Medicine* 21: 187–96.

MacAndrew, C. & Edgerton, R. B. (1969) *Drunken Comportment: A Social Explanation*, Chicago: Aldine.

McCarthy, R. G. (ed.) (1959) *Drinking and Intoxication*, Glencoe, IL: Free Press.

Manheimer, D., Davidson, S., Balter, M., Mellinger, G., Cisin, I., & Parry, H. (1973) 'Popular attitudes and beliefs about tranquilizers', *American Journal of Psychiatry* 130: 1246–53.

Melville, A. (1980) 'Reducing whose anxiety? A study of the relationship between repeat prescribing of minor tranquillisers and doctors' attitudes', in R. Mapes (ed.) *Prescribing Practice and Drug Usage*, London: Croom Helm.

Melville, A. & Johnson, C. (1982) *Cured to Death: The Effects of Prescription Drugs*, New York: Stein & Day.

Montagne, M. (1988a) 'The metaphorical nature of drugs and drug taking', *Social Science and Medicine* 26: 417–24.

Montagne, M. (ed.) (1988b) 'Philosophies of drug giving and drug taking', *Journal of Drug Issues* 18: 139–148.

Morgan, J. P. (1983) 'Cultural and medical attitudes toward benzodiazepines: conflicting metaphors', *Journal of Psychoactive Drugs* 15: 115–20.

Murray, J. (1981) 'Long-term psychotropic drug taking and the process of withdrawal', *Psychological Medicine* 11: 853–8.

Nations, M. K., Camino, L. A., & Walker, F. B. (1988) '"Nerves": folk idiom for anxiety and depression?', *Social Science and Medicine* 26: 1245–59.

Pekkanen, J. (1973) *The American Connection: Profiteering and Politicking in the 'Ethical' Drug Industry*, Chicago: Follett.

Pellegrino, E. D. (1976) 'Prescribing and drug ingestion, symbols and substances', *Drug Intelligence and Clinical Pharmacy* 10: 624–30.

Pelto, P. J. & Pelto, G. H. (1978) *Anthropological Research: The Structure of Inquiry*, 2nd edition, Cambridge: Cambridge University Press.

Pittman, D. J. & Snyder, C. R. (eds) (1962) *Society, Culture and Drinking Patterns*, New York: Wiley.

Prather, J. E. (1979) 'The mystique of minor tranquilizers', paper given at the Alcoholism and Drug Abuse Institute, University of Washington, Seattle, 25 January.

Prather, J. & Fidell, L. S. (1975) 'Sex differences in the content and style of medical advertisements', *Social Science and Medicine* 9: 23–6.

Public Citizen Health Research Group (1982) *Stopping Valium*, New York: Pantheon.

Radcliffe-Brown, A. R. (1952) *Structure and Function in Primitive Society*, New York: The Free Press.

Rhodes, L. A. (1984) '"This will clear your mind": the use of metaphors for medication in psychiatric settings', *Culture, Medicine and Psychiatry* 8: 49–70.

Rosenblatt, S. & Dodson, R. (1981) *Beyond Valium: The Brave New World of Psychochemistry*, New York: Putnam.

Rubin, V. (ed.) (1975) *Cannabis and Culture*, The Hague: Mouton.

Seidenberg, R. (1976) 'Advertising and drug acculturation', in R. H. Coombs, L. J. Fry, & P. G. Lewis (eds) *Socialization in Drug Abuse*, Cambridge, MA: Schenkman Publishing.

Shaffer, H. J. (1987) 'The epistemology of "addictive disease": the Lincoln–Douglas debate', *Journal of Substance Abuse Treatment* 4: 103–13.
Siegler, M. & Osmond, H. (1974) *Models of Madness, Models of Medicine*, New York: Macmillan.
Smith, M. C. (1980) 'The relationship between pharmacy and medicine', in R. Mapes (ed.) *Prescribing Practice and Drug Usage*, London: Croom Helm.
Smith, M. C. (1985) *Small Comfort: A History of the Minor Tranquilizers*, New York: Praeger.
Strug, D. L., Priyadarsini, S., & Hyman, M. M. (eds) (1986) *Alcohol Interventions: Historical and Sociocultural Approaches*, New York: Haworth.
Szasz, T. (1974) *Ceremonial Chemistry: The Ritual Persecution of Drugs, Addicts, and Pushers*, New York: Doubleday.
US House of Representatives, Select Committee on Narcotics Abuse and Control (1979) *Women's Dependency on Prescription Drugs*, Washington, DC: Government Printing Office.
US Senate, Committee on Labor and Human Resources (1979) *Use and Misuse of Benzodiazepines*, Washington, DC: Government Printing Office.
Veatch, R. M. (1974) 'Drugs and competing drug ethics', *Hastings Center Studies* 2: 68–80.
Veatch, R. M. (1977) 'Value foundations for drug use', *Journal of Drug Issues* 7: 253–62.
Waldron, I. (1977) 'Increased prescribing of Valium, Librium, and other drugs, an example of the influence of economic and social factors on the practice of medicine', *International Journal of Health Services* 7: 37–62.
Wallace, A. F. C. (1959) 'Cultural determinants of response to hallucinatory experience', *Archives of General Psychiatry* 1: 58–69.
Williams, P. (1983) 'Factors influencing the duration of treatment with psychotropic drugs in general practice: a survival analysis approach', *Psychological Medicine* 13: 623–33.
Williams, P., Murray, J., & Clare, A. W. (1982) 'A longitudinal study of psychotropic drug prescriptions', *Psychological Medicine* 12: 201–6.
Woods, J. H., Katz, J. L., & Winger, G. (1987) 'Abuse liability of benzodiazepines', *Pharmacological Reviews* 39: 251–419.
World Health Organisation (1981) *Assessment of Public Health and Social Problems Associated with the Use of Psychotropic Drugs*, Technical Report Series No. 656, Geneva: World Health Organisation.
Young, J. (1971) *The Drugtakers: The Social Meaning of Drug Use*, London: Paladin.
Zinberg, N. E. (1984) *Drug, Set and Setting: The Basis for Controlled Intoxicant Use*, New Haven, CT: Yale University Press.
Zinberg, N. E. & Harding, W. M. (eds) (1982) *Control Over Intoxicant Use*, New York: Human Sciences Press.

4 Long-term tranquilliser use: the contribution of epidemiology

Paul Williams and Cesario Bellantuono

INTRODUCTION

Drugs classed as tranquillisers are subdivided into major tranquillisers or antipsychotics, used in the management of psychosis, and minor tranquillisers, used primarily in the management of anxiety. We shall not be concerned at all in this chapter with major tranquillisers, and the term 'tranquilliser' will be taken to refer only to minor tranquillisers. At the present time, the most frequently prescribed minor tranquillisers in Britain and other industrialized countries are the benzodiazepines, a class of compound which includes diazepam, lorazepam, and alprazolam.

The relevance of epidemiology to the study of tranquilliser use has been recognized for some time: indeed, a major international symposium on this topic took place some eight years ago (Tognoni *et al.* 1981), although it did not focus specifically on long-term use, as does the present book.

THE NATURE OF EPIDEMIOLOGICAL ENQUIRY

The essential characteristic of epidemiology is that it is concerned with the occurrence, distribution, and determinants of health and disease in human groups or populations. As Morris described it,

> epidemiology may be contrasted with the clinical observation of patients or the controlled experiment in the laboratory . . . [epidemiology is] the study of the health and disease of populations and groups in relation to their environment and ways of living . . . it is the basic science of preventive and community medicine and is being applied to a variety of problems in health services as well as health.
>
> (Morris 1975: 3)

This relatively broad definition thus encompasses the application of epidemiological methods to a situation in which a health-related behaviour (such as long-term tranquilliser use) rather than a disease is studied, and in which the group of interest may consist in patients rather than the population as a whole.

Epidemiology is primarily a quantitative discipline. Often, an epidemiological investigation results in the specification – in statistical or mathematical terms – of a model to describe the relationship between a set of independent variables, or predictors, and a dependent variable (e.g. the occurrence of disease, long-term tranquilliser use). In so doing, one aim is to simplify – to produce as parsimonious a model as possible. Thus, relatively large quantities of data may be examined in order to extract general relationships between a few variables, a process in which a great deal of detail is inevitably lost. As Box (1979) has observed, 'all models are wrong, but some are useful'. The epidemiological method therefore stands in contrast to, and complements, those social science disciplines which are concerned with close and detailed interpretation of data.

Within epidemiology, a great deal of attention is paid to the definition of the dependent variable ('case definition'). In the present context, this would seem to require some threshold to distinguish between long- as opposed to short-term tranquilliser use. This is problematic, since, as Gabe and Williams (1986) have pointed out, becoming a long-term user of tranquillisers is a process and not simply a transition from one state to another. Even so, the reality is that thresholds do sometimes have to be defined for practical purposes, or for clinical or administrative reasons (Williams *et al.* 1980).

It should also be borne in mind that an accurate understanding of psychosocial epidemiology depends on realizing that it is characterized by 'context-dependent findings, not by pervasive laws' (Albrecht & Jackson 1985). There are also opportunities for investigators' preconceptions and biases to be reflected in their results. As Thunhurst (1984) has observed, 'statistical information is not a value-free instrument which somehow speaks for itself: it is socially constructed. Choice of data scrutinised, interpretation of information produced and even the technological procedures employed necessarily reflect the ideological perspective of the analyst'. Important aspects of psychosocial epidemiology, therefore, are the need for replication and the attempt to demonstrate convergent validity.

The major tools of epidemiological investigation are the cross-sectional survey, the longitudinal or cohort study, and the case-control study. In cross-sectional surveys, a population or a sample is investigated once only, so that such a survey provides information about the state of affairs at any given time. Such surveys have a major drawback in the present context, since categorizing a respondent as a long-term user must be done on the basis of retrospective recall, which is subject to a variety of biases. In contrast, a longitudinal study or cohort study provides information over several time points, allowing for inferences about duration, outcome, and prognostic factors. In a case-control study, a group defined by the presence of some relevant condition ('cases') is compared with a group without the condition ('controls') with respect to various characteristics of interest. Examples of each of these types of study will be used in the course of this chapter.

THE USES OF EPIDEMIOLOGY

In 1957, Jeremy Morris published *The Uses of Epidemiology*. In this book, which has since become a classic, he set out what in his view were the 'uses' to which epidemiological enquiry could be put.

Table 4.1 The uses of epidemiology and their relevance to long-term tranquilliser use

for community diagnosis	the extent of long-term tranquilliser use
for completing the clinical picture; for delineating new syndromes	describing long-term tranquilliser users
for historical study	investigation of trends in long-term tranquilliser use
for estimating the individual risks of acquiring disease; for establishing the causes of illness	risk factors for long-term use
for studying the workings of the health service	public health aspects of long-term tranquilliser use

Even though these were first put forward some thirty years ago and were set primarily in the context of cardiovascular disease, they are relevant to the present theme. The 'uses of epidemiology', as set out by Morris in the third edition of his book (1975), are community diagnosis; historical study; completing the clinical picture of disease; the delineation of new syndromes; estimating the individual risks of acquiring disease; establishing the causes of illness; and studying the workings of the health service.

Morris's seven 'uses of epidemiology' provide a framework from within which to explore the contribution of epidemiological enquiry to understanding and managing long-term tranquilliser use. Table 4.1 shows how the seven uses can be mapped to five categories relevant to the present theme: each of these categories will be discussed in turn.

THE EXTENT OF LONG-TERM TRANQUILLISER USE

Under the rubric 'community diagnosis', Morris wrote 'using epidemiological methods we can describe and try to diagnose the condition of the people. Indices are produced of health and well-being and the character and dimension of problems are charted' (Morris 1975: 27).

In the present context, charting the dimension of the problem means that information must be gathered as to the extent of long-term tranquilliser use. Table 4.2 shows studies which have attempted to do this, using a threshold for 'long-term' of around one year. The results are consistent in suggesting that 2–3 per cent of the UK population are long-term consumers of tranquillisers, that is, between one and one-and-a-half million persons. It can be seen from the results of Balter *et al.*'s (1984) community surveys that there is a great deal of between-country variation in the extent of long-term use. Belgium and France have very high rates, followed by Spain, while Sweden has a rate much lower than the remaining European countries.

DESCRIBING LONG-TERM TRANQUILLISER USERS

While it is important to know that some 2–3 per cent of the population are long-term users of tranquillisers, this is only the beginning. Who are the long-term users? In what way, if any, are they ill? What do they think of their treatment?

While studies of long-term users based on patients attending

Table 4.2 The extent of long-term tranquilliser use

		United Kingdom	
Stoll & Lader (1984)	community survey	'use of tranquillisers for one year or more'	1.5% of men
Balter *et al.* (1984)	community survey	'regular use of anti-anxiety/ sedative drugs for 12 months or more'	3.1% of popn.
Salinsky & Dore (1987)	prescribing audit, GP	'taking benzodiazepines regularly during the day for more than a year'	1.6% of registered patients
Rodrigo *et al.* (1988)	prescribing audit, GP	'prescription of benzodiazepines for one year or more'	2.2% of registered patients
		USA	
Mellinger & Balter (1981)	community survey, USA	'use of anti-anxiety agents for 12 months or more'	1.6% of popn.
Balter *et al.* (1984)	community survey, USA	'regular use of anti-anxiety/ sedative drugs for 12 months or more'	1.8% of popn.
		Europe	
Balter *et al.* (1984)	community survey	'regular use of anti-anxiety/ sedative drugs for 12 months or more'	
		Belgium	5.8%
		Denmark	1.3%
		France	5.0%
		Germany	1.6%
		Italy	1.6%
		Netherlands	1.7%
		Spain	3.8%
		Sweden	0.5%
		Switzerland	1.2% of popn.

specialist clinics may be useful, it is apparent that the full picture can be obtained only if the net is cast wider. As Morris noted, the epidemiological approach is important for completing the clinical picture:

> clinicians' experience of the chronic diseases is likely to be incomplete. In the less common conditions numbers may be too few,

> with attendant troubles of chance variation. But even when numbers are large his experience may be peculiar and his patients unrepresentative, i.e. the picture may be biased. Such limitations apply also to the work of a hospital or any other clinical facility. The epidemiologist, concerned with the total of defined cases in a defined population and not merely with patients who present in particular hospitals, clinics or practices, can help to provide a fuller picture than is obtainable in any or all of these. This fuller picture may prove to be a different one. The epidemiological method thus is helping to complete the clinical picture.
>
> (Morris 1975: 121)

There is general agreement from cross-sectional studies that long-term tranquilliser users are predominantly middle-aged and elderly women (Woodcock 1970; Parish 1971; Cooperstock 1976, 1978; Mellinger *et al.* 1984; Rodrigo *et al.* 1988; Catalan *et al.* 1988). Furthermore, long-term users of benzodiazepines and other tranquillisers report high levels of emotional distress. Mellinger *et al.* (1984) reported on sixty-eight respondents in a community survey who reported regular (daily for one year or more) use of anxiolytics. They found that half of these long-term users had high scores on their questionnaire measure of emotional distress, the Typology of Psychic Distress (PSYDIS – Mellinger *et al.* 1983), as compared with 20 per cent of the non-users. They noted, however, that in this respect 'the long-term users did not differ much from the other users', 45 per cent of whom were also high scorers.

In one study of long-term benzodiazepine users in a South London general practice, Rodrigo *et al.* (1988) found that twenty-four (38 per cent) of an interview sample of sixty-four patients were rated by psychiatrists as cases on the Standardised Psychiatric Interview (SPI – Goldberg *et al.* 1970), a semi-structured interview designed to quantify psychiatric disorder in non-psychiatric settings. While in absolute terms this is a substantial level of psychiatric morbidity, it is not very different from that which would be found in an unselected series of general practice attenders. For example, Marks *et al.* (1979) obtained a psychiatric case rate of 39 per cent in their study of patients attending ninety-one general practitioners in Manchester, and Boardman (1987) recorded a level of 43 per cent in eighteen south London general practices, in both cases using the Standardised Psychiatric Interview as the case criterion.

However, this seeming similarity in the extent of psychiatric disorder among long-term users and others may well be artefactual, since, in one of the few case-control studies in this area of research, Catalan *et al.* (1988) compared seventy long-term tranquilliser users drawn from an Oxfordshire health centre with seventy age and sex matched controls. Using the Present State Examination (PSE – Wing *et al.* 1974), they found that 43 per cent and 8 per cent of the long-term users and controls respectively were rated as cases.

In Rodrigo *et al.*'s (1988) study, the interviewing psychiatrists also assigned an ICD diagnosis to the twenty-four patients classified as cases. Eighteen (75 per cent of the cases, or 28 per cent of the whole sample) were classified under the rubric neurotic depression (ICD 300.4), none was assigned a diagnosis related to anxiety. Similarly, Catalan *et al.*'s (1988) case-control study found that neurotic depression was the commonest PSE diagnosis among the seventy long-term tranquilliser users that they studied.

There is other evidence to the effect that the use of tranquillisers is widespread for the treatment of depression in the community. For example, Weissman and Klerman (1977) studied 150 depressed women who had responded to tricyclic antidepressants and who had received eight months of maintenance treatment as part of a controlled clinical trial. When followed up one and four years after the maintenance treatment had ended, they were more likely to have received a minor tranquilliser than an antidepressant when they sought medical help. Similar findings emerged from a subsequent community survey, in which Weissman and her colleagues (1981) found that episodes of major depressive disorder in the community were more likely to be treated with tranquillisers than antidepressants.

This finding of an association between long-term benzodiazepine use and depression is related to Morris's concept of 'delineation of new syndromes'. As he noted, 'analysis may show that . . . the apparently unrelated may be linked because they are similarly distributed' (Morris 1975: 108).

The association between long-term tranquilliser use and physical illness may well be another example of this. *De novo* prescription of benzodiazepines and other tranquillisers frequently occurs in response to physical rather than psychological disorder (Solow 1975; Williams 1978), and a similar association has been found to occur in the context of long-term use. For example, Murray and her colleagues (1982) interviewed twenty-two patients who had been prescribed psychotropic drugs continuously for six months or more. They found that 'chronic physical complaints were common in the sample (diverticulitis, arthritis, hypertension, migraine) and 13 people were long-term users of non-psychotropic prescribed drugs'. Furthermore, in a questionnaire study of present and past long-term tranquilliser users (Murray 1981), only six out of 261 respondents were found to have no disability or physical symptoms as scored on the Belloc scale (Belloc *et al.* 1971). Mellinger *et al.* (1984), in a study of sixty-eight long-term consumers of anxiolytics, found that physical health distinguished between long-term users and other users more strongly than did any other factor they studied (including emotional distress). They noted that 'at least one-third of the long-term users reported four or more health problems – a rate twice that found among the other anxiolytic users and seven times that of the non users'. These differences persisted when age was controlled for, and they observed further that much of the difference between the long-term users and the others could be accounted for by cardiovascular disorders and arthritis.

Rodrigo *et al.*'s (1988) study in south London confirmed Mellinger *et al.*'s findings, in that the patients showed evidence of substantial physical morbidity. For example, twenty-seven (42 per cent) had consulted their GP during the previous month for a physical illness (other than coughs, colds, and influenza), and twenty-two (34 per cent) had attended medical or surgical out-patient clinics in the previous year. Catalan *et al.*'s (1988) case-control study also confirmed the relationship between long-term tranquilliser use and physical illness: 49 per cent of the index patients as compared with 27 per cent of the controls had been given general hospital out-patient appointments during the previous year.

What do long-term users of benzodiazepines think about their drugs? Surprisingly, it is only recently that researchers have begun to concern themselves with this issue. Epidemiological approaches include postal survey (Murray 1981), structured interviews and questionnaires (King *et al.* 1990), while sociological and anthropological studies (not reviewed in detail here – see Chapters 3 and 4) have been conducted using in-depth semi-structured interviews (Helman 1981; Gabe & Lipshitz-Phillips 1982, 1984; Gabe & Thorogood 1986) and group discussion techniques (Cooperstock & Lennard 1979).

Do long-term users regard their drugs as helpful? It appears that in a general sense, most do (Murray 1981; King *et al.* 1990). An important finding has been that when asked to specify the ways in which benzodiazepines and other tranquillisers are helpful, long-term users frequently mention aspects of social functioning and performance. Table 4.3 shows the activities for which respondents expressed a need for drugs, as reported in Murray's (1981) questionnaire survey of long-term psychotropic drug consumers and in King *et al.*'s (1990) interview study of long-term benzodiazepine consumers in a south London general practice. There are clearly marked differences between the two studies (which may well be accounted for by the nature of the samples and the methods used) but, taken together, they testify to the extent to which long-term users regard benzodiazepines and other psychotropic drugs as having a social as well as a purely clinical function. Sociological and anthropological studies have yielded similar results (Cooperstock & Lennard 1979; Helman 1981).

Table 4.3 Activities for which respondents expressed a need for tranquillisers

	current long-term users of psychotropic drugs (Murray 1981) n=183		*current long-term users of benzodiazepines (King et al. 1990)* n=68	
	n	%	n	%
travelling	81	(44)	7	(11)
shopping	78	(43)	4	(6)
mixing with people	75	(41)	7	(11)
running the home	65	(36)	8	(13)
work	61	(33)	16	(25)
family problems	61	(33)	1	(2)
marriage	40	(22)	3	(5)
money matters	20	(11)	2	(3)
housing problems	13	(7)	1	(2)

However, there is also evidence of considerable ambivalence: for example, 87 per cent of respondents in Murray's (1981) survey agreed with the statement 'I don't like taking these tablets but I could not manage without them' (further evidence of ambivalence has emerged from Gabe's studies – see Chapter 2).

Findings such as these raise the issue of dependence on benzodiazepines and other tranquillisers. Dependence is usually categorized as psychological or physical: psychological dependence is 'a condition in which a drug produces a feeling of satisfaction and a psychic drive that require periodic or continuous administration of the drug to produce pleasure or to avoid discomfort' (WHO 1974), whereas physical dependence can be defined as 'the development of an altered physiological state which requires continued administration of a drug to prevent the appearance of . . . [an] abstinence syndrome' (WHO 1974).

It is difficult to assemble an operational definition of psychological dependence and it would be even more problematic to develop a definitive instrument to measure it. However, the material assembled in Table 4.4 shows that substantial proportions of long-term tranquilliser users regard themselves as reliant on their tranquillisers, others refuse to consider withdrawal, while yet others enter a withdrawal regime and then default.

The existence of a withdrawal syndrome, the essential character-

Table 4.4 Findings related to dependence on tranquillisers

Of long-term tranquilliser users in a postal survey conducted by Murray (1981):		
33%	'would not be able to manage at all' without tranquillisers;	
40%	believed that they would 'always need to take the drugs'.	
Of long-term benzodiazepine users in general practice interviewed by King *et al*. (1990):		
40%	could think of no alternatives to benzodiazepines;	
18%	believed they 'could not be without' benzodiazepines.	
5% of	long-term tranquilliser users seen in general practice by Hopkins *et al*. (1982) and offered a withdrawal regime	refused to contemplate withdrawal
53% of	long-term tranquilliser users seen in GP-based psychiatric clinics by Tyrer *et al*. (1983) and offered a withdrawal regime	
45% of	long-term tranquilliser users entered into an acute withdrawal programme by Tyrer *et al*. (1981)	defaulted
17% of	long-term tranquilliser users entered into a four-week withdrawal programme by Hopkins *et al*. (1982)	
12% of	long-term tranquilliser users entered into a three-month withdrawal programme by Tyrer *et al*. (1983)	

istic of physical dependence, in response to the discontinuation of benzodiazepine tranquillisers is now well established, and the major clinical characteristics are shown in Table 4.5. However, there have been no large-scale epidemiological studies of this phenomenon, and all the evidence is derived from small-scale studies in selected samples. The occurrence of a withdrawal syndrome is known to be related to dosage and duration of treatment and to the method of withdrawal. Petursson and Lader (1984) estimated that after six months' continuous treatment with benzodiazepines at clinical doses, some 5–10 per cent of patients would exhibit a withdrawal syndrome after discontinuation of treatment; they also estimated that after two to four years' treatment the proportion would be 25–45 per cent, rising to 75 per cent after some six to eight years of continuous treatment.

Table 4.5 Frequency of benzodiazepine withdrawal phenomena reported in six studies (adapted from Schopf 1983)

Percentage of patients withdrawn from benzos. who experienced the symptoms	*Non-specific symptoms*	*Perceptual changes*	*Major phenomena*
>50%	sleep disturbance anxiety		
30–50%	irritability dysphoria muscle pains headache tremor nausea	hypersensitivity to noise	
10–30%	blurred vision	paraesthesia hypersensitivity to light, smell or touch kinaesthetic disturbance macropsia, micropsia depersonalization	
<10%		hyposensitivity to taste and smell	paranoid phenomena convulsions

INVESTIGATION OF TRENDS IN LONG-TERM TRANQUILLISER USE

Morris drew attention to the importance of epidemiological enquiry in the investigation of time trends as follows: 'historical statements in medicine are epidemiological (or ought to be); they relate to the frequency of events among populations at different points in time' (Morris 1975: 4).

The most well-known and frequently commented upon secular trend in tranquilliser use consists in the large and regular increases in the number of prescriptions for minor tranquillisers that occurred in many countries during the late 1960s and early 1970s. Subsequently there has been a levelling off and more recently a decrease in the numbers of prescriptions written for such drugs (Marks 1983a).

However, these data are not epidemiological, since they are not related to any particular population at risk. For example, six prescriptions could mean one prescription for each of six people, or six prescriptions for one person. Thus, the significance of trends in prescribing for understanding patterns of long-term use are unclear, since increases in prescribing could reflect an increase in the number of consumers as a whole, an increase in the number of prescriptions per consumer (whether due to increasing long-term use or to decreasing amounts of drug per prescription), an increase in the amount of drugs prescribed but not consumed, or any combination of these factors.

In order to investigate this, Williams (1983a) compared population- and general practice-based surveys of the extent of psychotropic drug consumption (of which tranquillisers constitute the bulk). Table 4.6 suggests that the increases in prescribing that occurred in the late 1960s and early 1970s were accompanied by an increase in the proportion of the population who received a prescription for a psychotropic drug. However, comparison of three population surveys of consumption of psychotropic drugs indicates that there was no comparable increase in the proportion of the population who reported consuming such drugs (these comparisons are predicated on the assumption that these surveys can be compared – see Murray *et al.* 1981 and Williams 1983a for evidence to support this assumption). Williams (1983a) collated evidence to indicate that the most likely explanation was a decrease in compliance and *an increase over time in long-term use*, an interpretation supported by Marks's (1983b) demonstration of substantial increases

Table 4.6 Surveys of psychotropic prescription and consumption

	n, place, year	*rate (%)*
One-year prevalence of prescribing:		
Parish (1971)	13259 Birmingham 1969	12.6%
Skegg *et al*. (1977)	36280 Oxfordshire 1974	19.3%
Two-week prevalence of consumption:		
Dunnell & Cartwright (1972)	1412 England 1969	11.0%
Murray *et al*. (1981)	5833 West London 1977	10.9%
Anderson (1980)	836 England 1977	12.0%

in the extent to which minor tranquillisers are prescribed on an 'unseen repeat' basis.

A similar explanation was put forward to account for increases in tranquilliser prescribing in Italy (Williams *et al*. 1986), based on data taken from Balter *et al*.'s (1974, 1984) population surveys. In each of these surveys (conducted in 1971 and 1981), a representative sample of Italian respondents was interviewed and asked whether (s)he had used tranquillisers or sedatives during the previous year. The one-year prevalence rates of tranquilliser consumption are shown in Table 4.7a. It is clear that there has been no appreciable increase in the prevalence of self-reported consumption during the ten-year period. Balter and his colleagues also collected data on prolonged use. Regrettably, they are largely presented in different ways in the two papers so that the comparisons are limited to those shown in Table 4.7b. Of these, it is prolonged tranquilliser use expressed as a proportion of any use that is both the most appropriate (since only users are at risk of becoming prolonged users) and the most interesting: the rates are 30 per cent and 42 per cent for 1971 and 1981 respectively. It can be estimated from these data that there were some 800,000 more prolonged users of tranquillisers in Italy in 1981 than in 1971.

Table 4.7 Tranquilliser consumption in Italy

Table 4.7a One-year prevalence of consumption

	1971	*1981*
males	9.8%	9.4%
females	12.6%	13.5%
total	11.2%	11.5%

Table 4.7b Prolonged tranquilliser use

proportion of population reporting daily tranquilliser use for one month or more during the previous year	3.4%	4.7%
proportion of tranquilliser users reporting daily use for one month or more in previous year.	30.0%	42.4%

Source: 1971 data from Balter *et al.* (1974); 1981 data from Balter *et al.* (1984)

RISK FACTORS FOR LONG-TERM USE

Above we used an examination of secular trends to exemplify Morris's use of epidemiology 'for historical study'. 'History' also has another meaning – 'a course of events: a life story' (*Chambers Twentieth Century Dictionary*, revised edition, 1972). The study of groups of respondents on more than one occasion – longitudinal, or cohort, studies – is central to the elucidation of factors which predict, or increase the risk of, some disease or disorder. The utility of epidemiological methods for exploring factors which increase the probability, or risk, of illness was outlined by Morris as follows: 'risks, chances, possibilities (of illness) for the individual can be predicted, on average, from analysis of the collective experience of large numbers of representative individuals with the characteristic in question' (Morris 1975: 98).

Who becomes a long-term user? A great deal of light can be thrown on this question by cross-sectional studies, as the previous section on 'describing long-term tranquilliser users' has demonstrated. However, it is the longitudinal prospective study that is paramount among methods for investigating risk factors.

Williams and his colleagues conducted such a study in a British general practice setting (Williams *et al.* 1982; Murray *et al.* 1982; Williams 1983b). Six general practitioners in five south London practices were asked to identify and provide information about those patients to whom they supplied a new prescription for a psychotropic drug. 'New' was defined so as to include first-ever prescriptions as well as those written for the treatment of a new episode of illness. Subsequent prescribing was monitored for six months.

One-hundred-and-fifty-four patients were entered into the study, and follow-up prescribing information was available for 124 (81 per cent) of these. For each patient, the duration of continuous treatment was calculated, defined according to the method of Parish (1971) as the length of time elapsing between the initiation of treatment and the day on which medication would have been used up if it had been taken according to prescription (this is of course not necessarily the same as duration of consumption). Survival curves were then plotted using these data on duration of treatment.

Figure 4.1 shows the survival distributions according to the type of psychotropic drug prescribed at inception into the study. It can be seen that after six weeks about one-third of the patients on tranquillisers (virtually all of which were benzodiazepines) were still receiving treatment. The figure also shows that just under 20 per

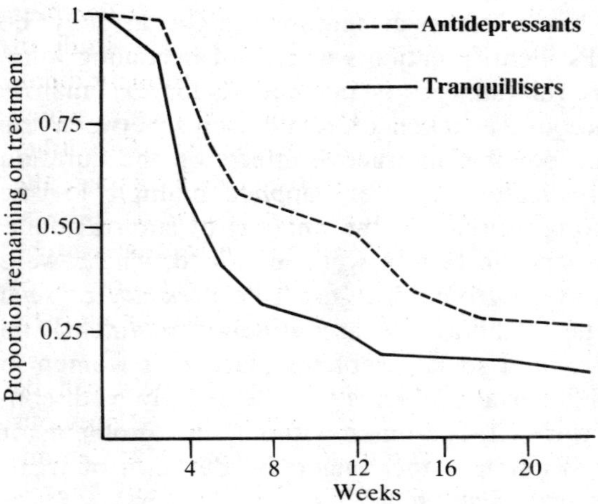

Figure 4.1 Survival distributions of duration of psychotropic drug use

cent of the tranquilliser recipients were prescribed drugs for the entire six-month period.

The investigators then used survival analysis techniques to investigate factors which predicted the duration of treatment with psychotropic drugs (Williams 1983b). They studied the effects of two characteristics of the patients (sex; age), two aspects of their health status (GPs' assessment of severity of symptoms at inception of treatment; presence or absence of physical illness), a measure of social functioning (GPs' assessment of social problems), three aspects of the treatment (type of psychotropic prescribed; past psychotropic drug use; whether or not drugs were requested by the patient), and the passage of time.

The effects of these factors on the survival distribution of drug use were first examined one at a time. At this level of analysis, they found that symptom severity, type of psychotropic, and previous psychotropic drug use were each related to duration of treatment (severe symptoms, prescribing of antidepressants, and a previous history of psychotropic drug use each being associated with a more prolonged duration of treatment). They also found an association between increasing age and duration of tranquilliser, but not antidepressant, use and a longer duration of treatment in women than men, but only in those patients assessed by the GP as having significant social problems.

Such an analysis is sufficient for descriptive purposes; that is, it allows us to answer questions such as 'do patients with characteristic X tend to receive treatment for longer than those without it?' Indeed, a checklist based on such features might usefully be developed to help GPs identify patients at risk of becoming long-term users. However, this analysis is inadequate for explanatory purposes, since no account is taken of relationships between the predictor variables and possible interactive effects on the duration of drug use. The investigators therefore applied multiple logistic regression techniques appropriate to the analysis of survival data.

Three significant prognostic factors were identified. These were a history of previous psychotropic drug use (the presence of such a history decreased the likelihood of discontinuing treatment), an interactive effect of sex and social problems (such that women in whom the GP identified social problems were less likely to discontinue treatment than were either women without such problems or men) and the passage of time – the longer the duration of treatment, the less the chance of stopping.

These findings applied equally to patients on antidepressants and

Table 4.8 Probability of discontinuing psychotropic drug treatment within the next two weeks (women only: estimated from the logistic model in Williams 1983b)

	Social problems	*Previous psychotropic use identified by GP*	
		no	*yes*
at the beginning of treatment	none or one	0.34	0.21
	two or more	0.45	0.11
after four months' treatment	none or one	0.12	0.05
	two or more	0.21	0.02

tranquillisers, and an example of the state of affairs predicted by the logistic model is given in Table 4.8. This shows the estimated probability of discontinuing psychotropic drug treatment within the next two weeks, at the beginning and after four months of continuous treatment. A woman with social problems who has previously been treated with psychotropics had, compared with other women, little chance of early discontinuation of treatment at the start, and a negligible chance after four months of drug treatment.

This finding that women with social problems are particularly at risk with regard to tranquilliser use has been confirmed in subsequent studies of tranquilliser prescription. Fiorio *et al.* (1989) studied the patients of three GPs in Verona (a city in northern

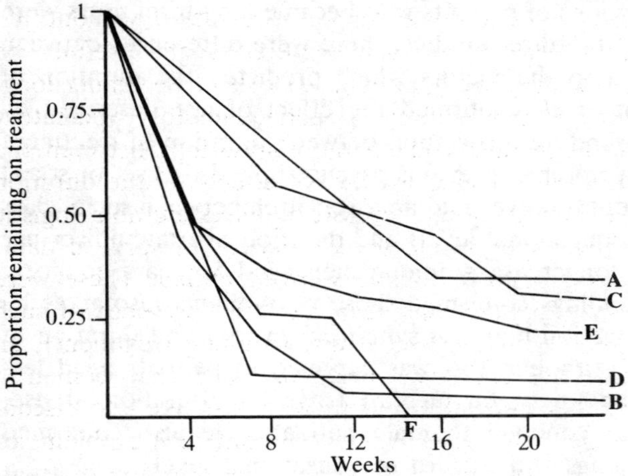

Figure 4.2 Survival distributions of duration of psychotropic drug use in patients of six general practitioners: between doctor differences

Italy) and found that women designated by the GP as having a social problem were much more likely to receive a prescription for a tranquilliser than women not so designated. The same finding emerged from a further study of some 1600 patients registered with ninety-two GPs in northern Italy (Bellantuono *et al.* 1989a) – the recognition of a social problem increased six-fold the chances of being prescribed a tranquilliser.

Returning to Williams's (1983b) longitudinal study, a further analysis was conducted to explore the differences between the doctors with regard to their patients' use of psychotropics. Figure 4.2 demonstrates these differences very clearly: while all Dr F's patients had stopped treatment within four months, about one-third of Dr A's patients were still receiving prescriptions after six months. Survival analysis indicated that these disparities were due to differences neither between the practices with regard to the characteristics of their patients, nor between the patients' clinical status, nor between specific aspects of the treatment. However, the effect of the passage of time on the probability of discontinuing treatment did vary between doctors, suggesting that some doctors interact with their patients in such a way as to encourage, albeit not consciously, long-term use of benzodiazepines and other psychotropic drugs (for further details, see Williams 1983b).

Longitudinal prospective studies of tranquilliser use have subsequently been conducted by Mant *et al.* (1988) and Fiorio (1988), each of whom used survival analyses similar to those of Williams. While the proportions of patients who became long-term users were similar in each of the three studies, there were differences between them with regard to the factors which predicted the duration of use. While Mant *et al.* confirmed the effect of age described by Williams, they found no association between duration of treatment and severity of symptoms, previous psychotropic drug use, or social problems. They did however find an association between social class (represented by educational level) and duration of tranquilliser use – less educated, longer use – among men aged 55 years or more. Fiorio's (1988) findings confirmed those of Williams insofar as he reported an association between symptom severity and duration of tranquilliser use (although this was confined to patients aged less than 44 years) and between increased age and duration of use, although this was confined to male patients. He also confirmed Mant *et al.*'s findings with regard to educational level.

PUBLIC HEALTH ASPECTS OF LONG-TERM TRANQUILLISER USE

It should be apparent from what has been described in this chapter that epidemiological enquiry has an important part to play in relation to planning and monitoring health services. Jeremy Morris believed that epidemiology could answer questions such as 'how are services working in reality as distinct from laws, plans and pronouncements about them? How are they adapting to the changing pattern of health and disease? To what extent is new knowledge being translated into medical care?' (Morris 1975: 71).

Despite dissenting opinions (e.g. Snaith 1984; Cohen 1987), short-term treatment with benzodiazepines and other tranquillisers continues to be accepted practice (Tyrer & Murphy 1987; Bellantuono *et al.* 1989b). The position with regard to long-term use is less clear, and is one in which benefits and risks need to be weighed up. There are few data which adequately address issues of risk and benefit, but Uhlenhuth *et al.* (1988) summarized the current state of affairs with regard to benzodiazepines as follows: 'some patients appear to derive continuing benefit from long-term treatment with benzodiazepines . . . [but] systematic data confirm that benzodiazepine addiction can occur when doses within the clinical range are taken regularly over a sufficient period of time'. These authors noted that the risks of 'dependence upon and addiction to' benzodiazepines are remarkably low in relation to the massive exposure to these drugs, and that benzodiazepine overuse has probably been exaggerated.

Even so, many believe that long-term use is to be avoided – for example, an expert committee of the UK Royal College of Psychiatrists (1988) has recommended that the duration of anxiolytic treatment with benzodiazepines should be limited to one month. Since only a minority of recipients become long-term users, the identification of risk factors for long-term use is of paramount importance. The work described here has identified a number of such factors, the relevance of which is enhanced by their being available at the beginning of treatment.

The extent to which steps should be taken to discontinue medication in an established long-term user is not so well established, although a number of studies testify that this is certainly possible (see Uhlenhuth *et al.* 1988). It is clear from the work described in this chapter that in such circumstances it is important to consider patients' own views about their drugs and drug treatment and the alternative resources available to them.

Even so, long-term use of benzodiazepines and other psychotropic drugs remains a major feature of medical practice. This chapter has illustrated the role that epidemiological enquiry can play, and studies from within this research tradition demonstrate that the phenomenon should not be conceptualized only within a pharmacological or even a strictly clinical context, and any approach to understanding and management needs to be grounded in recognition of the multifaceted nature of the problem.

REFERENCES

Albrecht, G. & Jackson, K. (1985) 'The social context of policy research', *Sociological Methods and Research* 13: 275–88.

Anderson, R. (1980) 'Prescribed medicines – who takes what?' *Journal of Epidemiology and Community Health* 34: 299–304.

Balter, M. B., Levine, J., & Manheimer, D. I. (1974) 'Cross-national study of the extent of anti-anxiety/sedative drug use', *New England Journal of Medicine* 390: 769–74.

Balter, M. B., Manheimer, D. I., Mellinger, G. D., & Uhlenhuth, E. H. (1984) 'A cross-national comparison of anti-anxiety/sedative drug use', *Current Medical Research and Opinion* 8(Suppl.4): 5–20.

Bellantuono, C., Arreghini, E., Adami, M., Bodini, F., Gastaldo, M., & Micciolo, R. (1989a) 'Psychotropic drug prescription in Italy: a survey in general practice', unpublished research report, Cattedra di Psicologia Medicia, University of Verona.

Bellantuono, C., Adami, M., & Fiorio, R. (1989b) 'I farmaci ansiolitici – le benzodiazepini e il buspirone', in C. Bellantuono & M. Tansella (eds) *Gli Psicofarmaci nella Pratica Terapeutica*, 2nd edition, Il Pensiero Scientifico, in press.

Belloc, N. B., Breslow, L., & Hochstim, J. R. (1971) 'Measurement of physical health in a general population survey', *American Journal of Epidemiology* 93: 328–36.

Boardman, A. P. (1987) 'The General Health Questionnaire and the detection of emotional disorder by general practitioners: a replicated study', *British Journal of Psychiatry* 151: 373–81.

Box, G. E. P. (1979) *Robustness in Statistics*, London: Academic Press.

Catalan, J., Gath, D. H., Bond, A., Edmonds, G., Martin, P., & Ennis, J. (1988) 'General practice patients on long-term psychotropic drugs: a controlled investigation', *British Journal of Psychiatry* 152: 399–405.

Cohen, S. (1987) 'Are benzodiazepines useful in anxiety?', *Lancet* II: 1080.

Cooperstock, R. (1976) 'Psychotropic drug use among women', *Canadian Medical Association Journal* 115: 760–3.

Cooperstock, R. (1978) 'Sex differences in psychotropic drug use', *Social Science and Medicine* 12B: 179–86.

Cooperstock, R. & Lennard, H. (1979) 'Some social meanings of tranquilliser use', *Sociology of Health and Illness* 1: 331–47.

Dunnell, K. & Cartwright, A. (1972) *Medicine Takers, Prescribers and Hoarders*, London: Routledge & Kegan Paul.

Fiorio, R. (1988) *Le Prescrizioni ed il Consumo di Psicofarmaci nella Medicina Generale: uno Studio Longitudinale*, unpublished PhD thesis, University of Verona.

Fiorio, R., Bellantuono, C., Arreghini, E., Leoncini, M., & Micciolo, R. (1989) 'Psychotropic drug prescription in general practice in Italy: a two-week prevalence study', *International Clinical Psychopharmacology*, in print.

Gabe, J. & Lipshitz-Phillips, S. (1982) 'Evil necessity? The meaning of benzodiazepine use for women patients from one general practice', *Sociology of Health and Illness* 4: 201–9.

Gabe, J. & Lipshitz-Phillips, S. (1984) 'Tranquillisers as social control?', *Sociological Review* 32: 524–46.

Gabe, J. & Thorogood, N. (1986) 'Tranquillisers as a resource', in J. Gabe & P. Williams (eds) *Tranquillisers: Social, Psychological and Clinical Perspectives*, London: Tavistock, pp. 244–69.

Gabe, J. & Williams, P. (eds) (1986) *Tranquillisers: Social, Psychological and Clinical Perspectives*, London: Tavistock.

Goldberg, D., Cooper, B., Eastwood, M. R., Kedward, H. B., & Shepherd, M. (1970) 'A standardised psychiatric interview for use in community surveys', *Journal of Preventive and Social Medicine* 24: 18–23.

Helman, C. (1981) 'Tonic, fuel and food: social and symbolic aspects of the long-term use of psychotropic drugs', *Social Science and Medicine* 15B: 521–33.

Hopkins, D. R., Sethi, K. B. S., & Mucklow, J. C. (1982) 'Benzodiazepine withdrawal in general practice', *Journal of Royal College of General Practitioners* 32: 758–62.

King, M., Gabe, J., Williams, P., & Rodrigo, E. K. (1990) 'Long-term use of benzodiazepines: the views of patients', *British Journal of General Practice* 40: 194–6.

Mant, A., Duncan-Jones, P., Saltman, D., Bridges-Webb, C., Kehoe, L., Lansbury, G., & Chancellor, A. H. B. (1988) 'Development of long-term use of psychotropic drugs by general practice patients', *British Medical Journal* 296: 251–4.

Marks, J. (1983a) 'The benzodiazepines: an international perspective', *Journal of Psychoactive Drugs* 15: 137–49.

Marks, J. (1983b) 'The benzodiazepines – for good or for evil', *Neuropsychobiology* 10: 115–26.

Marks, J., Goldberg, D., & Hillier, V. E. (1979) 'Determinants of the ability of general practitioners to detect psychiatric disorder', *Psychological Medicine* 9: 337–53.

Mellinger, G. D. & Balter, M. B. (1981) 'Prevalence and patterns of use of psychotherapeutic drugs: results from a 1979 national survey of American adults', in G. Tognoni, C. Bellantuono, & M. Lader (eds) *The Epidemiological Impact of Psychotropic Drugs*, Amsterdam: Elsevier, pp. 117–23.

Mellinger, G. D., Balter, M. B., Uhlenhuth, E. H., Cisin, I. H., Manheimer, D. I., & Rickels, K. (1983) 'Evaluating a household survey measure of psychic distress', *Psychological Medicine* 13: 607–21.

Mellinger, G. D., Balter, M. B., & Uhlenhuth, E. H. (1984) 'Prevalence and correlates of long-term regular use of anxiolytics', *Journal of the American Medical Association* 251: 375–9.

Morris, J. N. (1975) *The Uses of Epidemiology*, 3rd edition, Edinburgh: Churchill.

Murray, J. (1981) 'Long-term psychotropic drug taking and the process of withdrawal', *Psychological Medicine* 11: 853–8.

Murray, J., Dunn, G., Williams, P., & Tarnopolsky, A. (1981) 'Factors affecting the consumption of psychotropic drugs', *Psychological Medicine* 11: 551–60.

Murray, J., Williams, P., & Clare, A. W. (1982) 'Health and social characteristics of long-term psychotropic drug takers', *Social Science and Medicine* 16: 1595–8.

Parish, P. A. (1971) 'The prescribing of psychotropic drugs in general practice', *Journal of Royal College of General Practitioners* 21(Suppl. 4): 1–77.

Petursson, H. & Lader, M. H. (1984) *Dependence on Tranquillisers*, Oxford: Oxford University Press.

Rodrigo, E. K., King, M., & Williams, P. (1988) 'The health of long-term tranquilliser users', *British Medical Journal* 296: 603–6.

Royal College of Psychiatrists (1988) 'Benzodiazepines and dependence: a College statement', *Bulletin of the Royal College of Psychiatrists* 12: 107–9.

Salinsky, J. V. & Dore, C. J. (1987) 'Characteristics of long-term benzodiazepine users in general practice', *Journal of the Royal College of General Practitioners* 37: 202–4.

Schopf, J. (1983) 'Withdrawal phenomena after long-term administration of benzodiazepines', *Pharmacopsychiatry* 16: 1–8.

Skegg, D. C. G., Doll, R., & Perry, J. (1977) 'Use of medicines in general practice', *British Medical Journal* i: 1561–3.

Snaith, R. P. (1984) 'Benzodiazepines on trial', *British Medical Journal* 288: 1379.

Solow, C. (1975) 'Psychotropic drugs in somatic disorder', *International Journal of Psychiatry in Medicine* 6: 267–82.

Stoll, M. & Lader, M. (1984) Unpublished observations cited in H. Petursson & M. H. Lader, *Dependence on Tranquillisers*, London: Oxford University Press.

Thunhurst, C. (1984) 'Social inequalities in health – the medical empire strikes back', *Radical Community Health* September: 35–7.

Tognoni, G., Bellantuono, C., & Lader, M. (eds) (1981) *The Epidemiological Impact of Psychotropic Drugs*, Amsterdam: Elsevier.

Tyrer, P. & Murphy, S. (1987) 'The place of benzodiazepines in psychiatric practice', *British Journal of Psychiatry* 151: 719–23.

Tyrer, P., Rutherford, D., & Huggett, T. (1981) 'Benzodiazepine withdrawal symptoms and propranolol', *Lancet* II: 520–2.

Tyrer, P., Owen, R., & Dawling, S. (1983) 'Gradual withdrawal of diazepam after chronic therapy', *Lancet* I: 1402–6.

Uhlenhuth, E. H., DeWit, H., Balter, M. B., Johanson, C. E., & Mellinger, G. D. (1988) 'Risks and benefits of long-term benzodiazepine use', *Journal of Clinical Psychopharmacology* 8: 161–7.

Weissman, M. M. & Klerman, G. L. (1977) 'The chronic depressive in

the community: unrecognised and poorly treated', *Comprehensive Psychiatry* 18: 523–32.
Weissman, M. M., Myers, J. K., & Thompson, W. D. (1981) 'Depression and its treatment in a U.S. urban community', *Archives of General Psychiatry* 38: 417–21.
Williams, P. (1978) 'Physical ill-health and psychotropic drug prescription: a review', *Psychological Medicine* 8: 683–93.
Williams, P. (1983a) 'Patterns of psychotropic drug use', *Social Science and Medicine* 17: 845–51.
Williams, P. (1983b) 'Factors influencing the duration of treatment with psychotropic drugs in general practice: a survival analysis approach', *Psychological Medicine* 13: 623–33.
Williams, P., Tarnopolsky, A., & Hand, D. (1980) 'Case definition and case identification in psychiatric epidemiology – review and assessment', *Psychological Medicine* 10: 101–14.
Williams, P., Murray, J., & Clare, A. W. (1982) 'A longitudinal study of psychotropic drug prescription', *Psychological Medicine* 12: 201–6.
Williams, P., Bellantuono, C., Fiorio, R., & Tansella, M. (1986) 'Psychotropic drug use in Italy: national trends and regional differences', *Psychological Medicine* 16: 841–50.
Wing, J. K., Cooper, J., & Sartorius, N. (1974) *The Measurement and Classification of Psychiatric Symptoms*, Cambridge: Cambridge University Press.
Woodcock, J. (1970) 'Long-term consumers of psychotropic drugs', in M. Balint, M. Marinker, & J. Woodcock (eds) *Treatment or Diagnosis*, London: Tavistock, pp. 147–76.
World Health Organisation (1974) Expert Committee on Drug Dependence: 20th report, Technical Report Series No. 20, Geneva: World Health Organisation.

5 Long-term tranquilliser use: the contribution of health economics

Alan Shiell

INTRODUCTION

Advances in technology have contributed to the situation in which our ability to improve health far exceeds the available resources. It is not possible to do everything that is beneficial to health and therefore priorities must be set and choices made between alternative health care interventions. In short, the treatment of people with minor psychiatric disorders, for which minor tranquillisers are most commonly prescribed, must compete with other treatments for its share of resources.

A large part of health economics describes the application of techniques such as cost-benefit and cost-effectiveness analysis to problems of choice that arise in health and health care. But economic expertise is itself a scarce resource which must be allocated wisely and two pre-conditions must be fulfilled before an economic contribution to understanding the long-term use of minor tranquillisers is warranted. First, the problem being studied must be significant in terms of the resources currently (or potentially) devoted to its prevention, diagnosis, or management. Second, there must be available to the physician a variety of methods of managing the presenting illness, the relative merits of which are either unknown or uncertain. Together these pre-conditions justify the involvement of an economist and ensure that he or she will have something positive to offer.

The treatment of minor emotional disorders would appear to satisfy both pre-conditions. In both the United States and Britain up to one-third of consultations with general physicians are for complaints with a large psychological component (Regier *et al.* 1985; Shepherd *et al.* 1981; Anon 1979). Only a small proportion of these patients require referral for more specialist psychiatric support and most will continue to be managed by the general physician (Lesser 1983; Hankin *et al.* 1982; Skynner & Brown 1981). Many of these patients will receive a prescription for psychotropic medication, most commonly for a drug from the benzodiazepine group (Shepherd *et al.* 1981). Cross-national comparisons show the prevalence of tranquilliser use to range from 7.4 per cent to 17.6 per cent (Balter *et al.* 1984). In 1984, some 70 million scripts for such drugs were written in the USA (Baum *et al.* 1988) while in Britain there were 28 million prescriptions, costing the National Health Service over £30 million. Concerns about overuse have contributed to a fall in the number of prescriptions on both sides of the Atlantic (see Table 5.1) but the level of prescribing remains substantial.

Table 5.1 Prescriptions for minor tranquillisers (millions)

	United States	*United Kingdom*
1975	103	27
1976	100	29
1977	93	30
1978	84	31
1979	77	31
1980	70	29
1981	67	29
1982	67	30
1983	70	29
1984	71	28
1985	Not available	26
1986	Not available	25
1987	Not available	25

Sources: Baum *et al.* (1988); Hansard (1988) 128 Col 696W.

The resource consequences of current management practices are significant but there is sufficient doubt about the effectiveness of benzodiazepines to encourage the search for alternative treatments. Consequently, there is a sizeable, although almost exclusively British, literature which describes and evaluates non-drug therapies, in particular the attachment to general practice of counsellors from a variety of professional and non-professional backgrounds (for example see Wyld 1981).

The scope for economic appraisal is, therefore, high yet very little analysis of a specifically economic design has been carried out.

A recent international bibliography of health economics cites over 5000 references published before 1983, of which only seventy-five relate to psychiatry (Blades *et al.* 1986). Most of these studies compare community and in-patient treatments for people with more severe mental health problems and few are of direct relevance to the subject matter of this volume (Frank 1981). A number of papers have been published since 1983, in particular McGrath and Lowson's review of the economics of psychotherapy (McGrath & Lowson 1986) and Wagstaff and Maynard's study of illicit drug use and drug-enforcement policies (Wagstaff & Maynard 1988). The latter report contains a detailed explanation of the welfare economic foundations of policies to control the consumption of drugs, albeit in a slightly different context to the one discussed here. Both illicit drugs and minor tranquillisers share properties of dependence which mark them as distinct from the sort of commodity traditionally studied by economists and the problems this raises are discussed by Wagstaff and Maynard. However, an essential difference between the 'markets' for the two sorts of drug, apart from the legal status, is the mediating role of the general practitioner who, in the case of tranquillisers, acts both on the demand side (as the patient's agent) and on the supply side (as prescriber).

The total number of relevant studies, therefore, remains disappointingly small and a review of the contribution made by economists *per se* to understanding long-term tranquilliser use would be both short and unsatisfactory. However, much of the available literature has an economic feel about it, being concerned primarily with the effectiveness of alternative ways of managing minor affective disorders yet also considering to a greater or lesser extent their resource consequences. By reviewing this literature within the framework provided by economics this chapter might more accurately be described as an economist's interpretation of the contribution others have made to understanding the economic aspects of long-term tranquilliser use.

FORMULATING THE PROBLEM

The first step in any economic appraisal is a clear specification of the problem it should address. If the long-term use of tranquillisers is regarded as the problem then the most appropriate question is how best to wean from tranquillisers those users who have become dependent upon them (Hopkins *et al.* 1986; Ettore 1986; Nathan *et al.* 1986; Tyrer *et al.* 1985). An alternative approach, and one which is chosen here because it is the aspect to which most evaluative literature relates, is to focus on the conditions which precipitate the prescription of tranquillisers and consider how people who suffer from minor affective disorders are best treated. In this case, the distress caused by dependency and associated withdrawal may be regarded as one of the costs or, more accurately, one of the disbenefits of conventional drug-based therapies.

Potentially, there are a number of methods by which the physician could respond to the needs of those who present in some psychological distress but few of these have been the subject of stringent evaluation. Judged by the research literature, the main alternative to conventional management involving benzodiazepines is some form of counselling, though the term is used here in a broad sense to include a variety of predominantly psychological interventions ranging from simple advice to structured programmes of behaviour or psychotherapy. Published evaluations of other forms of intervention, such as self-help groups or learning packages (Kiely & McPherson 1986; Teare Skinner 1984) or alternative drug regimes involving non-benzodiazepine tranquillisers (Rakel 1987) or antidepressants (see Tyrer & Murphy 1987), are comparatively rare. Understandably, the focus of this literature is also strictly 'downstream', in the sense that 'upstream' measures such as political or social change designed to prevent or ameliorate psychological distress are not considered (McKinlay 1975).

In practice, counselling (in particular specialist counselling) will tend to supplement conventional GP management rather than replace it altogether. The correct focus for evaluation, therefore, is to identify what the new therapy *adds* to conventional management by way of cost and effect. The importance of this change in emphasis is best illustrated by means of a hypothetical example (see Table 5.2). In rows A and B, conventional GP management is compared to a new service involving the attachment to the practice of a specialist counsellor. The new service is more expensive than conventional GP care although the salary costs of the counsellor are partially offset by savings in GP consultations and drug prescriptions. The new service is also clearly more effective in reducing distress, measured very simply in this case by the number of people reported symptom-free at follow-up. The cost-benefit ratio summarizes these changes and shows the average cost of relieving the symptoms of one person. The ratio increases slightly with the introduction of the counsellor, showing that average costs have risen but the extra cost may be considered a small price to pay for the additional relief the new service brings. Row C shows what counselling *adds* to conventional care in terms of both cost and benefit. The marginal cost of extending the effectiveness of the service to bring relief to fifteen more people is far higher than implied by comparing averages and though it may still be decided that the extra price is worth paying, it is important for this value judgement to be made on the correct basis.

Table 5.2 Hypothetical evaluation of alternative methods of managing minor affective disorders

Programme	*Cost (£)*	*Benefit (Number of people symptom-free)*	*Cost:Benefit Ratio (Cost per person symptom-free)*
A. GP management	1200	60	20 : 1
B. GP and counsellor	1800	75	24 : 1
C. MARGIN of programme B over programme A	600	15	40 : 1

MEASURING EFFECTIVENESS

An economic appraisal must be based upon a sound technical evaluation of the effectiveness of the therapies being compared. An ineffective treatment is, by definition, also inefficient and its continued use represents both clinical and economic bad practice. However, even the use of an effective treatment may be considered inefficient if the requisite resources could be put to better (i.e. *more* effective) use elsewhere. The effectiveness of benzodiazepines, particularly in the long term, has been challenged (Committee on the Review of Medicines 1980; East of Ireland Faculty of RCGP and Department of Community Health 1983; Committee on the Safety of Medicines 1988; Royal College of Psychiatrists 1988), but there would appear to be sufficient doubt about these conclusions to continue regarding benzodiazepines as a feasible treatment, if only for short periods of time (Williams 1982; Oswald *et al*. 1982; Rickels *et al*. 1983; Uhlenhuth *et al*. 1988).

To establish the social value of treatment, benefits (as well as costs) must be defined as broadly as possible. The principal effect one seeks is improvement in the health status of patients, i.e. longer life expectancy and/or better quality of life, with the latter measured in terms of physical, psychological, and social functioning (Ryles 1986; Renshaw 1985). Health profiles reflect the multidimensional nature of outcome but can make it difficult to rank the effectiveness of treatments unless one therapy dominates the others across all dimensions. It may also be impossible to tell whether a treatment is beneficial at all if improvements in one dimension accompany reductions in another. These problems have led economists to get involved in the development of global health indices which summarize in a single number (the quality adjusted life year or QALY) the multidimensional health states which the indices encompass (Torrance 1986). The development of health indices is still in its infancy and existing measures have been criticized on theoretical, practical, and ethical grounds (Loomes & McKenzie 1989; Carr-Hill 1989; Mulkay *et al.* 1987; Donaldson *et al.* 1988; Smith 1987). Certainly, there are a number of issues to resolve before such measures become operational but they do have the advantage of using lay, rather than clinical, valuations of health outcome and will facilitate comparisons of cost-effectiveness of treatments across a wide range of conditions.

Further factors to consider are the health of carers and close family members and any change in productive output caused by reduced absenteeism from work. In contrast to improvements in the health state of patients and their carers, changes in output are often and erroneously termed an 'economic' benefit merely because they are easy to express in monetary terms. The inclusion of such effects is justified on the grounds that, other things being equal, we prefer more goods and services to less, but actual changes in output are rarely demonstrated and, in times of unemployment, may not occur. Wage rates are commonly used to value changes in production, which builds into the appraisal bias in the labour market and discriminates against therapies benefiting women and the elderly. The inclusion of production gains (or losses) therefore remains a controversial issue with no consensus of opinion among economists.

MEASURING COSTS

Economic costs are equivalent to sacrifices and relate to the value of the treatment resources in their most favoured alternative use. An economic appraisal is therefore the equivalent of comparing the benefits or outcome of doing one thing with the benefits or outcome of doing another. The evaluation of cost is often less problematic than for benefits because the price paid to secure the use of a resource usually reflects its economic cost. An exception worthy of mention is the time patients and relatives give up to participate in treatment which has a value to the people concerned but is often ignored in evaluations of cost because it has no explicit price.

The most significant resources required by a counselling service include the salary and travel costs of the counsellor, office rental and equipment, and time and travel costs of patients and relatives. Initial training costs need to be considered and could be large if a new specialist service is to be developed. GP consultations, drug prescriptions, and hospital services may still be required but possibly to a lesser extent than with conventional GP management. The additional costs of the new service may therefore be reduced slightly by savings achieved in conventional care but the extent of these savings depends on the marginal value of the resources actually released. Marginal savings will tend to be lower than the average costs of facilities and services, partly because some resources do not vary in response to small changes in utilization. Unfortunately, average costs tend to be easier to calculate and are therefore used more frequently in appraisals.

HOW EFFECTIVE IS COUNSELLING COMPARED TO TRANQUILLISERS?

Assessing the relative merits of counselling compared to tranquillisers is difficult because of flaws in study design. Effectiveness is best determined by using randomized trials to control for selection bias and other extraneous factors that might otherwise affect the results, but few published studies attain this ideal and many employ no control group or have inadequate controls such that it is difficult to ascribe the observed changes in outcome to the particular intervention under scrutiny (Beldon *et al*. 1985). The studies chosen for review (see Table 5.3) have the merit of comparing alternative forms of treatment using randomized or matched controls to cope with extraneous sources of bias.

These studies have used a variety of instruments to evaluate the effectiveness of the alternative methods of managing minor psychological ill-health with differing results. Johnstone and Shepley (1986) used the General Health Questionnaire (GHQ) to show that a practice-based health visitor could be just as effective as the GP in treating patients with a neurotic disorder. Catalan and his colleagues (1984) compared alternative forms of management by the GP using

Table 5.3 Evaluation of alternatives to conventional management of patients with minor affective disorders

Study	*Alternative treatment*	*Sample population*	*Effectiveness measures*	*Resource measures (£): valued in cash terms*
Robson *et al.* (1984)	Psychologist and GP	GP referrals n=429	Severity of problem Effect on sufferer Effect on family	Psychologist (£) GP consultations Prescriptions (£)
Earll & Kincey (1982)	Psychologist and GP	GP referrals n=50	Emotional distress Life satisfaction Locus of control	GP consultations Prescriptions
Cooper *et al.* (1975) Shepherd *et al.* (1979)	Social worker and GP	GP referrals (chronic neurotic illness) n=189	Psychiatric (PSE) Social	
Johnstone & Shepley (1986)	Health visitor	Hidden neurotic illness (GHQ<20) n=58	General Health (GHQ)	
Ginsberg *et al.* (1984) Marks (1985)	Nurse therapist	Neurotic patients (phobic and obsessive compulsive) n=92	Problem ratings Work/leisure ratings Phobic anxiety	Treatment cost (£) Patient costs (£) Lost production (£)
Catalan *et al.* (1984)	GP (non-drug)	New minor affective disorders n=91	General Health (GHQ) Mood (POMS) Social adjustment (SAS-M) Satisfaction	GP consultations Prescriptions

a battery of instruments including the GHQ, the Profile of Moods States (POMS), and the Social Adjustment Scale (SAS-M). Patients presenting for the first time with new episodes of minor affective disorder were assigned at random to one of two groups. In the control group, the physician could treat in whichever way he or she thought best. In the experimental group, the physician was *initially* constrained to using non-drug therapies although no training in such techniques was given. Drugs could be prescribed after this initial period only if the patient had not responded to treatment. After seven months both groups had improved and there were no significant differences in outcome between them. However, patients in the experimental group reported higher levels of satisfaction with the treatment they had received.

More effective results appear to be gained if the counsellor to whom patients are referred has some training or professional experience in aspects of psychotherapy. Cooper *et al.* (1975) describe the attachment of a specialist social worker to a general practice and suggest, in terms of both psychiatric and social functioning, that some benefit is conferred upon those who use the service. Marks (1985) evaluated the use of behaviour therapy administered by specially trained psychiatric nurses in the treatment of patients suffering from phobic or obsessive compulsive disorders. Significant improvements along each of three outcome measures – reflecting presence of symptoms, severity of problem, and work/leisure difficulties – were made by the patients in the experimental group and these were maintained for the twelve months to follow-up. Satisfaction with treatment was also higher among this group. Finally, control patients who had not received behaviour therapy showed improvements similar to the original experimental group when, after twelve months, they were referred to the nurse for behaviour therapy.

Psychologist-attachments to general practice have been the subject of a number of studies. Robson *et al.* (1984) showed, using scales reflecting the severity of problems and effects on both client and family, that patients attending the new service initially fared better than those managed conventionally, although, at twelve months, there were no significant differences in outcome between the two groups. Earll and Kincey (1982) found that patients referred to a psychologist fared no better than a control group at follow-up seven months after referral, although they were more satisfied with treatment and received fewer prescriptions.

From this evidence it would appear that counselling is at least as effective as drug therapy and may be more so, depending upon who is responsible for delivering care. The gains from counselling are not sustained into the very long term though recovery is accelerated (a positive benefit) and such intervention is preferred by patients. A number of studies (Marks 1985; Cooper *et al.* 1975; Freeman & Button 1984) also mention the improvements to GPs' conventional management of patients which derived from them having a specialist therapist on hand to offer advice and guidance. Such 'crossover' effects are a positive and practical advantage of specialist placements in primary care.

WHAT DOES EACH ALTERNATIVE COST?

Unfortunately, few studies address the question of cost and therefore in most cases no recommendations can be made about which alternative therapy is most cost-effective.

In comparison to staff-intensive therapies, such as counselling, drugs are likely to be relatively cheap. The average net ingredient cost of benzodiazepines is probably less than £2 per prescription (Taylor 1987) to which needs to be added the costs of dispensing and physician consultations. This is an average cost and, to the extent that fixed costs of production exist, it will overstate the marginal savings to be achieved from reducing the scale of prescribing. In comparison, the cost of employing a full-time social worker or psychologist is currently in the region of £15,000 per annum. In the experimental service originally examined by Cooper *et al.* (1975) and re-evaluated by Shepherd *et al.* (1979), the social worker was involved in the treatment of sixty-one families, seeing each family, on average, on 6.6 occasions. Assuming that he or she was employed full-time and using current salary scales, this translates into an average cost per contact of £37 and per course of treatment (or family seen) of £245. However, this figure may overestimate the costs of the new service, as it may ascribe only to patients actually seen by the social worker time he or she spent in support of the practice as a whole.

Robson *et al.* (1984) help overcome this problem by specifying the time the psychologist spent in contact with patients. The mean duration of treatment was 154 minutes which, allowing for related administrative duties, implies the cost of the new service to be £30 per patient episode. The authors also suggest that about one-third of the costs of the new service could be offset against savings resulting from the reduced level of prescribing, but as the average, and not the marginal, cost of drugs was used to arrive at these figures these savings have probably been overestimated. Contact time was probably lower in this study than might be expected elsewhere and so costs will normally be higher. For example, Earll and Kincey (1982) found the mean duration of treatment to be 7.7 sessions and if each session is assumed to last for one hour including administration etc., then the cost of treatment is closer to £65 per patient.

Catalan and his colleagues (1984) made reference to the resource consequences of withholding anxiolytics but did not attempt to value them explicitly. As would be expected, patients who were counselled initially received fewer prescriptions but over the whole period of the study the difference between the two groups was not so great as to be statistically significant at conventional levels. Similarly, there were no significant differences in consumption of alcohol, tobacco, or other non-prescribed drugs. The mean number of consultations with GPs was also the same in both groups but, as only the duration of the initial consultation is reported, it is not possible to check the validity of the authors' conclusion that withholding anxiolytic medication from patients does not lead to unreasonable demands on the time of general practitioners. On this evidence, physicians can alter their own treatment practices in favour of counselling without a significant increase in the use of resources.

The one exception to the general neglect of cost is the study by Ginsberg *et al.* (1984) which considered the costs of the nurse therapist service evaluated by Marks (1985). This paper purports to be a cost-benefit analysis although the outcomes of treatment are not valued. Instead, the study is a (near) comprehensive evaluation of the resource consequences of the new service in which its costs are offset against resource savings made elsewhere from increased economic activity and reduced demands for conventional care. The new service is estimated to cost about £340 per patient (1986 prices) but, by considering a wide range of factors, including reduced absence from work, Ginsberg and his colleagues allege that the service will pay for itself after two years. The numbers involved, especially for some categories of resource use, are quite small and there are substantial, yet unexplained, differences in baseline costs even though the two groups of patients were supposedly allocated at random. Even so, Ginsberg's conclusions are powerful because they suggest that the improvements in outcome observed by Marks can be achieved in the long run at no extra cost.

Ginsberg's attempt to cost the alternative therapies is to be commended but as it is the sole such example of relevance to this volume it is hard not to single it out for criticism. For example, a notable though, in context, possibly minor omission is the value of time given up by patients to participate in treatment. This was ignored, except where it involved absence from work, because of the difficulty of valuation.

More important problems arise from the methods adopted to value changes in resource use. The largest single element offsetting the costs of the nurse therapy service are the productive gains allegedly made because of reduced absence from work. The assumptions that such gains actually occur and that labour markets are the most appropriate source of value are therefore critical. The second largest element related to lower utilization of health service facilities among the treatment group. The savings supposedly achieved were valued at average cost which will overstate the marginal value of any resources actually released by reduced utilization. Taken together, these two resources are responsible for most of the savings allegedly arising from nurse therapy. The method of valuing changes in their use therefore has a significant effect on final estimates of the efficiency of the new service. If production changes are ignored and the marginal savings of reduced hospital utilization assumed to equal 50 per cent of average cost, then the savings reported by Ginsberg *et al.* all but disappear. Far from paying for itself, the nurse therapy service may cost as much as £300 per patient.

ECONOMIC EFFICIENCY

Given the shortage of studies quantifying both costs and effects it is impossible to determine with any degree of confidence which is the most efficient means of treating people with minor affective disorders. The value of specialist counsellors is unproven. Counselling tends to be preferred by patients, may accelerate relief from distressing symptoms, and offers the GP benefits in his or her conventional management of patients. It may also reduce long-term dependency on tranquillisers and the resource costs and distress which go with it, but this has not yet been assessed. However, symptomatic relief tends to be short-lived and the benefits outlined above are expensive to obtain as specialist counselling may cost from £30 to £300 more per patient than conventional care. Evidence that some, if not all, of this additional cost could be recouped from savings in drug and GP costs is not convincing.

The most persuasive evidence is provided by Catalan and his colleagues (1984) who show that people can be managed through the acute phase of their illness with less recourse to drugs and at apparently no extra cost. As both methods were equally effective in terms of reducing symptoms but counselling was preferred by patients, this is clearly the more efficient option. However, irrespective of their initial treatment, a number of people went on to develop chronic problems which required long-term management *including* the use of drugs. Simple reassurance and advice from GPs would therefore appear to be the most cost-effective way of treating new cases of minor affective disorders but there is little evidence to suggest that it alone will reduce the level of long-term tranquilliser use.

A ROLE FOR ECONOMICS IN THE FUTURE?

This economic reinterpretation of the available literature has probably served only to confirm what many already believed; that counsellors have some beneficial impact but may be expensive and that GPs can be just as effective in the short term without the use of drugs as with them. Little insight into the long-term use of tranquillisers has been gained and the question of how best to manage people who suffer from chronic emotional problems remains unanswered (Tyrer 1988). In addressing this question there are two areas in which economics might contribute in the future. The first is in further evaluation of alternative treatment options. If people who are liable to develop chronic problems can be identified at an early stage (Catalan *et al.* 1984) it may be possible to target services accordingly. However, the precise form such intervention should take remains unclear. Specialist counselling from a social worker or psychologist has been shown to have some effect but it is not known which of the various activities of the counsellor contribute most to outcome (Shepherd *et al.* 1979). This suggests that it may be possible to rationalize counselling practice to concentrate on those activities which have a demonstrable effect on patient welfare.

Other forms of intervention, including alternatives to counselling, also warrant evaluation. In Britain, there has been a spontaneous and uncoordinated growth in the number of psychiatrists attached to general practice (Strathdee & Williams 1984). The advantages of this development include better liaison, continuity of care, and reduced hospital utilization but evaluations of economic cost and client outcome are notably absent (Tyrer *et al.* 1984). The work of community psychiatric nurses (CPNs) also remains largely unevaluated, although it was the subject of one of the few economic appraisals in mental health. Mangen *et al.* (1983) looked at the management of people with chronic neuroses, severe enough to warrant referral to a psychiatrist, and compared traditional outpatient psychiatric care with management by the CPN. They found no significant differences in total cost or clinical and social outcomes but higher levels of patient satisfaction with treatment by the CPN service. On balance therefore, the authors concluded that community psychiatric nursing was beneficial for this particular patient group. A comparison of the relative merits of CPN and GP management of people with long-standing but relatively minor emotional disorders is therefore worthy of attention.

Finally, non-professionals such as voluntary or self-help groups must also be considered. Volunteer counsellors may be better placed to help people whose anxieties arise primarily from social problems (Waydenfield & Waydenfield 1978), while self-help groups may have a role, not only in support of people during the process of withdrawal from tranquillisers, but also in providing an alternative means of managing the original emotional distress (Ettore 1986). Such support has the additional advantage of minimizing the risk of dependency on professionals as well as on drugs.

Each of these alternatives has the potential to improve the quality of life of people who suffer from psychological distress but each also has resource consequences which cannot be ignored. Decisions about the relative value of health care interventions cannot be made on the basis of cost or outcome alone. Both must be considered so that scarce health care resources can be allocated to the activities in which they have most effect. In short, each alternative must be subject to an economic appraisal.

The second area in which economics might contribute is in identifying the incentives and constraints which are generated by different systems of financing and providing health care and which may explain why some treatments are more likely to be prescribed than others (Hornbrook & Rafferty 1982). In most health care systems, the patient and physician are insulated from the need to consider costs by the existence of insurance schemes and/or government programmes. In the United States, where fees per item of service and full reimbursement of hospital costs still predominate, the effect has been to encourage overutilization and escalating expenditure (Enthoven 1977). Private insurance schemes also suffer from the problem of adverse selection and, in an attempt to screen out what are perceived to be poor risks, tend to limit coverage, especially for people with psychological problems (Muszynski *et al.* 1983). Total expenditure is more tightly controlled in the United Kingdom and comprehensive coverage eliminates adverse selection, but the financial system still tends to punish efficiency and acts to encourage the shifting of costs on to the budgets of other agencies (Enthoven 1985). Such cost-shifting can influence the type of care provided. For example, in contrast to the costs of counselling which must usually be met from cash-limited and often over-stretched NHS reserves, the costs of GP drug therapy fall mainly on the patient and an unlimited Family Practitioner budget. The physician's own-time costs can also be reduced by allowing the receptionist to issue repeat prescriptions. In addition, current financial inducements to encourage GPs to employ their own staff have had a limited effect on the number of counsellors because fees paid on the number of vaccinations and cervical smear tests make the employment of practice nurses more lucrative (Tudor Hart 1985). The combined result provides a strong incentive to GPs to prescribe rather than counsel.

Policy initiatives to improve cost-consciousness centre on the introduction of patient charges and the encouragement of competition between the providers of health care. Not surprisingly, increasing the amount patients must contribute to their treatment has been shown to reduce the numbers seeking help and those subsequently hospitalized (Manning *et al.* 1987; Keeler *et al.* 1988). Successive increases in prescription charges have also been associated with a fall in the number of tranquillisers dispensed in the UK (Taylor 1987). However, such analyses rarely consider the characteristics of the people deterred from seeking help or the effect this has on health outcome. Unless patients are assumed to be the best judges of the usefulness of tranquillisers, increased charges are as likely to deter those on low incomes as those for whom such drugs have least effect.

Incentives are better aimed at the physician as it is he or she who initiates treatment and is best, though by no means perfectly, able to assess the effect it will have on a patient's health. Proposals to cap drug expenditure and introduce budgets from which general practitioners will be expected to provide or purchase care represent an attempt to introduce a more rational incentive structure into primary care in the UK (Maynard 1985; Maynard *et al.* 1986; Pirie & Butler 1988). These proposals draw heavily upon recent experience in the United States where pressure to contain costs is contributing to a reshaping of the health care system along more competitive lines. Prospective payment systems such as Diagnostic Related Groups (DRGs) provide a direct incentive to the emerging health care organizations to contain costs, though perhaps at the expense of quality of care and patient outcome, both of which are more difficult to measure.

The new financial systems will present a number of challenges to those concerned with the treatment of people with psychological difficulties (Sharfstein & Beigel 1984). To set prospective payments and negotiate contracts for care, it will be necessary to devise patient classification systems from which to predict the costs of treatment. This in turn will generate new incentives, appropriate and otherwise (Schumacher *et al.* 1986). The medical and psychiatric professions will need to specify more clearly which sorts of treatment they are able to offer and for whom they are more appropriate. Finally, if the proposals are to result in improvements in efficiency and not just lower expenditure, it will be necessary for physicians to monitor their treatment activities and assess the effect their care has on patients' health state.

CONCLUSIONS

In a recent review of the economics of mental health care, Wilkinson and Pelosi (1987) concluded 'The most cost-effective way to deliver mental health care is not clear'. This conclusion is echoed here, for there has been very little economic appraisal in psychiatry and most tends to focus on institutional comparisons of hospital versus community provision. The role of the primary care physician in providing mental health care is largely ignored. This lack of evaluation is to be regretted given the substantial expenditure on drugs, the investment of time by general practitioners and mental health professionals, and the distress felt by those who suffer or care for someone who suffers from a long-term psychological disorder.

Whatever the reasons for this neglect, one consequence is the lack of knowledge about the best means of treating people with minor but chronic affective disorders and of reducing the risks of long-term dependency on tranquillisers. However, there is no lack of ideas about what can be done and a brief research agenda has been mapped out. If past mistakes are to be avoided, it is highly desirable, if not essential, that this agenda includes an economic component.

REFERENCES

Anonymous (1979) 'Behavioural problems in general practice', *Journal of Royal College of General Practitioners* 29: 323–7.

Balter, M. B., Levine, J., & Manheimer, D. I. (1974) 'Cross-national study of the extent of anti-anxiety/sedative drug use', *New England Journal of Medicine* 290: 769–74.

Balter, M. B., Manheimer, D. I., Mellinger, G. D., & Uhlenhuth, E. H. (1984) 'A cross-national comparison of anti-anxiety/sedative drug use', *Current Medical Research and Opinion* 8(Suppl. 4): 5–20.

Baum, C., Kennedy, D. L., Knapp, D. E., Juergens, J. P., & Faith, G. A. (1988) 'Prescription drug use in 1984 and change over time', *Medical Care* 26(2): 105–14.

Beldon, B. D., Braukmann, C. J., & Wolf, M. M. (1985) '"Psychology as a health care profession": how healthy was APA's case for the cost-effectiveness of psychological health care?', *Psychological Reports* 56: 391–401.

Blades, C. A., Culyer, A. J., Wiseman, J., & Walker, A. (1986) *The International Bibliography of Health Economics: A Comprehensive Guide to English Language Sources since 1914*, Brighton: Harvester.

Carr-Hill, R. (1989) 'Assumptions of the QALY procedure', *Social Science and Medicine* 29(3): 469–77.

Catalan, J., Gath, D., Edmonds, G., Ennis, J., Bond, A., & Martin, P. (1984) 'The effects of non-prescribing of anxiolytics in general practice', *British Journal of Psychiatry* 144: 593–610.

Committee on the Review of Medicines (1980) 'Systematic review of the benzodiazepines', *British Medical Journal* 280: 910–12.

Committee on the Safety of Medicines (1988) *Current Problems* 21.

Cooper, B., Harwin, B. G., Depla, C., & Shepherd, M. (1975) 'Mental health care in the community: an evaluative study', *Psychological Medicine* 5: 372–80.

Donaldson, C., Atkinson, A., Bond, J., & Wright, K. (1988) 'Should QALYs be programme specific?', *Journal of Health Economics* 7: 239–57.

Earll, L. & Kincey, J. (1982) 'Clinical psychology in general practice: a controlled trial evaluation', *Journal of Royal College of General Practitioners* 32: 32–7.

East of Ireland Faculty of RCGP and Department of Community Health (1983) 'A double-blind randomized control trial of diazepam', *Journal of Royal College of General Practitioners* 33: 635–6.

Enthoven, A. (1977) 'Consumer choice health plan (part 1)', *New England Journal of Medicine* 298(12): 650–8.

Enthoven, A. (1985) *Reflections on the Management of the National Health Service*, London: Nuffield Provincial Hospitals Trust.

Ettore, E. M. (1986) 'Self-help groups as an alternative to benzodiazepine use', in J. Gabe & P. Williams (eds) *Tranquillisers: Social, Psychological and Clinical Perspectives*, London: Tavistock.

Frank, R. (1981) 'Cost benefit analysis in mental health services: a review of the literature', *Administration in Mental Health* 8(3): 161–76.

Freeman, G. K. & Button, E. J. (1984) 'The clinical psychologist in general practice: a six-year study of consulting patterns for psychosocial problems', *Journal of Royal College of General Practitioners* 34: 377–80.

Ginsberg, G., Marks, I., & Waters, H. (1984) 'Cost-benefit analysis of a controlled trial of nurse therapy for neuroses in primary care', *Psychological Medicine* 14: 683–90.

Hankin, J. R., Steinweichs, D. M., Regier, D. A., Burns, B. J., Goldberg, I. D., & Hoeper, E. W. (1982) 'Use of general medical care services by persons with mental disorders', *Archives of General Psychiatry* 39: 225–31.

Hopkins, D. R., Sethi, K. B. S., & Mucklow, J. C. (1986) 'Benzodiazepine withdrawal in general practice', in J. Gabe & P. Williams (eds) *Tranquillisers: Social, Psychological and Clinical Perspectives*, London: Tavistock.

Hornbrook, M. & Rafferty, J. (1982) 'The economics of hospital reimbursement', *Advances in Health Economics and Health Services Research* 3: 79–115.

Johnstone, A. & Shepley, M. (1986) 'The outcome of hidden neurotic illness treated in general practice', *Journal of Royal College of General Practitioners* 36: 13–415.

Keeler, E. B., Manning, W. G., & Wells, K. B. (1988) 'The demand for episodes of mental health services', *Journal of Health Economics* 7: 369–92.

Kiely, B. G. & McPherson, I. G. (1986) 'Stress self-help, packages in primary care: a controlled trial evaluation', *Journal of Royal College of General Practitioners* 36(288): 307–9.

Lesser, A. L. (1983) 'Is training in psychiatry relevant for general practice?', *Journal of Royal College of General Practitioners* October: 617–18.

Loomes, G. & McKenzie, L. (1989) 'The use of QALYs in health care decision-making', *Social Science and Medicine* 28(4): 299–308.

McGrath, G. & Lowson, K. (1986) 'Assessing the benefits of psychotherapy: the economic approach', *British Journal of Psychiatry* 150: 65–71.

McKinlay, J. B. (1975) 'A case for refocusing upstream: the political economy of sickness', in A. Enelow (ed.) *Applying Behavioural Science to Cardiovascular Risk*, New York: American Heart Association.

Mangen, S. P., Paykel, E. S., Griffith, J. H., Burchell, A., & Mancini, P. (1983) 'Cost-effectiveness of community psychiatric nurse or outpatient psychiatrist care of neurotic patients', *Psychological Medicine* 13: 407–16.

Manning, W. G., Newhouse, J. P., Duan, N., Keeler, E. B., Leibowitz, A., & Marquis, M. S. (1987) 'Health insurance and the demand for medical care: evidence from a randomised experiment', *American Economic Review* 77: 251–77.

Marks, I. (1985) 'Controlled trial of psychiatric nurse therapists in primary care', *British Medical Journal* 290: 1181–4.

Maynard, A. (1985) 'Performance incentives', in G. Teeling-Smith (ed.) *Health Education and General Practice*, London: Office of Health Economics.

Maynard, A., Marinker, M., & Gray, D. P. (1986) 'The doctor, the patient and their contract: III. Alternative contracts, are they viable?', *British Medical Journal* 292: 1438–40.

Mulkay, M., Ashmore, M., & Pinch, T. (1987) 'Measuring the quality of life: a sociological invention concerning the application of economics to health care', *Sociology* 21(4): 541–64.

Muszynski, S., Brady, J., & Sharfstein, S. S. (1983) *Coverage for Mental and Nervous Disorders: Summaries of 300 Private Sector Health Insurance Plans*, Washington, DC: American Psychiatric Press.

Nathan, R. G., Robinson, D., Cherek, D. R., Simon Sebastian, C., & Hack, M. (1986) 'Alternative treatments for withdrawing the long-term benzodiazepine user: a pilot study', *International Journal of the Addictions* 21(2): 195–211.

Oswald, I., French, C., Adams, K., & Gilham, J. (1982) 'Benzodiazepine hypnotics remain effective for 24 weeks', *British Medical Journal* 284: 860–3.

Pirie, M. & Butler, E. (1988) *The Health of Nations: Solutions to the Problems of Finance in the Health Care Sector*, London: Adam Smith Institute.

Rakel, R. (1987) 'Assessing the efficacy of antianxiety agents', *American Journal of Medicine* 82(5A): 1–6.

Regier, D. A., Burke Jr., J. D., Manderscheid, R. W., & Burns, B. J. (1985) 'The chronically mentally ill in primary care', *Psychological Medicine*, 15: 265–273.

Renshaw, J. (1985) *Care in the Community: Measuring Outcomes for Mentally Ill People*, PSSRU discussion paper no 310/2, University of Kent.

Rickels, K., Case, G., Downing, R. W., & Winokur, A. (1983) 'Long-term diazepam therapy and clinical outcome', *Journal of American Medical Association* 250(6): 767–71.

Robson, M. H., France, R., & Bland, M. (1984) 'Clinical psychologist in primary care: controlled clinical and economic evaluation', *British Medical Journal* 288: 1805–7.

Royal College of Psychiatrists (1988) 'Benzodiazepines and dependence: a College statement', *Bulletin of the Royal College of Psychiatrists* 12(3): 107–9.

Ryles, A. (1986) 'Efficacy of treatment of mental illness in primary care settings', in M. Shepherd, G. Wilkinson & P. Williams (eds) *Mental Illness in Primary Care Settings*, London: Tavistock.

Schumacher, D. N., Namerow, M. J., Parker, B., Fox, P., & Kofie, V. (1986) 'Prospective payment for psychiatry – feasibility and impact', *New England Journal of Medicine* 315(21): 1331–6.

Sharfstein, S. S. & Beigel, A. (1984) 'Less is more? Today's economics and its challenge to psychiatry', *American Journal of Psychiatry* 11: 1403–8.

Shepherd, M., Harwin, B. G., Depla, C., & Cairns, V. (1979) 'Social work and primary care of mental disorder', *Psychological Medicine* 9: 661–9.

Shepherd, M., Cooper, B., Brown, A. C., & Kalton, G. (1981) *Psychiatric Illness in General Practice*, Oxford: Oxford University Press.

Skynner, A. C. R. & Brown, D. G. (1981) 'Referral of patients for psychotherapy', *British Medical Journal* 282: 1952–5.

Smith, A. (1987) 'Qualms about QALYs', *Lancet* I: 1134–6.

Strathdee, G. & Williams, P. (1984) 'A survey of psychiatrists in primary care: the silent growth of a new service', *Journal of Royal College of General Practitioners* 34: 615–18.

Taylor, D. (1987) 'Current usage of benzodiazepines in Britain', in H. Freeman & Y. Rue (eds) *The Benzodiazepines in Current Clinical Practice*, Royal Society of Medicine Services.

Teare Skinner, P. (1984) 'Skills not pills; learning to cope with anxiety', *Journal of Royal College of General Practitioners* 34(262): 258–60.

Torrance, G. (1986) 'Measurement of health state utilities for economic appraisal', *Journal of Health Economics* 5: 1–30.

Tudor Hart, J. (1985) 'Practice nurses: an under-used resource', *British Medical Journal* 290: 1162.

Tyrer, P. (1988) 'Prescribing psychotropic drugs in general practice', *British Medical Journal* 296: 588–9.

Tyrer, P. & Murphy, S. (1987) 'The place of benzodiazepines in psychiatric practice', *British Journal of Psychiatry* 151: 719–23.

Tyrer, P., Seivewright, N., & Wollerton, S. (1984) 'General practice psychiatric clinics: impact on psychiatric services', *British Journal of Psychiatry* 145: 15–19.

Tyrer, P., Murphy, S., Oates, G., & Kingdon, D. (1985) 'Psychological treatment for benzodiazepine withdrawal', *Lancet*, I: 1042–3.

Uhlenhuth, E. H., Dewit, H., Balter, M. B., Johnson, E. E., & Mellinger, G. D. (1988) 'Risks and benefits of long term benzodiazepine use', *Journal of Clinical Psychopharmacology* 8(3): 101–7.

Wagstaff, A. & Maynard, A. (1988) *Economic Aspects of the Illicit Drug Market and Drug Enforcement Policies in the United Kingdom*, Home Office Research and Planning Unit Report Study 95, London: HMSO.

Waydenfield, D. & Waydenfield, S. W. (1978) *Counselling in the General Practice Setting*, London: North London Marriage Guidance Council.

Wilkinson, G. & Pelosi, A. J. (1987) 'The economics of mental health services', *British Medical Journal* 294: 139–40.

Williams, P. (1982) 'The GP and the specialist: psychiatry', *British Medical Journal* 284: 876–7.

Wyld, K. L. (1981) 'Counselling in general practice: a review', *British Journal of Guidance and Counselling* 19(2): 129–41.

6 Decoding advertising: the role of communication studies in explaining the popularity of minor tranquillisers

Jane E. Prather

How did tranquillisers become so popular throughout the world that one brand, Valium, became the most frequently used drug in the world (Smith 1985; Krupka & Vener 1985)? What was the symptomatology that resulted in physicians prescribing so many minor tranquillisers? Did anxiety and tension become the most common international health problems? Why did so many women, but not men, become long-term users of minor tranquillisers?

This chapter offers some answers to these questions by reviewing the contribution of communication studies in analysing the impact of pharmaceutical advertising. An interdisciplinary field, communication studies has eclectically derived research techniques to decode both the content and the meaning of advertisements. Although the primary function of advertising is said to be to provide essential information to introduce and to promote consumer goods to the public, communication studies has revealed that contemporary advertising has become more and more involved in the manipulation of social values and attitudes (Dyer 1982: 2). Seen from this perspective, ads in modern society operate like myths in primitive cultures. The ads impart simple stories and explanations which convey values and ideas that assist people in making sense out of their world (Dyer 1982: 2). As will be shown in this chapter, advertisements for minor tranquillisers have also been perceived as suggesting a simplistic solution of medication to alleviate complex sociopsychological problems that prevail in modern society. The purpose of this chapter, then, is to describe the contributions of communication studies in investigating the impact of pharmaceutical advertising upon the popularity of tranquillisers and the resultant long-term usage of these drugs. To develop this argument four topics will be discussed: 1) an overview of pharmaceutical advertising as related to minor tranquillisers; 2) a review of content analysis studies of pharmaceutical advertising; 3) a summary of semiotic approaches for comprehending the meaning of the ads; and 4) a summary of the effects of advertising on physicians' prescribing patterns.

THE ROLE OF ADVERTISING IN LONG-TERM MINOR TRANQUILLISER USAGE

Following the Second World War drug innovations doubled and pharmaceutical sales increased at unprecedented rates (Statman 1983: 7). The major multinational pharmaceutical companies headquartered in Great Britain, the United States, West Germany, France, and Switzerland were embroiled in fierce competition to create new drugs. As the market for pharmaceuticals began to reach saturation, any drug introduced had to feature unique qualities (Statman 1983: 7). Since, by the mid–1950s, medications had already been developed to conquer many of the leading life-threatening diseases, and since the fields of psychology and psychiatry were gaining recognition, the timing was right for the innovation of drugs to alleviate mental illness. Major tranquillisers were the first on the market (Serpasil, 1953; Thorazine, 1954), followed by minor tranquillisers (Miltown and Equanil, 1956; Librium, 1960) and the most popular, Valium, in 1973 (Silverman *et al.* 1981: 49). What was significant about these drugs was not only their chemical innovation but also the clever advertising techniques pharmaceutical companies designed. Symptoms of psychological illness – tension, anxiety, insomnia, and depression – were, according to the ads, designated as 'diseases' which all physicians, not just psychiatrists, could treat with the new drugs (Silverman *et al.* 1981: 48). Since these psychological problems or mental illnesses often persisted for years, long-term drug therapy might be recommended.

The history of psychopharmacology thus reveals extremely aggressive promotion of the mood-modifying drugs under the guise of education. Since many physicians, even in the best of medical schools, may receive limited formal training in psychopharmacology (Gottlieb *et al.* 1978), they become highly susceptible to the pharmaceutical companies' promotional materials. Keeping abreast of new drugs is even more acute a problem for Third World physicians (Melrose 1982) who frequently have minimal pharmacological education and also may practise in remote areas with limited access to other colleagues (Greenhalgh 1987). Regardless of governmental attempts to regulate the marketing of ethical drugs, pharmaceutical companies incorporate highly competitive if not cutthroat marketing strategies and levy powerful lobbying pressure against changes in governmental control. For example, in spite of regulations prohibiting pharmaceutical companies from enticing physicians with lavish gifts, American pharmaceuticals may offer such incentives as expenses-paid trips to resort islands to attend a medical conference. The actual time allotted for medical education, however, might be only a few hours and the training might be the introduction of a new medication (see Silverman *et al.* 1981). Promotional techniques are even more aggressive in the developing countries where pharmaceutical companies may offer physicians scarce household appliances such as refrigerators, televisions, air conditioners, or even cars (Silverman *et al.* 1982).

The significant person in drug promotion is the detail person or pharmaceutical sales representative (PSR). Typically, the PSR has little formal training in medicine or pharmacology. With each physician visit, the PSR brings a host of commercial information under the semblance of scientific data, including prescribing guides, drug reference books, drug pamphlets, and drug samples. Ironically, pharmaceutical companies concentrate their promotion efforts in communities with the fewest physicians. Consequently, there are proportionally more pharmaceutical sales representatives (PSRs) per physician in developing countries than in wealthier nations. Whereas in Great Britain there is approximately one PSR for every eighteen physicians and in the United States a ratio of one for every eight physicians, in Latin American countries there is one PSR for every three physicians (UN data cited in Melrose 1982: 67).

In developing nations the pharmaceutical sales representatives may make frequent trips to both offices and homes of physicians (Silverman *et al.* 1982). PSRs are so persistent that a Brazilian physician reported that within twenty-one working days he had seen PSRs sixty-nine times and received 452 samples plus twenty-five gifts (Ledogar cited in Melrose 1982: 67). General practitioners in the Philippines reported up to twenty PSR contacts per day (Hardon 1987). Third World physicians may have no other sources for information about drugs except the commercial reports acquired from the PSRs (Greenhalgh 1987).

Even more important than physicians in developing countries are drug vendors who sell ethical drugs without prescriptions in market stalls, shops, or small pharmacies (see Van der Geest 1987a, and 1987b for descriptions of various drug suppliers). Having limited, if any, professional knowledge about drugs, the vendors rely upon advertising distributed by the PSRs and report frequent interaction with these sales representatives (Wolffers 1987).

Pharmaceutical advertising is omnipresent to the medical profession. Regardless of whether the physician reads a brochure accompanying drug samples, receives direct mail literature, scans a medical journal or medical business magazine, refers to the Physician's Desk Reference, hears an audio cassette or attends a symposium sponsored by the pharmaceutical companies – the advertising messages and the format are the same (see Ferm and Smith in Smith, M.C. 1983: 369). In the Third World pharmaceutical advertising for both ethical and over-the-counter medications is aimed at the masses. Magazines, newspapers, flyers, billboards, television, and radio – all feature pharmaceutical advertising for all drugs (Wang'Ombre & Mwabu 1987). Perhaps most effective among the poor and illiterate are the radio messages which have the potential to reach every village even though health care cannot (Silverman *et al.* 1982: 10).

Pharmaceutical advertising promotes brand name recognition. Brand loyalty may even be more pronounced in developing countries where physicians, drug sellers, and patients are suspicious of generic drugs because they lack sufficient knowledge about pharmacology and they fear and/or find generic substitutes are inferior (Greenhalgh 1987; Wang'Ombre & Mwabu 1987). The experiences of poverty and of drug scarcity lead the people to confer a mystique on brand name drugs which they may credit with producing miraculous cures (Hardon 1987). Whether generic drugs are as effective and are subjected to the same quality control as brand names is being debated in the United States. Attempts to curb ever-increasing costs of providing medical care in the United States have led both private and public medical insurance programmes to advocate use of generic drugs. The major pharmaceuticals have responded through advertising. For example, advertisements for Valium in the 1980s have featured a variety of ads advising physicians to specify the brand name of the minor tranquilliser they prescribe.

Budgets for advertising and other promotions for pharmaceuticals are immense. The American pharmaceutical industry spends an estimated $1.3 billion a year on advertising (Mendelsohn 1982) and the annual promotional budgets of British pharmaceuticals are approximately £35 million (Stimson 1977). In spite of their claims that the high cost of research raises drug prices, United States pharmaceutical corporations spend an average of 13 per cent of their total revenue on advertising, in contrast to 9 per cent for research and development (Mendelsohn 1982: 60).

Perhaps no other drug advertisements have been scrutinized as have those for the minor tranquillisers. On the other hand, perhaps no class of pharmaceuticals has been promoted to the same extent as have these drugs. In the following sections of this chapter, the numerous studies of tranquilliser advertisements will be reviewed.

CONTENT ANALYSIS STUDIES OF PHARMACEUTICAL ADVERTISEMENTS

Much of the relevant research on the advertising of minor tranquillisers has encompassed all kinds of psychotropic medications. Therefore, this literature review presents in chronological order the findings of research on the promotion of all classes of psychotropic drugs. These studies for the most part have concentrated on pharmaceutical advertising published in western European, American, or Australian medical journals.

The first investigations of pharmaceutical advertisements incorporated the methodology of content analysis. In this procedure each ad is analysed according to descriptive categories that have been defined and operationalized so that multiple judges are able to arrive at the same classification. Statistical analyses can then be performed to describe the relationships between categories. (For further information about content analysis methodology in advertising, see Leiss *et al.* 1986.)

One of the first published commentaries about minor tranquilliser advertising was actually a case study by a marketing specialist, Moskowitz (1960), who investigated how Librium had within three months become the leading minor tranquilliser. He described the range of commercial publicity physicians received about the drug. This included forty separate direct mailings, in addition to long-playing phonograph records (a novelty in the 1960s) containing physicians' testimonials of wondrous drug results. Eight-page advertisements appeared in leading medical journals. The significance of Moskowitz's study is that it was the first to document the importance of advertising for the success of tranquilliser sales.

In 1971, Robert Seidenberg (1971a, 1971b), an American psychiatrist, published a harsh critique of psychotropic drug advertisements. Although his original work contained few methodological details, Seidenberg claimed to have analysed ten years of twenty-four medical and psychiatric journals. He was one of the first to admonish the ads for medicalization, which he defined as the 'extension of drug use', implying ordinary conditions of living are pathological and, therefore, necessitating medication. Seidenberg was also the first scholar to call attention to the sexism in pharmacological advertising. He denounced the presentation of women as the sicker sex and the promotion of derogatory and demeaning images of women. He speculated about the motives of the pharmaceutical industry for condoning drug dependency among adults at the same time as society was fighting drug abuse among the young. Furthermore, Seidenberg criticized advertisers' recommendations of prescribing drugs without considering alternatives. In a later article Seidenberg (1974) described the difficulties he encountered in publishing his critique of psychopharmacology advertisements, which was rejected by over twenty journals before being accepted by one that did not solicit drug advertising. Seidenberg questioned whether scholarly journals dependent upon drug advertising could be objective in their selection of which research to publish.

Hemminki (1973) examined psychotropic ads in Finnish medical journals. Representing one of the most scholarly of these studies, Hemminki's work included precise definitions of categories and sampling techniques. In her investigation of three time periods (1959, 1965, 1971) she concluded that emotional appeals (use of humour, sex, or empathy rather than technical information) were more common in ads for psychotropics than non-psychotropics. She analysed the appeals in both the texts and the pictorials. If the sales appeal was emotional it was judged to be unprofessional. In contrasting the 1959 ads with those of 1971, Hemminki found minor tranquillisers were increasingly advertised with little text, with unprofessional pictures and captions, and with sparse information about drug functions or chemical structure. Like Seidenberg, she noted the tendency of advertising to recommend psychotropics for ordinary conditions of everyday life – tiredness, apathy, sensitivity. Hemminki concluded there was no significant difference in the ads regardless of whether the journals were Finnish, German, or Danish.

Stimson (1975a, 1975b) studied both psychotropic advertisements featured in British medical publications (1973–74) and the promotional literature distributed to general practitioners' offices. He objected to the vague and inconsistent drug indications presented in the ads for minor tranquillisers. The same minor tranquilliser compound (benzodiazepines) was advertised under three brand names with each ad recommending the drug for a different symptom. In addition, psychological terms such as 'anxiety', 'tension', or 'emotional' were misleading and could be subject to interpretation. Stimson's major criticism concerned the promotion of 'at-a-glance diagnosis' – the inference that a wide range of social and environmental stresses could be defined as individual problems meriting psychological treatment including medication. Confirming previous research, Stimson identified that women outnumbered men in psychotropic ads and that the reasons for prescribing drugs differed according to sex: women required psychotropics because of marital difficulties or housewife problems; men because of problematic work situations.

Prather and Fidell (1975) reviewed the pharmaceutical ads in three major American medical journals and one psychiatric journal for five years (1968–72). Ads were categorized according to whether a drug was for a psychogenic symptom or a physical illness. The study disclosed that women were more likely than men to be pictured in ads for psychotropic drugs and women were under-represented in advertisements for drugs prescribed for physical illness. Women were stereotyped as having imaginary or emotional problems while men were labelled as suffering from actual physical illness. Sex differences were also found in the reasons given for using psychotropic drugs. Physicians should prescribe psychotropics to men when tension accompanied physical disability or work obstacles and practitioners were advised to dispense psychotropics, especially minor tranquillisers, to women displaying symptoms of diffuse anxiety, tension, or depression.

Mant and Darroch (1975) analysed pharmaceutical advertising in Australian medical journals, investigating approximately 500 drug advertisements that appeared in seven years (1969–75). Randomly selecting one journal for each year, the researchers coded every advertisement according to whether a patient was shown, the sex of patient, the drug class, and the type of appeal. A scientific appeal was defined as including clinical information, scholarly references, or prescribing information. Significant differences were found between the ads for mood-modifying drugs and ads for all other drugs. Approximately 12.5 per cent of all the pharmaceutical ads were for mood modifiers. However, pictorials in the mood-altering drug ads most frequently included stereotyped females. Women were shown nude or as decorative illustrations. They appeared as helpless, foolish, seductive or as the harassed housewife. Women's psycho-emotional illnesses inconvenienced others. Men, on the other hand, were rarely belittled. Their ailments were shown as painful interruptions of normal life and work. The authors concluded that ads for all pharmaceutical varieties contained little scientific or professional appeal. Furthermore, they admonished that consistently advertising women as psychotropic drug users might reinforce the physician's expectation that female patients require such medications.

Mosher's (1976) work was a commentary on previous research on pharmacological advertising. She voiced concern about the sexism in prescription and proprietary psychotropic advertisements and she labelled the portrayal of women by the pharmaceutical advertiser as medical betrayal. In her view, the stereotyping of female patients reduced the need for complete medical diagnosis and, in turn, promoted unwarranted prescribing of mood-altering drugs.

Smith and Griffin (1977) obtained slides from a commercial agency of all psychotropic advertisements (no duplicates) that appeared during 1974 in major medical journals. The total sample of 329 ads was classified by drug categories: anti-anxiety, antipsychotics, and antidepressants. Smith and Griffin differentiated the appeals as either rational or non-rational. Rational appeals supplied information about the product, its clinical use, other practitioners' testimonials, or the reputation of the company. Irrational appeals suggested humour, ludicrous situations, sex appeal, or curiosity. Pharmacy students rated the rationality or irrationality of three ad components: illustration, caption, and text. Gender differences were discovered in ad appeals, with non-rational appeals associated with female patients, rational appeals with males. In the illustrations for all drug categories both males and females were depicted with non-rational appeals but females much more frequently than males. Only in the textual components of the ads were rational appeals consistently found for both males and females. Unlike in previous studies, the researchers did not confirm a significant association between the drug advertised and the sex of the patient depicted. They accounted for their unique findings as being due to the exclusion of duplicates and/or the possibility that the ads had changed. In conclusion, the authors (1977: 413) speculated that, even though sexism did occur in pharmaceutical advertising, ads may actually be less of an influence upon medical practice than a mirror reflecting it.

Thompson (1979) studied all pharmaceutical ads in the *New England Journal of Medicine* and the *Journal of the American Medical Association* for one year (1975). She classified ads according to drug-use conditions: psychogenic, organic, and functional. The unique finding of her study was that males were over-represented and females under-represented in the psychotropic drug ads. Thompson based her analysis on estimates of actual numbers of men and women in the US who suffered from a particular ailment or illness using data from the National Health Survey. Since these surveys reported that more females than males claimed they suffered from anxiety, insomnia, and depression, Thompson reasoned that the ads should include a higher percentage of women than men. Thompson evaluated her conclusions positively. By viewing proportionally more males than females in the psychotropic ads, physicians might become sensitized to the notion that men as well as women suffer from emotional disorders. The author did not address whether women are actually experiencing more emotional problems than men or are more willing to admit these psychological symptoms. This issue has repeatedly been raised by Cooperstock (1971, 1974), who questioned the legitimacy of the higher proportion of psychotropic prescriptions written for women than men.

King (1980) investigated all psychotropic advertisements (including duplicates or repeats) for seventeen years that appeared in the *American Journal of Psychiatry*. Her work confirmed and elaborated upon the sex stereotyping of earlier studies. The symptoms described in the ads were compared according to patients' gender and drug classification. Ads mentioning anxiety and depression most frequently featured a female patient and advised antidepressants in combination with major/minor tranquillisers. Anxiety and tension, on the other hand, elicited a portrayal of a male patient with a recommendation of prescribing a minor tranquilliser. Psychotropic ads most frequently depicted females as patients and these ads were repeatedly rerun, which she argued intensified their impact. Antidepressant ads featured women 82 per cent of the time while men were shown as the primary patients in ads for anticonvulsants, psychostimulants, and alcohol aversives. Examining the themes presented in the captions, the researcher uncovered gender differences in the presentation of symptoms. For example, a caption 'problems – real or imagined', she contended, cast doubt on the female patients' symptoms. Gender stereotypes abound in the captions and in the depictions of male and female patients. Ads displayed the female sufferer as helpless, passive, or ridiculous while the male was illustrated as encountering stress from job pressure, physical illness, or alcoholism. By contrast, the stereotyped females had problems caring for children, fulfilling their housewifely obligations, or coping with being single. Women also required medication because they were causing difficulties for others, such as a retarded child or a retired husband. The stereotyped advertising, according to King, instructed physicians to assist males to be productive again and to help females become more responsive. The ads reinforced gender stereotypes of ageing: older males worried about loss of health and physical vitality while elderly females feared loss of attractiveness.

King expressed concern about the 'before–after' ads which alluded to the physician as 'miracle-worker'. In these situations, the stereotyped female patient would be miserable, depressed, and estranged from her family. But after drug therapy she not only wore a happy face but acquired an attentive husband. Thus, according to King, writing a prescription allowed the physician to perform miracles that benefited both patient and spouse and enhanced his own self-esteem.

From a historical perspective M.C. Smith (1985) chronicled how minor tranquillisers were described in the mass media, in advertisements, and by regulatory agencies. Referring to his own research that traced the promotion of minor tranquillisers in American medical journals from 1964 to 1981, he contended that over time tranquilliser advertising had changed, possibly in response to governmental regulations or public outcries. The number of minor tranquilliser advertisements had decreased significantly since the drugs were introduced. Ad appeals had changed. Ads recommending tranquillisers for treating anxiety associated with disease began to replace ads advocating minor tranquillisers for coping with everyday living.

Gabe and Pelosi (forthcoming) conducted the most recent content analysis on all psychotropic drug advertisements appearing in four selected years (1965, 1973, 1978, 1983) of the *British Journal of Psychiatry*. Four features were observed: the nature of the prescribing information, rational vs. non-rational appeals, personal imagery, and impersonal imagery. (Rational/non-rational categories were based upon Smith and Griffin's definitions; personal imagery meant including human attributes such as a hand or face vs. impersonal which might incorporate symbols, objects, or animals.) Ads were designated as unprofessional if their appeal was emotional in contrast to a rational or technical perspective. Several findings merit comment. Psychotropic advertising increased during the years 1965–78 and then decreased. Over time more ads appeared for major tranquillisers but fewer advertisements were present for minor tranquillisers. More rational appeals occurred than non-rational. In the majority of cases when references were cited, the research was unpublished or available only by request. When the gender of a patient was depicted, 62 per cent of the ads included a picture of a woman, usually young. If portrayed, men were most likely illustrated in their middle years. What had not changed was the finding that twice as many women as men were employed in domestic capacities. In recent years advertisements have relied upon fewer patient pictorials but have included more impersonal imagery such as clinical settings of equipment, medical records, or tablet bottles. Also, newer ads featured tranquil imagery – flowers, lakes, or crossroads. (The meaning of these trends will be discussed in the next section of this chapter.) In conclusion, the authors commented on the racism, classism, and sexism featured in the ads. No blacks were depicted and most patients were represented as middle class. Physicians were characterized as male with nurses stereotyped as female. Emotional appeals were most often associated with images of females. In reflecting upon the significance of their findings, the researchers pondered whether the ads reflected or reinforced medical opinion and practice.

In summary, communication studies of the content analysis of psychotropic drug advertisements raise two significant concerns that might influence long-term tranquilliser use. The sexism concern is based upon the findings that women were typically illustrated as the patients in psychotropic advertisements and posed as ridiculous, passive, or incompetent. Although newer studies suggest that the inclusion of patients in drug ad pictorials appears to have decreased over time as has the degree of sex stereotyping, the imagery of a female taking minor tranquillisers may have formed an indelible image that continues to have consequences upon prescribing behaviour. The second concern that emerged from the content analysis research is that psychotropic ads promote medicalization – the defining of everyday tribulations as benefiting from medical attention. The minor tranquilliser ads in particular have presented medication as a solution to alleviating stresses as varied as coping with work roles or dealing with ageing. In this respect, critics (Lennard *et al.* 1971; Stimson 1977; Zola 1972) warn that these ads imply that physicians with a quick diagnosis and a simple prescription can solve a whole host of problems patients encounter daily or are causing others. From this perspective, the medicalization concern has serious ramifications for long-term prescribing of minor tranquillisers.

IDEOLOGICAL AND SEMIOTIC PERSPECTIVES ON DRUG ADVERTISING

With content analysis, communication studies had the methodology for rigorously comparing advertisements and for discovering patterns of similarities and differences. Subsequently, scholars in communication studies have begun to incorporate semiology, the study of signs, to decode advertising messages. In the semiotic perspective, signs consist of two components: 1) the signifier which is the actual object or item eliciting meaning and 2) the signified which is the meaning conveyed by the object (Leiss *et al.* 1986: 153). Using semiological techniques, the researcher can obtain an in-depth interpretation of the various messages ads convey to different audiences.

Semiotics has become even more important for analysing advertising in the last decade during which the format of advertising has changed (see Leiss *et al.* 1986). Previously, ads consisted of a more or less direct presentation of the product and information, even though the content might be misleading or exaggerated. Early ads contained many lines of text and featured small pictorials. Since the late 1970s advertising has consisted of a larger proportion of picture to text. There is often a complicated and indirect description of the product involving symbols for the setting, activity, and consumers. The text is either concise or non-existent. Captions may make implications rather than explicit statements. The ads imply – but do not directly communicate – that using the product will enhance the consumer by locating him/her in an idyllic setting surrounded by desirable people as the right feelings or moods emerge. The consumer or reader of the ad may need to study the ad's symbolism, to complete the abstraction, or to transform the product into a sign in order to comprehend the meaning. The more times the reader views the ad to grasp the meaning, the greater the probability he/she will remember the ad and hence become familiar with the product.

Pharmaceutical advertisements, too, began to reflect this indirect and complex use of symbols and two studies have been published that decode the meanings of psychotropic advertisements: Chapman (1979) and Goldman & Montagne (1986). Chapman's article described eight case studies of psychotropic advertisements printed in Australian medical journals. Theoretically, Chapman argued that an ad presented a problem and then offered a promise which was energized or made salient by a myth. A myth represented a recurring dominant theme or character type that embodied cultural ideals or evoked deep-felt emotions (1979: 751). Chapman decoded each ad according to the problem described, the promises made, and the cultural myths reinforced in three areas: doctors and doctoring, patients and their symptoms, and drugs or cures.

What persuades a physician to consider prescribing a particular drug? According to Chapman, the physician might harbour negative feelings about being the supplier of drugs, or about not being the healer he/she would like to be, or about making a diagnostic mistake or mis-prescribing. The physician might be experiencing typical problems of low self-esteem, poor people-relating skills, or doubts about sex appeal. Ads could then promise to resolve any of these problems. For example, by producing testimonials from other physicians, an ad offers reassurance to a sceptical or insecure physician. According to Chapman, when an ad appeals to a physician, a process occurs in which he/she feels gratified in seeing an aspect of himself (herself) – a fear, fantasy, or an attitude – objectified and made even more real through the physical ad (1979: 753).

Just as the content analysis studies disclosed that more women were portrayed in psychotropic advertisements, Chapman's analysis concentrated on five ads of women in stereotyped roles. Two ads featured housewives who were promised help in completing routinized chores and in making themselves and their families happy if they obtained mood-modifying drugs. According to Chapman, these ads attracted a (male) physician who perceived that the woman depicted might be like his wife; hence, he, too, could appreciate how husbands would like a happy and competent homemaker. Thus, the ad reinforced and normalized myths about the role of women that the physician might also believe.

To illustrate how ads used sex appeal to entice a physician, Chapman decoded an ad featuring a beautiful, young, seductive woman who complained her sleeping pills were ineffective. By recommending another drug, the ad implied that writing the prescription would not only increase the patient's respect for the physician, but also the patient would trust him, believe in him, and even perceive him as sexually appealing. While previous researchers (Seidenberg 1974; Mosher 1976) using content analysis criticized the pharmaceutical ads for creating psychological diseases out of everyday problems, Chapman's analysis illuminated why these ads were effective. For the medical reader the ads first presented a problem, then offered a solution which would be easy to perform through writing the prescription, and finally the ads affirmed some age-old myths or beliefs upheld by the physician. Furthermore, this perspective also explained why these ads have conveyed reassuring messages to internists and general practitioners, the major prescribers of psychotropics. As the physicians who first encountered patients with vague symptoms, the general practitioners sought ways to diagnose difficult symptoms. The ads suggested a simplistic solution – the 'diagnosis at a glance'. Testimonials or before–after images provided even further reassurance that the physician made a wise decision.

Chapman's works raised several important considerations for understanding advertising and long-term tranquilliser use. Advertisements were effective because they proposed promises in response to problems that mirrored myths important to physicians' beliefs. Successful medical advertising, by definition, reproduced the ideologies of physicians. Thus, by presenting minor tranquillisers as solving female patients' problems the ad promised the practitioner such things as self-esteem, sex appeal, and reassurance, at the same time reinforcing the physician's stereotyped ideas about women. In addition, Chapman speculated that journal editors or other regulators have, 'an extraordinarily naive view of the persuasion process' (1979: 763). When guidelines focused on the 'good taste' test for evaluating ads, the real impact or significance of the ad might be ignored.

Goldman and Montagne (1986) used a semiotic perspective to investigate how advertisements communicated with physicians through use of abstract visual metaphors and symbols. They argued ads conveyed simplistic, reductionist views about psychiatric illness by implying the illness can be quickly diagnosed and simply treated by a chemical formula. According to the authors, the ads ignored the complex socio-cultural roots of psychiatric illness and the unique configuration of factors that may produce the symptoms in any individual.

To illustrate their assertions, the researchers decoded two ads for antidepressants: Ludiomil and Desyrel. The introductory ad for Ludiomil incorporated the symbol of a dewy red rose growing out of a dry, parched surface that supported a surrealistic facial mask. According to the authors, the rose depicted in all Ludiomil ads represented a promise of a new drug for depression while the parched earth symbolized the depressed mind. The physician linked the rose with effective drug therapy. In the Desyrel ad the symbols were a solar eclipse signifying darkness and 'the new light' of the sun representing the drug that would lift the darkness.

In their analysis three interpretative procedures were evoked by the ads: abstraction, equivalency, reification. Abstraction was illustrated by the use of the symbols being detached from their normal context so that the readers accepted new meanings or invented their own. Abstract art or surrealistic images such as the mask and the parched earth were designed to 'hook' the reader to contemplate the pictorial to ascertain its meaning. Not only was an ad more effective the longer it grasped the reader's attention, but the more the ad could promote the reader to particularize the ad to her/his experience, the more effective would be the selling power. Equivalency referred to the metaphoric qualities of the symbol. Thus, the nature symbol such as the rose became equivalent to the qualities produced by the antidepressant drug. Thus, psychotropic drug advertisements often included binary oppositions – one symbol portraying the pain/anguish of the mental illness and the other symbol representing the opposite of this mental state, implying that the drug can cause the transference, the replacement of one state by the other. By repeating the same symbol, the ad persuaded the physician to make this transference: the symbol representing the product that in turn would transform the mental state of the patient. The symbolized product was thus interchangeable with a symbolized feeling – the two were equivalent and exchangeable for each other. Symbolism eliminated the need for additional information and allowed the physician as viewer to make further inferences. The third interpretative procedure was reification: the process by which acts reinforced physicians' beliefs and realities. Through reification, the ads perpetuated such common societal notions as the omnipotence of the physician's role, the mystique of drugs to heal, or the typifications of patients' symptoms. Analysing minor tranquilliser ads by these interpretative procedures reveals how a physician might be persuaded to write prescription re-fills for minor tranquillisers without recognizing that repeatedly performing this act may be leading to long-term usage, if not dependency.

In summary, semiological analysis has resulted in three major contributions to the study of psychotropic advertisements. First, semiotic studies have clarified the well-documented findings (Prather & Fidell 1975; Gabe & Pelosi forthcoming) that pharmaceutical advertising usually depicted only male physicians with white, middle-class patients. Just as advertisements for any consumer item imply that the purchase of a product will enhance one's social status, the pharmaceutical ad illustrated the preferred patients – the ones the physician would like to include in his/her practice – which typically means those who are white and middle class. These attributes might symbolize a patient who was educated or in other respects shared a similar value system, thus facilitating communication. When applicable to a fee for service health system, this patient also signified someone likely to have financial resources to pay the physician's bill. The inclusion in psychotropic ads of seductive young women alludes to the (male) physician's fantasies (as imagined by the advertisers) of being sexually attractive to beautiful women. Illustrations of a seductive female patient imply that the sexy woman is the practitioner's reward for prescribing the drug. Other ads employ symbols that insinuate that the physician is a magician or miracle worker by illustrating before and after use of the drug: a transformation in a patient's mood occurs because the physician dispensed the appropriate drug. In these ads benefits accrued to both the consumer (patient) and the prescriber (doctor). Thus, the physician identifies with the advertisement projecting that his patients, like those in the ads, are white and middle class and will provide him with financial rewards as well as psychic benefits for solving their problems.

Second, semiology has emphasized that the significant appeal of ads is conveyed through understanding the signs presented in the ads. The belief systems, the meanings, the ideologies of a society are embedded in the signs or symbols that may be either directly or abstractly represented in the ads. The underlying messages effectively reinforce beliefs that may be at a latent or non-conscious level for the reader. Tranquilliser ads thus contain many covert messages that reify cultural beliefs and stereotypes about anxious or frustrated women, emotional stress accompanying disease, the hectic pace of daily living, or the peaceful qualities of nature. Long-term tranquilliser usage, according to this perspective, would be reinforced more by the symbolism than the content of the ad.

The third contribution of semiology has been in the realm of regulation. The semiologists have advocated that agencies or researchers concerned about pharmaceutical advertising should direct their attention to the messages relayed through abstract symbols and visual metaphors. Cosmetic alterations in the pictorials or captions will not improve the validity of the advertising message, unless the significant symbols are also changed.

THE IMPACT OF PHARMACEUTICAL ADVERTISING

How effective, then, is pharmaceutical advertising? Although some scholars assert a correlation exists between drug promotion and drug sales (Melrose 1982: 64; Hemminki 1973, 1975; Krupka & Vener 1985; Lexchin 1987) others argue that the relationship remains inconclusive (Snell 1982; Mackowiak & Gagnon 1985). In her literature review, Hemminki (1975) advocates that prescribing practices can best be improved through changes in advertising and education rather than attempts to alter characteristics of patients and physicians. She also recommends that not only journal advertising but all forms of pharmaceutical promotional literature, including data conveyed through PSRs and the drug information services, should be analysed for their impact upon prescribing. The role of pharmaceutical companies in sponsoring medical research has also been questioned. Researchers (O'Malley & O'Hanrahan 1982) warn that medical professionals (including the authors) receiving sponsorship from pharmaceutical corporations need to recognize that they are sacrificing independence in conducting their studies and that this relationship merits continuous review.

In an investigation (Peay & Peay 1988) of physicians' decisions to prescribe a newly marketed minor tranquilliser, the majority (68 per cent) stated they first heard about the new tranquilliser from commercial sources obtained from detailmen. Promotional materials were cited by 57 per cent of the physicians as having the most influence in their decision to first prescribe the drug. Moreover, physicians who mentioned commercial sources as their usual forum for drug information prescribed the tranquilliser earlier and were more likely to prefer it to other alternatives than were those who did not rely upon commercial resources. Thus, the authors (Peay & Peay 1988) concluded that pharmaceutical promotional data are more significant than professional sources in the initial decision to prescribe a minor tranquilliser.

When Valium was featured in more advertisements in medical journals than any other prescription drug (1972–77) Valium became the most widely prescribed drug in the world (Krupka & Vener 1985). The correlation confirmed that advertising of prescription drugs in professional journals was of financial benefit to pharmaceutical companies. Furthermore, it was speculated that advertising of minor tranquillisers, such as Valium, may be even more important for influencing sales than promotionals for drugs that alleviate specific physiological conditions, since physicians may experience more ambivalence about prescribing mood-modifying drugs (Krupka & Vener 1985).

An ad effectiveness study revealed that if physicians recalled an advertisement there was a very high probability they would prescribe the drug within sixty days (Walton 1980 cited in Ferm & Smith 1983: 394–5). Most physicians, however, deny they can be swayed by promotional pressures (Melrose 1982: 64). In an interesting case of professional projection, psychiatrists argued they would *not* be influenced by psychotropic ads but that other medical specialists might be persuaded (McRee *et al.* 1974). The majority (55 per cent) of these psychiatrists indicated that their thinking would not be influenced at all by drug advertisements of any type. Yet a large majority (74 per cent) thought that physicians, who knew little about psychiatry, would believe ads *that implied* that more women than men had mental illness symptoms requiring medication.

Pharmaceutical companies capitalize on the difficulties that most physicians experience keeping abreast of new drugs. The situation is exacerbated because the majority of drugs currently marketed were not developed fifteen years ago (Mumford 1983: 463) and, hence, physicians frequently prescribe drugs which were unknown to them during their medical training (Hemminki 1973). A literature review (Krupka & Vener 1985) ascertained that as few as 6 per cent in one study and as many as 62 per cent of physicians in another article stated medical advertising provided their first knowledge about new drugs. Among American general practitioners surveyed, 73 per cent claimed advertising in medical journals was very important or somewhat important as an informational source about new medicines (Linn & Davis 1972). Even if physicians prefer to believe they are not influenced by advertising, pharmaceutical companies and advertising firms remain unconvinced. As an executive of the Canadian Pharmaceutical Manufacturers Association stated, 'If advertising doesn't influence doctors then a hell of a lot of people are wasting a lot of money' (Cocking 1977 as reported in Lexchin 1987). After investigating a pharmaceutical company that suffered severe financial setbacks when it distributed announcements rather than advertisements about new drugs, a Canadian study concluded that the most effective way to expand sales of any drug is to increase the promotional budget. In the case cited, the pharmaceutical company recovered economically only when it launched an aggressive advertising campaign (Pazderka *et al.* cited in Lexchin 1987).

Although most western countries have governmental regulations (British Medicines Act 1968) or manufacturers' codes (Association of British Pharmaceutical Industry code of practice) to monitor pharmaceutical promotions, enforcement of these rules remains lax or difficult (Lexchin 1987; Stimson 1975a; O'Malley & O'Hanrahan

1982; Dyer 1987; Millstein 1983). As the semiology researchers have demonstrated, regulatory agencies typically focus on the blatant content rather than the subtler message, scrutinizing factual details while ignoring the implied promises. The problems of regulating advertisements are exacerbated in Third World countries where governmental controls over the transnational pharmaceuticals are extremely ineffective (Greenhalgh 1987; Smith, G.T. 1987; Lilja 1983; Taylor 1986).

Pharmaceutical advertisements have been criticized, for while they purport to be informative, they may actually contain few data upon which the practitioner can make a professional decision (Stimson 1975a, 1975b, 1975c; O'Malley & O'Hanrahan 1982). Specifications about contraindications, side effects, and special precautions are often lacking and ads contain inaccurate or inadequate information (Hemminki 1973). The psychotropic ads include testimonials of questionable clinical value (Lexchin 1987: 84) or refer to research that is unpublished or available only upon request (Gabe & Pelosi forthcoming). Advertisements distributed in the Third World have been criticized for their inaccurate content in which they minimize or totally ignore hazards, exaggerate claims, overstate indications, and contain pretentious or fictitious testimonials (Gereffi 1983; Silverman *et al.* 1982). Not uncommon are advertisements for potentially dangerous drugs with little space devoted to side effects (Lilja 1983). Ads promote psychotropic drugs, including tranquillisers, for a wide range of indications such as pain, fever, nonspecific abdominal symptoms, and trivial complaints (Greenhalgh 1987). When scientific results are presented, they frequently do not contain evidence to support the claims being made (Lilja 1983). Both multinational and indigenous pharmaceutical companies are guilty of these practices among developing nations (Lilja 1983). Advertising to the masses in developing countries creates demands for medications by both rich and poor who want to emulate the perceived superior health status of the developed countries (Smith, G.T. 1987). They want the so-called 'white people's medicine' (Bledsoe & Goubaud 1985). Since most other aspects of western health care are unavailable, attractively packaged drugs are sought even if the medications do not directly solve their health problems (David cited in Melrose 1982: 92). Minor tranquillisers are one of these wondrous drugs in high demand in developing countries. Among the top ten in imported pharmaceuticals, minor tranquillisers are one of the five most common drugs in combination medications in the Third World (Greenhalgh 1987).

Pharmaceutical advertising plays a much more significant role in the developing countries than in wealthier nations since advertising may be the only information that patients, pharmacists, drug vendors, and physicians in the Third World receive about drugs. Concern over the lack of accurate information to developing countries has led critics (Lionel and Herxheimer cited in Melrose 1982) to assert that the ethical drug problems these countries experience are exacerbated by pharmaceutical advertising, which, to a great extent, has been responsible for the problems of excessive and irrational prescribing of drugs, including minor tranquillisers.

Thus, in both modern and developing countries there is concern about whether the ads are more persuasive than informative and about whether ads, especially for minor tranquillisers, are promoting long-term drug use. The most recent outcries about pharmaceutical advertising have come from the most significant audience: physicians. In articles and in letters to the editor in the major medical journals, western physicians have been increasingly writing to deplore the pharmaceutical industry's promotional practices (Finucane 1987; Smith, R. 1986) or to warn about the potential negative impact of direct consumer advertising (Morris *et al*. 1986) or to suggest guidelines for controlling pharmaceutical advertising (Carter 1987).

CONCLUSION

In this chapter I have shown how communication studies has provided the methodological tools for analysing the ways in which psychotropic drugs are advertised. Content analysis has revealed that these advertisements have a history of gender stereotyping women as the patients most often necessitating all classes of psychotropics and insinuating that their gender predisposes them to psychological illness. Only the most recent content analysis studies have reported a decrease in sex stereotyping. Semiotics has been instrumental in decoding advertisements to reveal the covert messages which imply that drugs such as minor tranquillisers will perform miracles in transforming a patient's mood and, in turn, the physician's capabilities. Semiotic analysis has uncovered the ads' appeal to physicians – a fantasy that she/he may become more competent, more omnipotent, or more sexually attractive. Communication studies has also helped explain why the popularity of tranquillisers has rapidly increased in developing countries where health needs and advertising regulations are distinct from those in developed nations.

Communication studies has demonstrated how ineffective regulatory agencies are because of their myopic focus upon the few blatant fraudulent advertisements, while dismissing the majority of ads conveying misleading, if not deceptive, assertions.

Most importantly, communication studies has elucidated the contribution of advertising in potentially promoting long-term tranquilliser use, especially among female patients. By initially advertising that female patients could benefit from taking minor tranquillisers for surviving in their hectic everyday worlds, the pharmaceutical companies established a target population of users. When the most advertising space was purchased for minor tranquillisers, the most prescriptions were filled (Krupka & Vener 1985). The prescribing patterns reflected the advertising message and twice as many women as men received prescriptions for minor tranquillisers (Balter *et al.* 1984). Even though the advertisements of the late 1980s may contain less of the sexual stereotyping of an earlier decade and in many cases do not contain a pictorial of a patient, these trends do not signify that the advertising of minor tranquillisers is not having an impact on long-term usage of these drugs. Instead, the contemporary tranquilliser ads are attempting to target different populations and to convey new messages in order to increase or, at best, sustain sales. To now include more men than women in the minor tranquilliser ads can be viewed as a way to multiply sales by extending the market to another population (see Krupka & Vener 1985: 195). Semiologists would argue that there are important prescribing messages implied in the gender-neutral and nature symbols found in the most recent minor tranquilliser ads. The message to specify brand names in the minor tranquilliser ads is in response to both generic prescribing and the patent expiry of two leading minor tranquillisers, Valium and Librium. As communication studies have revealed, what becomes important in decoding tranquilliser advertising is interpreting not only the illustration but also the illusion; not merely the overt message but also the covert symbolism. Although presumably it was not intended that advertisements would promote long-term minor tranquilliser usage, this may, in fact, have been the result. For, through a host of various promotional messages, pharmaceutical companies may have established a justification for long-term prescribing of these drugs.

REFERENCES

Balter, M. B., Manheimer, D. I., Mellinger, G. D., & Uhlenhuth, E. H. (1984) 'A cross-national comparison of anti-anxiety/sedative drug use', *Current Medical Research Opinion* 8(Suppl. 4): 5–20.

Bledsoe, C. H. & Goubaud, M. F. (1985) 'The reinterpretation of Western pharmaceuticals among the Mende of Sierra Leone', *Social Science and Medicine* 21: 275–82.

Carter, I. E. (1987) 'Canadian Psychiatric Association Guidelines in relating to the pharmaceutical industry', *Canadian Journal of Psychiatry* 32: 476–80.

Chapman, S. (1979) 'Advertising and psychotropic drugs: the place of myth in ideological reproduction', *Social Science and Medicine* 13A: 751–64.

Cooperstock, R. (1971) 'Sex differences in the use of mood-modifying drugs: an explanatory model', *Journal of Health and Social Behavior* 12: 238–43.

Cooperstock, R. (1974) 'Some factors involved in the increased prescribing of psychotropic drugs', in R. Cooperstock (ed.) *Social Aspects of the Medical Use of Psychotropic Drugs*, Toronto: Addiction Research Foundation.

Dyer, C. (1987) 'The penalties of issuing misleading advertisements', *British Medical Journal* 294(February 14): 426–7.

Dyer, G. (1982) *Advertising as Communication*, New York: Methuen.

Ferm, M. A. & Smith, M. C. (1983) 'Advertising', in M. C. Smith (ed.) *Principles of Pharmaceutical Marketing*, Philadelphia: Lea & Febiger.

Finucane, T. (1987) 'Drug company-sponsored symposia: pros and cons, letter to the editor', *American Journal of Medicine* 83: 811–12.

Gabe, J. & Pelosi, A. (forthcoming) 'Trends in psychotropic drug advertising: a study of the *British Journal of Psychiatry*'.

Gereffi, G. (1983) *The Pharmaceutical Industry and Dependency in the Third World*, Princeton, NJ: Princeton University Press.

Goldman, R. & Montagne, M. (1986) 'Marketing "mind mechanics": decoding antidepressant drug advertisements', *Social Science and Medicine* 22: 1047–58.

Gottlieb, R., Nappi, T., & Strain, J. (1978) 'The physician's knowledge of psychotropic drugs', *American Journal of Psychiatry* 135: 29–32.

Greenhalgh, T. (1987) 'Drug prescription and self-medication in India: an exploratory survey', *Social Science and Medicine* 25: 307–18.

Hardon, A. P. (1987) 'The use of modern pharmaceuticals in a Filipino village: doctors' prescription and self medication', *Social Science and Medicine* 25: 277–92.

Hemminki, E. (1973) 'The quality of drug advertisements in two Finnish medical journals: a comparison between psychotropic and other drug advertisements', *Social Science and Medicine* 7: 51–9.

Hemminki, E. (1975) 'Review of literature on the factors affecting drug prescribing', *Social Science and Medicine* 9: 111–15.

King, E. (1980) 'Sex bias in psychoactive drug advertisements', *Psychiatry* 43: 129–37.

Krupka, L. R. & Vener, M. A. (1985) 'Prescription drug advertising: trends and implications', *Social Science and Medicine* 20: 191–7.

Leiss, W., Kline, S., & Jhally, S. (1986) *Social Communication in Advertising*, New York: Methuen.
Lennard, H., Berstein, L., & Ransom, D. (1971) *Mystification and Drug Misuse*, San Francisco: Jossey-Bass.
Lexchin, J. (1987) 'Pharmaceutical promotion in Canada: convince them or confuse them', *International Journal of Health Services* 17: 77–89.
Lilja, J. (1983) 'Indigenous and multinational pharmaceutical companies', *Social Science and Medicine* 17: 1171–80.
Linn, L. S. & Davis, M. S. (1972) 'Physicians' orientation towards the legitimacy of drug use and their preferred source of new drug information', *Social Science and Medicine* 6: 199–203.
Mackowiak, J. I. & Gagnon, J. P. (1985) 'Effects of promotion on pharmaceutical demand', *Social Science and Medicine* 20: 1191–7.
McRee, C., Corder, B. F., & Haizlip, T. (1974) 'Psychiatrists' responses to sexual bias in pharmaceutical advertising', *American Journal of Psychiatry* 131: 1273–5.
Mant, A. & Darroch, D. B. (1975) 'Media images and medical images', *Social Science and Medicine* 9: 613–17.
Melrose, D. (1982) *Bitter Pills, Medicines and the Third World Poor*, Oxford: Oxfam.
Mendelsohn, R. S. (1982) *Malpractice*, Chicago: Contemporary Books.
Millstein, L. G. (1983) 'The regulation of prescription drug advertising', *American Pharmacy* NS23: 54–7.
Morris, L., Brinberg, D., Klimberg, R., Millstein, L., & Rivera, C. (1986) 'Consumer attitudes about advertisements for medicinal drugs', *Social Science and Medicine* 22: 629–38.
Mosher, E. (1976) 'Portrayal of women in drug advertising: a medical betrayal', *Journal of Drug Issues* 6: 72–7.
Moskowitz, M. (1960) 'Librium: a marketing case history', *Drug and Cosmetic Industry* 87: 460–1, 566–7.
Mumford, E. (1983) *Medical Sociology*, New York: Random House.
O'Malley, K. & O'Hanrahan, M. (1982) 'Drug promotion and the doctor', *British Journal of Clinical Pharmacology* 14: 661–4.
Peay, M. Y. & Peay, E. R. (1988) 'The role of commercial sources in the adoption of a new drug', *Social Science and Medicine* 26: 1183–9.
Prather, J. E. & Fidell, L. S. (1975) 'Sex differences in the content and style of medical advertisements', *Social Science and Medicine* 9: 23–6.
Seidenberg, R. (1971a) 'Drug advertising and perception of mental illness', *Mental Hygiene* 55: 21–31.
Seidenberg, R. (1971b) 'Advertising and abuse of drugs', *New England Journal of Medicine* 284: 789–90.
Seidenberg, R. (1974) 'Images of health, illness and women in drug advertising', *Journal of Drug Issues* 4: 264–7.
Silverman, M., Lee, P. R., & Lydecker, M. (1981) *Pills and the Public Purse*, Berkeley: University of California Press.
Silverman, M., Lee, P. R., & Lydecker, M. (1982) *Prescriptions for Death: The Drugging of the Third World*, Berkeley: University of California Press.
Smith, G. T. (1987) 'The economics of essential drug programmes', *Social Science and Medicine* 25: 621–4.

Smith, M. C. (1983) *Principles of Pharmaceutical Marketing*, Philadelphia, PA: Lea & Febiger.
Smith, M. C. (1985) *Small Comfort: A History of Minor Tranquilizers*, New York: Praeger.
Smith, M. C. & Griffin, L. (1977) 'Rationality of appeals used in the promotion of psychotropic drugs: a comparison of male and female models', *Social Science and Medicine* 11: 409–14.
Smith, R. (1986) 'Doctors and the drug industry: too close for comfort', *British Medical Journal* 293: 905–6.
Snell, E. S. (1982) 'Drug promotion and the doctor – a reply', *British Journal of Clinical Pharmacology* 14: 664–6.
Statman, M. (1983) *Competition in the Pharmaceutical Industry*, Washington, DC: American Enterprise Institute for Public Policy Research.
Stimson, G. V. (1975a) 'Information contained in drug advertisements', *British Medical Journal* iv: 508–9.
Stimson, G. V. (1975b) 'The message of psychotropic drug ads', *Journal of Communication* 25: 153–60.
Stimson, G. V. (1975c) 'Women in a doctored world', *New Society* 1: 265–7.
Stimson, G. V. (1977) 'Do drug advertisements provide therapeutic information?', *Journal of Medical Ethics* 3: 7–13.
Taylor, D. (1986) 'The pharmaceutical industry and health in the third world', *Social Science and Medicine* 22: 1141–9.
Thompson, L. (1979) 'Sexual bias in drug advertisements', *Social Science and Medicine* 13A: 187–90.
Van der Geest, S. (1987a) 'Pharmaceuticals in the Third World: the local perspective', *Social Science and Medicine* 25: 273–6.
Van der Geest, S. (1987b) 'Self-care and the informal sale of drugs in South Cameroon', *Social Science and Medicine* 25: 293–305.
Wang'Ombre, J. K. & Mwabu, G. M. (1987) 'Economics of essential drugs schemes: the perspectives of the developing countries', *Social Science and Medicine* 25: 625–30.
Wolffers, I. (1987) 'Drug information and sale practices in some pharmacies of Colombo, Sri Lanka', *Social Science and Medicine* 25: 319–21.
Zola, I. K. (1972) 'Medicine as an institution of social control', *Sociological Review* 20: 487–504.

7 The political economy of long-term minor tranquilliser use

Larry Ray

This chapter develops an approach to the long-term use of benzodiazepines, drawing upon literature in the political economy of the pharmaceutical industry. This is a highly controversial area, and it is not difficult to see why. A globally organized, highly profitable industry allocates major health goods as commodities, subject to market rationality. Pharmaceuticals are high-technology products, the safety and efficiency of which consumers (the patients) have to take largely on trust. An industry driven by research and development (R&D) and extensive product rather than price competition is exceptionally secretive, as the case of Hoffman-La-Roche and Stanley Adams indicated. Estimations of the social value of the industry thus vary widely. George Teeling-Smith (Director of the industry-sponsored Office of Health Economics), for example, recently voiced the view that the industry was under siege:

> a series of organizations purporting to represent the broad public interest have launched a massive and concerted attack on the activities of the pharmaceutical industry throughout the world. These organizations include Oxfam, War on Want, the World Council of Churches, and Social Audit, as well as Health Action International. These are supported by politically motivated doctors.
>
> (Wells 1985: 72)

On the other hand, John Braithwaite, whose *Corporate Crime in the Pharmaceutical Industry* (1984) is one of the most remarkable pieces of corporate 'whistle blowing' in recent years, claims: 'Bribery and corruption, fraud in the testing of drugs, criminal negligence in the manufacture of drugs, dubious advertising claims – the pharmaceutical industry has a worse record of law-breaking than any other industry' (Braithwaite 1986: 19).

Political economy raises the question not only of unethical practices in the pursuit of profit, but also of the commodification of health needs, of how these needs are constituted, and by what ideological strategies markets for tranquillisers are reproduced. Indeed, it is the attempt to grasp the totality of social relations – economic, institutional, and ideological – through which capital is reproduced that distinguishes political economy from social science in general. In relation to tranquilliser use, it is necessary to consider the central tendencies of the industry in the context of the movement of capital as a whole – towards internationalization, oligopolistic market segmentation, the realization of value through specialist agencies (such as physicians and pharmacies), and the maintenance of sponsorship. It is also necessary to look at sites of struggle around these processes, in particular at consumer activism and litigation (organized in the UK for example by Tranx or the Council for Involuntary Tranquilliser Addiction), and the pressure this exerts on government for additional regulatory control. This discussion will also consider how the state (as both executive and legislative) exercises a dual function as both regulator of capital and guarantor of its profitability. First, though, let us look at the framework of a political economy of the pharmaceutical industry.

POLITICAL ECONOMY OF THE PHARMACEUTICAL INDUSTRY

J. B. McKinlay (1984) suggests that the value of political economy lies in its ability to render explicable the 'seemingly illogical and inexplicable system of the medical-industrial complex', as the ideologies and activities that support it are considered in terms of the 'logic of capitalist expansion' (McKinlay 1984: 2). Central to this view is the notion that profitability is driven by competition, accumulation, reinvestment, and technological development. The continual drive to create new markets and reduce costs (thus offsetting the tendency of the rate of profit to fall)[1] involves, if necessary, deceptive advertising, minimal standards of product safety,[2] and a 'commodified fetishistic culture'. By this he means that transforming use-values into commodities creates, along with the market, a form of consciousness in which the social relations of exploitation are hidden, and in which needs are articulated in terms of the ability to pay.

Indeed, as commodities, pharmaceuticals enjoy a number of advantages over many other products. There is a large and captive market, guaranteed by the doctor, who acts as gatekeeper of consumption structures (Lennard & Cooperstock 1980; Bodenheimer 1984). Drugs have a near total consuming public, since almost everyone in developed societies takes prescription and over the counter (OTC) drugs at some time. The state acts as guarantor of profit, both as major purchaser and as licensing authority. These advantages have given rise to disputes over levels of profitability, the abuse of monopoly power, and the social costs or benefits of high R&D costs. Disputes surround the necessity for stringent regulatory control (e.g. through the Food and Drugs Administration (FDA) in the USA), the relationship between high profit margins and incentives to innovation, and control over technology and information flows.

One of the central issues here is that of the monopolization of therapeutic sub-markets by drug transnational corporations (TNCs). At first glance, the industry does not appear highly concentrated. In Britain the top five firms accounted for only 26.6 per cent of pharmaceutical sales in 1973 (Slatter 1977: 47). No company globally has more than 10 per cent of the total market (Melville & Johnson 1983: 47). What is crucial here is the degree of market segmentation – since competition takes place within therapeutic categories, in which there is very low cross-elasticity of demand, i.e. an increase in the price of sex hormones will not cause doctors to substitute with antibiotics and *vice versa*. Thus ICI's heart pills, Beechams's antibiotics, or Hoffman-La-Roche's tranquillisers are not in competition. Within these therapeutic sub-markets, though, concentration is relatively high: of fifty-one chemical entities making up two-thirds of US prescription sales, twenty-seven had only one producer; eight had two; and three, less than seven (Melville & Johnson 1983: 47). Further, in 1973 the degree of concentration among the four leading firms for tranquillisers was 86 per cent, topped only by anti-arthritics (96 per cent) and antidiabetics (98 per cent).

The extent of monopolization in the industry was investigated in the Kafauver Hearings in the US in the early 1960s, which found that: i) indirect demand, where the doctor constituted the demand but did not carry the cost, created inelastic demand; ii) monopolization occurs in sub-markets through patents that create false product differentiation (e.g. Librium, Valium, and Mogadon, which have the same chemical properties); iii) patenting favours concentration, since for small firms a patent is merely an invitation to costly litigation; iv) advertising economies of scale favour large firms which can disparage the products of small firms; v) patents therefore act as a barrier to competition (Steele 1962, 1964; Egan *et al.* 1982). These findings have been strongly contested by industry economists, who have argued that: viewed over time entry barriers to market segments are not excessive; patenting (and high profits) are justified by the overall welfare they create; and, if R&D is costed as capital investment rather than capital expense, and is depreciated, then rates of profitability will be lower than they appear (e.g. Egan *et al.* 1982). These arguments will be considered in due course, but it is notable that, as Comanor (1986) points out, the locus of debate since the Kafauver Hearings has shifted from issues of monopoly and competition to the effects of regulation on innovation.

For political economy, though, the logic of profit maximization is such that decision making in TNCs is seldom influenced by awareness of social needs or social costs, but will on the contrary ruthlessly ignore these where necessary. Thus the industry markets unsafe and untested drugs in parts of the world that lack regulatory controls[3] and for which palliative medicine is largely inappropriate anyway. Chien complains that 'excessive proof of efficacy and safety has raised the cost and uncertainties of research to such an extent that participation by smaller companies has been inhibited; government policies also appear to have reduced the rate of return for such investment below opportunity costs' (Chien 1979: vi). However, Grabowski and Vernon are reassuring: the multinational structure of the industry enables it to respond 'to the more stringent regulatory conditions in the USA, by testing drug products in foreign markets where regulatory conditions are less stringent, and performing R&D abroad'. In 1974, 80 per cent of US firms tested their new drugs abroad, whereas before 1964 (i.e. before the FDA's stringent regulations) 'virtually all clinical testing was done in the USA' (Grabowski & Vernon, in Chien 1979: 48–9).[4]

Political economy then takes minor tranquillisers for what they are: potentially dependency-forming mood-altering drugs that are marketed by complex and powerful global organizations in pursuit of profit. In this way, political economy strips away the halo of 'sophisticated advertising institutions and public relations activities' that 'project a false image of conspicuous benevolence' around the industry (McKinlay 1984: 5). However, the ideological halo with which the industry attempts to surround itself does more than just promote brand names and sustain a market. It is argued that tranquillisers are a special type of commodity, in that they also represent the process of medicalization, in which social and political issues are depoliticized into questions of medical diagnosis. Their role in the symbolic exchange between doctors and patients brings into play powerful social relations of gender and social class, which are harnessed in the economic reproduction of the industry (see, for example, Mosher 1976; Chapman 1979; or Prather, Chapter 6 in this volume).

COMPETITION, OLIGOPOLY, AND PRICE

In 1978 world-wide, 68 million prescriptions were issued for benzodiazepines, of which 44.6 million were for Valium. Librium and Valium were, during the 1970s, the most widely prescribed ethical drugs in the world. One in ten adults in the US used Valium or Librium during any three-month period during the 1970s, and 15 per cent of Americans used minor tranquillisers of some kind each year (Koumjian 1981). Benzodiazepines became part of life for millions of people. While all prescriptions increased by 44 per cent between 1964–70 in the US, those for tranquillisers increased by 78 per cent, largely replacing barbiturates as drugs of choice for anxiety (Silverman & Lee 1974: 293). The picture was similar in the UK: according to Lall and Parish (1976), one in five of all NHS prescriptions in the mid–1970s were for minor tranquillisers of which 70 per cent were for Librium and Valium. In 1971, 47.8 million prescriptions for psychotropic drugs were dispensed, of which 38 per cent were for tranquillisers and 41 per cent for hypnotics. Again in the UK, between 1961 and 1971 barbiturate prescriptions fell by 23 per cent, and prescriptions for minor tranquillisers rose by 197 per cent, against an overall increase in NHS prescribing of 48 per cent (Lall & Parish 1976; Slatter 1977). World-wide, some 100 million people were thought to be taking minor tranquillisers each day during the peak of their sales around 1978–79 (Melville & Johnson 1983). Since then sales in the UK have declined by about 16 per cent in volume, but they remain among the most widely selling drugs in the world. Tables 7.1 and 7.2 show the overall increase and decrease in UK prescriptions of leading benzodiazepines. The anxiolytics diazepam (Valium) and chlordiazepoxide (Librium) both decline in relation to temazepam (hypnotic) and lorazepam (Ativan/Wyeth). The decline in brand-name benzodiazepines was encouraged further by the 1985 limited list in the UK, which requires doctors to prescribe listed benzodiazepines generically on the NHS, as part of an overall policy of encouraging the use of generic prescribing. The current proposals in the White Paper on the NHS (1989) for 'indicative' drug budgets for GPs, would involve a further shift towards generic substitutes for brand names. The pharmaceutical industry (along with the British Medical Association) have indicated that they will vigorously resist this (e.g. *Scrip* 1384, February 1989).

Table 7.1 Number of prescriptions for seven leading benzodiazepines, UK, 1976–86 (in millions)

Product	*1976*	*% change*	*1986*
Temazepam	–	–	7.2
Nitrazepam	9.6	−42.7	5.5
Diazepam	11.3	−54.0	5.2
Lorazepam	1.0	>100	3.1
Triazolam	–		2.0
Chlordiazepoxide	3.6	−69.4	1.1
Oxazepam	0.8	–	0.8

Source: *Scrip* 1296, 1 April 1988.[a]

During the period of their world market dominance though, Hoffman-La-Roche were producing 60 per cent of minor tranquillisers, and ranked as the largest drug company in the world, earning $1.5 billion in revenue from Librium and Valium alone (Lall & Parish 1976). Roche's profit rate (based on tax returns) ran at 19 per cent overall, which was about average for the industry in 1980, but was well above average profit rates of 5–6 per cent for manufacturing industry as a whole in OECD countries. Returns on Librium and Valium ran at 100–150 per cent on capital deployed over ten years. Since 1955 pharmaceuticals have ranked first or second in profitability among all industries, with returns of 30–40 per cent not unusual (Linsday 1978; Braithwaite 1984).

Economists defending the industry's profit levels have argued that recorded profits artificially inflate the true rate of return on investment (e.g. Teeling-Smith 1972; Chien 1979; Reekie & Weber 1979; Egan *et al.* 1982; Wells 1985). 'Excessive profits', they argue, reflect the tax-accounting practices by which R&D expenditures are not treated as investment capital, but are seen as an outlay deducted from income. Some, such as Egan or Comanor, would regard advertising too as an asset, yielding 'goodwill' and consumers' knowledge over a number of years (Egan *et al.* 1982: 86; Comanor 1986). As a research-led 'sunrise' industry, intangible assets are high relative

Table 7.2 Share of UK prescriptions of seven leading benzodiazepines, 1972–85

	1972	*1973*	*1974*	*1975*	*1976*	*1977*	*1978*	*1979*	*1980*	*1981*	*1982*	*1983*	*1984*	*1985*
N=('000):	19,673	22,106	24,617	26,540	28,719	29,658	30,568	30,871	29,073	29,495	29,738	28,748	28,044	25,711
Product	*% share:*													
Temazepam	-	-	-	-	-	-	1	2	5	7	10	13	15	24
Nitrazepam	30	32	34	34	33	33	33	33	31	28	26	25	23	23
Diazepam	40	42	41	41	39	38	36	34	30	27	24	22	19	21
Lorazepam	-	-	2	3	3	5	6	7	8	10	12	12	12	12
Triazolam	-	-	-	-	-	-	-	1	2	4	4	4	5	6
Chlordiazepoxide	24	19	16	13	13	11	10	9	7	7	6	5	5	5
Oxazepam	4	4	3	3	3	3	2	2	2	3	3	2	2	3

Source: DHSS Statistics and Research Division, 1986

to total assets and are costed in the year incurred, rather than capitalized and then depreciated. Because of the long lead time of R&D, between investment and return (which is made longer by what industry economists regard as excessive regulatory controls), advertising and R&D are outlays that must be charged against future income streams generated by those (few) expenditures that produce a successful marketed product. These time lags, in which advertising and R&D are tied up, involve opportunity costs, and, unless these are costed, declared profit rates will be exaggerated (Egan *et al.* 1982). If advertising and R&D expenditures were regarded instead as capital investment, then, in the calculation of profitability, the denominator (capital employed) would increase, and the numerator (revenue) would decrease, producing a lower rate of return (Reekie & Weber 1979: 164).

One problem with this is that 'corrected' rates of return do not necessarily work out as significantly less than declared profits. Pfizer's 'corrected' rate was only 0.04 per cent lower than their declared rate for 1973, while that for sterling fell by 7.8 per cent (Egan 1979: 86). Comanor (1986) doubts whether adjusted rates of return will be 'hugely different' from published rates. Whether the mass of profit rises or falls depends upon the relative sizes of depreciation charges against R&D assets and R&D expenditures which would normally be charged against profits. More significantly perhaps, industries with high intangible assets pay lower corporation taxes than firms with more tangible assets. Writing off R&D in the year in which it occurs reduces tax liability and the industry is effectively receiving a tax subsidy from the present system (Weiss in Chien 1979: 130).[5]

Again, it is argued that drug development is a risky business, and the patent which provides the innovating firm (e.g. Roche's Librium, Valium, and Mogadon) with an oligopolistic position for 10–20 years (depending on national patenting lengths) is a legitimate return for risk. Further, it is argued that products have rapid obsolescence and that, viewed over time, the industry is not oligopolistic, even in segmented sub-markets. Thus Reekie and Weber claim, '50 per cent in any one period is neither reasonable nor unreasonable. It must be looked at in the context of the company over time' (Reekie & Weber 1979: 128). There are two issues here – the welfare benefits alleged to accrue from patent protection and the extent of competition over time in the industry. Both are relevant to long-term tranquilliser use.

First, the monopoly rent that follows from patent protection is regarded as an incentive to innovation, and therefore as 'socially optimal for the difference between price and marginal cost to be greatest where demand elasticity is less' (Comanor 1979: 93).[6] Monopoly price can exceed marginal cost by ten to twenty times in minor tranquillisers (Murray 1981: 167–9). Where the product is dependency forming, as with benzodiazepines (or cigarettes, alcohol, or narcotics), demand elasticity will be low. It will be low anyway where doctors' prescription decisions are made according to therapeutic criteria rather than price (although there is disagreement as to whether choices in prescription medicine are price related: Weston (1979) argues they are; Silverman and Lee (1974) and Melville and Johnson (1983) that they are not).

The 'welfare' argument, though, presupposes that Roche's patent on Librium, Valium, and Mogadon was in the public interest because these drugs added to human welfare. However, the welfare benefits of minor tranquillisers need to be weighed against their harmful effects. The latter include, in addition to physical dependency, such things as: impairment of judgement; interference with motor skills; aggressive reactions; increased risk of road accidents, thought to rise by five times when tranquillisers are taken over consecutive days (Skegg *et al.* 1979). Thus the social cost of minor tranquilliser use has been compared with that of alcohol abuse (Melville & Johnson 1983: 108). Further, even if the welfare benefits of tranquilliser use have outweighed their costs, the effect of patent protection has been to encourage competing firms to direct scarce research talent and money at 'me-too' substitutes rather than to therapeutic advances. 'Me-toos' are molecularly distinct but therapeutically identical products that attempt to get round the legal monopoly. Chlorpromazine is one of the most modified chemical entities on the market, produced in at least eighteen generic forms, stimulated by the enormous success of Roche. 'Me-too' research has occasionally stumbled upon significant therapeutic advances (e.g. prednisone from cortisone), but, as Braithwaite asks, 'how much more of value might these scientists have discovered if their goal had been the maximum advancement of medicine instead of finding a loophole around a patent?' (Braithwaite 1984: 164).

Second, it is often argued by industry economists that pricing structure does not indicate monopolization, even within therapeutic sub-markets. Yet critics of the patenting system claim that patents allow firms to resist price reductions while maintaining market dominance, even after the expiry of the patent. Evidence can be adduced for both views, because pricing behaviour is complex, and is far removed from the expectations of micro-economic models. Pricing structures and market dominance need to be looked at in both the long and the short term, and related to the behaviour of high-tech industries.

Industry economists argue that in the short-term view the industry looks monopolized in market segments, but that over time product obsolescence and innovation put downward pressure on prices and make entry competitive. One could call this 'serial monopolization'. Thus, when Roche marketed Librium in 1960, sales of 'Miltown' (Carter-Wallace) began to decline and, after Valium appeared in 1973, Carter's profits fell to −23.5 per cent by 1973. This was partly because Roche produced a low 'limit entry' price for Librium and Valium to exclude competitors, thereby maintaining market dominance for most of the 1970s (Chien 1979). Eventually, Roche too was to lose market dominance, something Roche Products (UK) tried to forestall by lowering the price of Valium by 36 per cent to defend their market position when Berk Pharmaceuticals introduced its own diazepam (Slatter 1977: 91).

Moreover, it is argued that the price structure of pharmaceuticals indicates competitiveness over time and complex substitutabilities between and within sub-markets (e.g. benzodiazepines for barbiturates). Further, it is argued that product competition is in any case more important in the industry than price competition (e.g. Chien 1979; Reekie & Weber 1979; Egan *et al.* 1982). To some extent though, the latter argument undermines the former. It is true that there has at times been downward pressure on prices, at least in some parts of the world: prices for Roche psychopharmaceuticals in the US fell by 15.6 per cent between 1962–71, against a rise in the consumer price index of 30 per cent (Weston 1979). But this does not indicate, as some economists would have it, that the industry is price competitive. The fortunes of Roche indicate that price reductions do not necessarily increase or defend market share. When they attempted to defend their Valium market against Berk, Roche incurred a greater loss of profit than had they sold Valium at its former price while receiving royalty on their remaining market share (Slatter 1977). Berk gave promotional expenditure priority – despite a turnover of only 2.3 million in 1970 against Roche's £9 million, Berk employed fifty-eight detailers, nearly matching Roche's sixty-six. Price competition proved less effective for Roche than product competition in the form of advertising, detailers, and 'seller services'. In the UK, DDSA produced a generic chlordiazepoxide priced 25 per cent lower than Librium, but had only 3 per cent of the market (Lall & Parish 1976). Thus, 'it does not normally make sense for a pharmaceutical manufacturer with a major product to engage in price competition' (Slatter 1977: 92).[7] Competition is geared towards defending monopoly position.

There is evidence from international price variations for minor tranquillisers that monopoly holders charge whatever the market will bear, and conceal excessive profits through transfer pricing.[8] The price of Librium varied by 250 per cent within the USA in 1965, and cost twice as much in Australia, and six times as much in Switzerland, as in the UK (Lall & Parish 1976). In Colombia diazepam has been imported at a price 6400 per cent higher than the lowest price elsewhere, and in Argentina it has been overpriced by 150 per cent (Geriffi 1984: 196). Patented tranquillisers cost far more than generics: for example, 1000 400mg tablets of meprobamate sold at $68.21 as Equanil (Wyeth), and at $4.90 as Meprobamate (Interstate) in 1972, a differential ratio of 13.9:1 (Silverman and Lee 1974: 34). Table 7.3 indicates price differentials for Librium and Valium in six selected countries, and examples of such arbitrary pricing abound in the literature (e.g. Melville & Johnson 1983; McCraine & Murray 1978; Murray 1981; Melrose 1982; Patel 1983; Braithwaite 1984; Lexchin 1987). These price differentials indicate monopoly power within sub-markets at a point in time, which is of course subject to change.

Table 7.3 Prices of Librium and Valium (100 tablets), 1975 in USD, wholesale

			Indexed	
	Librium	*Valium*	*Librium*	*Valium*
UK	0.83	0.63	100	100
FDR	4.38	5.35	528	849
Switzerland	4.75	5.44	572	908
USA	5.80	6.89	699	1093
Mexico	4.42	6.03	532	957
Costa Rica	7.03	9.13	847	1449

Source: Geriffi 1984: 194.

The tendency of capital in the twentieth century to form global monopolies has eroded market pricing. From raw material inputs, through manufacture, to marketing of the product, prices within the TNC are set administratively, i.e. they are transferred through the organization. TNC global intra-firm trade means that an increasing volume of world trade occurs through administered pricing rather than market forces. By 1970, 39 per cent of US exports and 50 per cent of imports took the form of intra-firm transfers (Murray 1981: 2). This has a number of implications. First, it strikes at the basis of the main assumptions of traditional pricing theory. Second, the operations of TNCs can be extensively hidden from governments. Third, government policies – e.g. currency devaluation or taxation changes – will have unpredictable effects since they will be absorbed and transferred within the firm to maximum advantage.[9] Finally, the TNC has considerable power to manipulate world prices and influence the economies of countries in which it operates (especially in the Third World). It also uses this 'global reach' as Barnet and Muller (1984) call it, to accumulate capital by selling in rich markets but developing technology and manufacture where labour is cheap. Thus growth within the pharmaceutical industry as a proportion of total world GNP increased between 1960–80 from 0.58 to 0.78 per cent, and this growth was concentrated in the six 'core' countries – the USA, FRG, Japan, UK, Switzerland, and France (Currie 1986: 431). The industry economists discussed above largely avoid these issues of globalization, and prefer to remain on the safer ground of micro-economic theory.

The transfer of value through the pharmaceutical TNC has implications not only for the price of tranquillisers, but also for the social relationships between private capital, governments, workers, and consumers. As prices are fixed administratively, so struggle arises between these social actors around the distribution of profit, the role of the state, and regulation, in a complex international division of labour. The remainder of this chapter will be concerned with these issues.

STATES, REGULATION, AND STRUGGLES FOR CONTROL

Political economy understands the state and ideological structures as sites of struggle over the reproduction of capital. Pharmaceutical companies are among the most powerful institutions in the world, able to move resources globally, in often bitter struggle to maintain profitability and market dominance. The drug TNCs organize globally but state regulatory practices are more often local than international. The capitalist state moreover plays a contradictory role in both generalizing the 'public interest' (in quality and safety control and monopoly limitation) and securing the private interests of capital (patenting, and guaranteeing the market).[10] In the developed countries, and increasingly in the Third World too, organized consumer pressure demands further regulatory control – though as Lall and Bibile (1982) indicate, the degree of success of such initiatives is likely to depend on the political complexion of the local government.

The 'extraordinary international structure of market power' of the drug TNCs, 'seems inviolable to all the market, social or political forces which might challenge it' (Lall & Parish 1976: 4). In the late 1960s the British Government began an investigation into Roche Products that started a dispute which, when resolved in the mid–1970s, illustrated both the potential and limitations of public opinion and government regulation. Roche had inflated its costs for raw materials and overheads, so that the true costs for the active ingredients of Librium and Valium were £9 per kg and £20 per kg, respectively, compared with transfer prices of £370 and £922. This reduced the gross profit margin in their published returns from actual levels of 86.9 per cent and 90 per cent to 40.5 per cent and 40 per cent respectively for Librium and Valium. In 1970 Roche paid the Government £900,000, but created a market for Valium in after-care at the same time, by providing Valium free to NHS hospitals! The following year, however, Roche refused to repay excessive profits earned in 1970, and was referred by the DHSS to the Monopolies Commission. Finding evidence of real profit rates of nearly 60 per cent on Librium and Valium, the Commission ordered Roche to reduce the price of Librium to 40 per cent, and Valium to 25 per cent of the 1970 price. Roche appealed to the High Court, and the matter was eventually resolved in January 1975, when Roche repaid £12 million for excess profits earned between January 1970 and April 1973, and reduced prices to half their 1970 levels (Slatter 1977; Murray 1981; Braithwaite 1984; Melville & Johnson 1983).

However, direct government pressure to lower the price of drugs is unusual (Slatter 1977: 89), and even when undertaken by governments with public support (as with UK vs Roche) is often only partially successful.[11] The effect of Roche's repayments to the UK Government was limited moreover by Roche's ability to trade off currencies. Reekie and Weber point out, with evident satisfaction, that between Roche's repayments and the period in which the profits accrued, sterling had depreciated by 30 per cent against the Swiss Franc. Since the profits were remitted to Basle at the higher rate of exchange, but repaid in sterling at the depreciated rate, the costs to Roche will have been one-third less than the money paid (Reekie & Weber 1979: 77).

In an administered system of pricing and oligopolistic global organization, the distribution of profit is subject to the political balance of power, and the interest of the government in the product. This can be illustrated with reference to the relationships between governments and the industry in the developed and developing world. The imposition of FDA regulations on product testing, advertising, labelling, and export was met by what Epstein (1979) calls a 'flight from regulation'. This involves the movement of assets into Third World countries with less strict regulatory controls (or without prescriptive controls at all). By the early 1970s, repatriated foreign earnings of the US drug TNCs exceeded the dollar outflow of fresh capital investment: the industry became a net importer of capital (McCraine & Murray 1978). Direct foreign investment evades regulatory controls in the US and transfers value from low-wage sectors of the international division of labour to the parent company.

A study of 2400 patients in an Indian urban centre illustrates this. Greenhalgh found that drugs such as diazepam were sold over the counter for trivial conditions, and for inappropriate indications, such as 'body pains', 'abdominal symptoms', and 'fever'. A short course of diazepam was prescribed by a GP for 'fever' in 26 per cent of cases. Tranquillisers were found in irrational combinations, often hidden for example in combination with analgesics, cough mixtures, antispasmodics, and anti-asthmatics (Greenhalgh 1987). These irrational combinations are dangerous and irrelevant to people's health needs in countries where the main causes of morbidity and mortality are related to the synergy of infection and malnutrition. They reflect the global relations of unequal exchange between the developed and developing worlds, and contribute to worsening health status in the latter, not only as a result of harmful side effects, but also by absorbing high proportions of family budgets and health resources. Yudkin found that the sums spent on Valium and Melleril (thioridazine) at Muhimbili Hospital (Dar es Salaam), where 10 per cent of out-patient prescriptions contained benzodiazepines, would have provided malaria prophylaxis for 350,000 children (Yudkin 1980).

The situation arises because of the 'drug colonialism' of both the industry and the western medical profession. Drug promotion in developing countries reflects the western market, and local practitioners acquire the ideology of 'developed' curative medicine.

Thus the WHO estimated in 1976 that tropical disease R&D in the industry was only 2 per cent of that on anti-cancer drugs. Third World doctors are susceptible to drug promotion not only because of the detailers who in rural areas might be their only source of professional contact (Greenhalgh 1987), but also because of the influence of drug companies in the medical curriculum (especially through sponsorship). Drug colonialism could be prevented by the states of the exporting countries, but they have little interest in doing so, preferring to resort instead to the notion of 'informed consent' (Norris 1982).[12] When Dr Barbara Moulton requested that the FDA insist on 'addiction' warnings being placed on tranquilliser labels of exports, this was refused on the grounds that the policy of 'friendliness' with the industry would be interfered with (McCraine & Murray 1978). Western governments are reluctant to interfere with the export earnings of home-based companies, whose interests are protected by powerful lobbies such as the Pharmaceutical Manufacturers' Association in the US and the Association of British Pharmaceutical Industries (reckoned by Lang (1974) to be generally successful in their objectives).

In developed countries, however, drug TNCs face greater regulatory control, and growing public accountability. In the UK, for example, the industry faces a challenge from radicalized consumer groups such as Tranx and the Council for Involuntary Tranquilliser Addiction (Gabe & Williams 1986). More than a hundred legal firms have formed an association called the Benzodiazepine Solicitors Group to co-ordinate the research for legal action against tranquilliser manufacturers and doctors. The Group estimates that over 500 tranquilliser patients might consider filing law suits against the manufacturers for allegedly supplying benzodiazepines without due warning of the risk of dependence, or against doctors for alleged negligent prescribing (*Scrip*, 1286, 1988: 6)[b]. This action is directed initially at Ativan (lorazepam/Wyeth), which has high reported adverse reactions in relation to its market share (see Table 7.4), although product liability action is likely to be extended to other products including Valium, in due course (*Scrip* 1339, 1988: 2)[d]. If successful, product liability action can have devastating effects on a company, as the Dalkon Shield (H. A. Robins) case shows,[13] and Wyeth has already applied for a UK product licence for a lower dosage of Ativan, which would be 'a desperate attempt to keep in the market' as one Group solicitor commented (*Scrip*, 1337, 1988: 13)[e].

However, it is yet to be seen whether the threat of product

Table 7.4 Adverse reports, benzodiazepines, UK, 1978–87

	All benzodiazepines	*Lorazepam*	*%ARR*	*% market share*
1978	201	36	18	6
1979	218	29	13	7
1980	232	31	13	8
1981	166	24	14	10
1982	266	24	11	12
1983	274	35	13	12
1984	243	20	8	12
1985	179	29	16	12
1986	143	21	15	12
1987	100	16	16	12

Source: *Scrip* 1291, March 1988[c]

liability litigation will regulate the industry. Following widespread concern in the UK over minor-tranquilliser dependence, and the use of repeat prescriptions, the Committee on Safety of Medicines recommended in 1988 (following an earlier report in 1980) that benzodiazepines should not be prescribed for more than six weeks. But a spokesperson for Wyeth placed the responsibility for long-term use with the doctors: 'Treatment of the patient is the responsibility of the physician and doctors should be well aware of the information available concerning long-term prescription of benzodiazepines' (*Observer* 21 February 1988). Moreover, problems of threatened litigation have not prevented Roche from making a bid to emerge as a 'renewed force' in the industry with the intravenous benzodiazepine sedative Versed (midazolam), which earned $41 million during 1987–88 from 30 million prescriptions (*Scrip* 1296, 1988: 8)[f]. This has been the subject of a campaign by the US Public Citizen Health Research Group to persuade the FDA to restrict the use of Versed, but so far without success (*Scrip* 1285, 1988: 8)[g]. None the less, the industry takes consumerist activities seriously if only because they threaten its corporate image.[14]

It seems doubtful whether this strategy of control will have much success in the Third World. The level of compensation payments in developing countries tends to be dramatically lower than in the US, so product litigation in the Third World is less of a threat to the industry's profits. Moreover, the difficulty that Third World governments have in controlling the drug TNCs hardly augurs well for the potential influence of consumerist groups. Such groups include the Consumer Association of Penang, the Association of

People for Practical Life Education (Ghana), the People's Health Centre (Gonoshastrama Kendra, Bangladesh), the All India Drug Action Network, as well as international pressure groups such as Health Action International or the International Organization of Consumer Unions. Although Lall is correct to suggest that (as the Bangladesh Essential Drugs Law 1981 indicates) Third World governments can control the supply of pharmaceuticals, it is still the case that political will can be overridden by other factors.

For example, in Mozambique the introduction of a national formulary and state pharmaceutical company (MEDIMOC) had considerable success around 1976–78. Costs were reduced in real terms, imports were restricted to the WHO Essential Drugs List – the price of diazepam was reduced by two-thirds (Marzagáo & Segall 1983). But, as Cliff points out, 'One essential prerequisite for a sovereign pharmaceutical policy is . . . a solvent economy' (Cliff *et al*. 1986: 11). Destabilization by South Africa (especially its support for MNF terrorists, for whom rural health posts are a priority target) and by the IMF and World Bank (which insist on an expanded private sector and TNC investment) has raised medical costs and allowed the return of dangerous and irrational drugs (Cliff *et al*. 1986). Local states and pressure groups are often caught up in the global military-economic complex over which they have no control, but which capital will use to reassert its interests.

Further, Geriffi argues that 'foreign control is an inherent part of the structure of the [pharmaceutical] industry' and, following Stepan's model of the State-Foreign Capital Bargaining Cycle, he argues that the degree of control available to local states varies with the degree of priority with which the product is regarded against the status of foreign capital prior to bargaining: in particular whether it is new or already 'sunken' (Geriffi 1984: 155–7). If states accord benzodiazepine use low priority, they could negotiate with the drug TNCs for their removal, at least from irrational combinations. But there would be political and economic costs since drug TNCs' capital is already sunken, and will not readily withdraw from profitable products.

Geriffi's focus though is on foreign capital *vis-à-vis* the national bourgeoisie, in which, as White (1983) also argues, the latter has some room for manoeuvre in the formulation of pharmaceutical products stage, but little where entry barriers are high, at the R&D stage. Thus Roche's leading position in minor tranquillisers in Mexico was eroded with the entry, in the mid–70s, of local firms marketing generic substitutes for Librium and Valium. There is no guarantee, though, that local capital will observe safety regulations or will manufacture essential drugs – especially since their markets will be predominantly those of the westernised élites. Local firms might be more amenable to state regulation than TNCs, but the general ambivalence of the role of the state here is heightened by the 'revolving door syndrome', in which consultants or employees of drug regulatory bodies, medical education specialists, and doctors will at some time be on the payroll of the industry.

MEDICALIZATION AND IDEOLOGY

Political economy attempts to integrate structural analysis of the industry with the ideology-effects of the reproduction of markets and a fetishized commodity culture. Many writers have, for example, examined the ways in which medical practices reify social, domestic, and psychological stresses into diagnoses, and thereby suggest that conflicts (particularly over gender roles) can be resolved into a scientifically neutral bio-technological fix. Literature on medicalization, then, argues that the 'medical-industrial complex' serves as a powerful agent of social control, and that this is particularly apparent in relation to psychopharmaceuticals (see for example, Lennard & Cooperstock 1980; Melville 1980; Koumjian 1981; or Gabe in Chapter 2 of this volume). The culture of a 'pill for every ill' brings into play powerful ideologies, especially the patriarchal belief in women's psychological inferiority, which Prather discusses in Chapter 6 in relation to an analysis of tranquilliser advertisements. Integrating the promotional activity of the industry with the social structure capital, Bodenheimer (1984) suggests that doctors (along with company researchers, administrators, university researchers, and government bureaucrats) constitute an 'intermediate strata', responsible for the ideological and economic reproduction of capital. Yet, as such, medicine also becomes a site of struggle over definitions of the body, gender, and authority.

Two examples should illustrate this. First there is the interrelationship between the excess prescription of minor tranquillisers to women as opposed to men and gender stereotyping in adverts for minor tranquillisers. Although the differential tends to narrow in older age groups, women are in general prescribed minor tranquillisers about twice as often as men, in both the UK and USA (Mosher 1976; Cooperstock & Lennard 1986; Taylor 1987). Anthony Clare, in discussing Taylor, suggests that this is the 'mirror image' of gender differentials, in that our social structure encourages men to relieve stress through alcohol use, while women visit their GP. Yet it is also necessary to understand the more deeply held expectation that women will be 'help seekers', in a way that confirms women's dependence on male authority structures and generates markets for minor tranquillisers. Thus, analysis of the content of benzodiazepine advertising indicates a tendency to portray women as 'emotional', unable to cope with the stresses of family and job, and making demands on the doctor (e.g. Chapman 1979; Lexchin 1987), although there is some evidence now of a shift towards more abstract representation (see Prather, Chapter 6).

These images, Chapman says, are 'myths that reproduce the ideologies of those to whom they appeal', notably doctors, 'to the ongoing commercial benefit of those producing the advertised products' (Chapman 1979: 762). Yet this is not necessarily a process without conflict, in which the role of the drug TNCs is drawn into a political arena. Gabe and Lipshitz-Phillips (in Gabe & Williams 1986) argue that the 'social control' thesis does not take enough account of 'pre-existing oppositional consciousness', in which women use benzodiazepines, without 'acquiescence in the structure of a male dominated society' (Gabe & Williams 1986: 278). Thus, prescriptions should be seen as sites of struggle over socially induced stresses and medical definitions. Yet the physiological dependence on benzodiazepines reproduces the social dependence of women in patriarchal structures, and does so objectively, even if users are subjectively aware of their dependency effects. It is one of the consequences of consumerist activism, though, to politicize this oppositional consciousness.

A second important issue here is the way in which the apparently scientifically objective diagnoses of stress and anxiety are constructed through drug company promotion to match the conditions for which drugs are available (Silverman 1977). Hence the concepts of 'panic attack' or of the 'sleep cripple' have been constructed by Roche in their marketing of Valium and Mogadon respectively. Again, for 'bed-wetting' Ciba-Geigy marketed Tryptizol (imipramine), which caused fatalities in children under five in the UK in the late 70s. These illness entities serve to collapse social distress into individualized problems while changing nothing in the conditions that give rise to stress but guaranteeing markets for pharmaceutical products. An aspect of the political critique of the medical-industrial complex has emphasized non-pharmacological forms of stress-reduction, such as counselling or relaxation therapies (Waldron 1977).

CONCLUSIONS

A commodity, as Marx said, is at first sight a simple thing, but on reflection is a most peculiar thing, in that it apparently has life and properties of its own. For political economy, commodities as exchange values embody the social relations of exploitation that enter into their production. Thus, as health commodities, pharmaceuticals 'behave' exactly like other commodities – they are sold at the highest price that the market will stand, they are produced for profitable markets, rather than according to need, and indeed, with benzodiazepines, effective demand is generated at least in part by promotion and by their dependency-forming properties. Benzodiazepines are peculiar moreover in that they embody the relations of a commodified culture, in a set of relations between doctors, patients, and the drug TNCs, and stand at the intersection of ideology and economy, body and society, surrounded by the aura of a false image of 'conspicuous benevolence' of the pharmaceutical industry.

Tranquillisers are among the most profitable commodities in the world, produced by TNCs that can be ruthlessly competitive in their struggle to achieve or defend an oligopolistic position in therapeutic sub-markets. Thus political economy understands the long-term use of benzodiazepines in terms of the dominant tendencies of capital in the twentieth century. These have involved in particular increasing monopolization and internationalization (Baran & Sweezy 1966), the shift of markets to non-regulating countries in the flight from state regulation in advanced capitalist states, and the consequent transfer of value through organizations largely unaccountable to national authorities. These tendencies have further favoured the growth of high-tech 'sunrise' industries that are R&D led, and which have the capacity to transfer resources around the world with relative ease. Not that the marketing of minor tranquillisers has been without political controversy. On the contrary, the globalization of capital places the national state in an ambiguous relation – of both ensuring the conditions of the reproduction of capital and representing the public interest in fiscal control and product safety. Benzodiazepines are becoming politicized, as consumer groups press litigation against tranquilliser manufacturers, and as international pressure mounts for increased regulation and for ethical conduct from the drug TNCs. Whether these struggles will be effective in regulating the activities of the industry, in the absence of a fundamental restructuring of global social relations, however, remains to be seen.

NOTES

1 The tendency for the rate of profit to fall is an economic theorem that follows from the increasing fixed costs of capital (the organic composition of capital). As the proportion of surplus value going to fixed costs (e.g. interest payment, rent, fuel, maintenance) rises, so the ratio of value added to capital by living labour declines relative to total value realized, and the rate of profit must fall. Capital therefore seeks to offset this tendency (e.g. by moving to labour reserve areas; through cartelization or globalization: taking advantage of differential costs in the world economy).

2 Braithwaite (1984) cites many examples of this in the pharmaceutical industry.

3 Documentation of the 'dumping' of unsafe drugs or testing of new drugs in the Third World is legion. For example, Melrose (1983), Mapes (1980), Muller (1982), Norris (1982). Norris refers to the climate of 'benign neglect' in which governments in developing countries allow drug companies to expand. That pharmaceuticals respond to market pressure rather than need is indicated by their response to the Indian Government's price reductions in drugs in 1979. Following the restriction of profit mark-ups to 40–50 per cent on essential drugs, many firms stopped selling 'unprofitable' compounds such as anti-TB drugs, and increased production of food substitutes and vitamins (Greenhalgh 1987).

4 Actually, Comanor (1986) suggests that the time lag between submission of tranquillisers to the FDA and their approval increased by an average of only 0.8 months between 1962–69.

5 It should be remembered, though, that the profits of drug TNCs are likely to be massively under-declared as a result of transfer pricing, and that this is as important as arguments about corrected rates of return. This is discussed below.

6 In a perfect market, with perfect competition, price should equal marginal cost, the cost of an additional unit of supply. But in a monopolized market, producers earn excess profit (monopoly rent), which is set by the slope of the demand curve to the extent that the more inelastic is demand, the higher is the excess monopoly rent.

7 Although, at the 'bottom end' of the market, where fragmentation is greater and there is a greater dependency on generic sales, price competition might be more effective. 'Seller services' include direct mailings to physicians, free samples, sponsorship of medical education, and medical journals.

8 This is in addition to illegal price-fixing cartels, see Braithwaite 1984: 172.

9 For example, devaluation of a currency might not make exports cheaper and imports more expensive if the TNC transfers value between curren-

cies to maximum advantage. Similarly, profits will be under-declared in areas of high taxation and over-declared in areas of low taxation. See S. Lall, 'The international pharmaceutical industry', *Oxford Bulletin of Economics and Statistics* (August 1974). Lall, who was during the 1970s one of the leading critics of the drug TNCs, seems now to have made his peace. See his essay in Wells (1985).

10 J. Habermas, *Legitimation Crisis*, London, HEB, 1976, discusses the contradiction between the state as a forum for public interests and its function in maintaining the conditions of profitability of capital.

11 In 1976, the UK Labour Health Minister, David Ennals attempted to restrict tax exemptions on adverts to those in reputable medical journals (*Lancet*, *BMJ*, and the *Practitioner*), but abandoned this in return for an agreement from the industry to reduce advertising by 10 per cent by 1979.

12 Informed consent is discussed by Norris (1982). The recipient acknowledges that the product (e.g. drugs) is prohibited for sale in the exporting country or is untested there.

13 Dalkon Shield was an intrauterine contraceptive marketed in the early 1970s by A. H. Robins. The product was later found to have caused injuries and birth defects, and the company has to find $2 billion to compensate 50,000 women. Robins might sell out to American Home Products for $3 billion (*Financial Times* 8 November 1988).

14 The increasingly hostile environment in which drug TNCs operate, including the pressure of consumer activism, was attributed, along with price controls, regulation, and patent life erosion, with having motivated Roche's (unsuccessful) bid for Stirling. This was regarded in the industry as having 'broken the unspoken agreement that hostile bids were not in the industry's best interests' since Roche had set a precedent for increased aggressiveness (*Scrip* 1296, April 1988: 9. Even so, Dexter Tiranti is optimistic as to the possibilities for improvements in marketing practices among drug TNCs, in response to adverse publicity (*New Internationalist* 165, November 1986: 6).

REFERENCES

Baran, P. & Sweezy, P. (1966) *Monopoly Capital*, New York: Monthly Review Press.

Barnet, R. J. & Muller, R. E. (1984) *Global Reach: The Power of Multinational Corporations*, London: Jonathan Cape.

Bodenheimer, T. S. (1984) 'The transnational pharmaceutical industry and the health of the world's people', in T. B. McKinlay *Issues in the Political Economy of Health Care*, London: Tavistock.

Braithwaite, J. (1984) *Corporate Crime in the Pharmaceutical Industry*, London: Routledge & Kegan Paul.

Braithwaite, J. (1986) 'The corrupt industry', *New Internationalist* 165: November.

Chapman, S. (1979) 'Advertising and psychotropic drugs', *Social Science and Medicine* 13A(6): 751–64.

Chien, R. I. (ed.) (1979) *Issues in Pharmaceutical Economics*, Lexington, Mass.: Lexington Books.

Cliff, J., Kamji, N., & Muller, M. (1986) 'Mozambique health holding the line', *Review of African Political Economy* 36: September.
Comanor, W. S. (1979) 'Competition in the pharmaceutical industry', in R. Chien (ed.) *Issues in Pharmaceutical Economics*, Lexington, Mass.: Lexington Books.
Comanor, W. S. (1986) 'The political economy of the pharmaceutical industry', *Journal of Economic Literature* XXIV(Sept): 1178–217.
Cooperstock, R. (1978) 'Sex differences in psychotropic drug use', *Social Science and Medicine* 12(13): 179–86.
Cooperstock R. & Lennard, H. (1986) 'Some social meanings of tranquilliser use', in J. Gabe & P. Williams (eds) *Tranquillisers: Social, Psychological and Clinical Perspectives*, London: Tavistock.
Currie, K. (1986) Review of N. Wells, 'Pharmaceuticals among the sunrise industries', *Social Science and Medicine* 23(4): 430–2.
Egan, J. W., Higinbottom, H. N., & Weston, J. F. (1982) *Economics of the Pharmaceutical Industry*, New York: Praeger.
Epstein, S. (1979) *The Politics of Cancer*, New York: Sierra Club Books.
Gabe, J. & Williams, P. (1986) *Tranquillisers: Social, Psychological and Clinical Perspectives*, London: Tavistock.
Geriffi, G. (1984) *The Pharmaceutical Industry and Dependency in the Third World*, Princeton, NJ: Princeton University Press.
Greenhalgh, T. (1987) 'Drug promotion and self-medication in India', *Social Science and Medicine* 25(3): 307–18.
Koumjian, K. (1981) 'The use of Valium as a form of social control', *Social Science and Medicine* 15E(3): 245–9.
Lall, S. & Bibile, S. (1982) 'The political economy of controlling the transnationals: the pharmaceutical industry in Sri Lanka 1972–76', in V. Navarro (ed.) *Imperialism, Health and Medicine*, London: Pluto Press.
Lall, S. & Parish, P. (1976) *The Price of Tranquillity – The Manufacture and Use of Psychotropic Drugs*, London: MIND Occasional Paper 4.
Lang, R. W. (1974) *The Politics of Drugs*, Lexington, Mass.: Lexington Books.
Lennard, H. L. & Cooperstock, R. (1980) 'The social context and functions of tranquilliser prescribing', in R. Mapes (ed.) *Prescribing Practice and Drug Usage*, London: Croom Helm.
Lexchin, J. (1987) 'Pharmaceutical promotion in Canada: convince them or confuse them', *International Journal of the Health Services* 17(1): 7–89.
Linsday, C. (1978) *The Pharmaceutical Industry*, New York: Wiley.
McCraine, N. & Murray, M. J. (1978) 'The pharmaceutical industry – a further study in corporate power', *International Journal of the Health Services* 8(4): 573–88.
McKinlay, J. B. (1984) *Issues in the Political Economy of Health Care*, London: Tavistock.
Mapes, R. (ed.) (1980) *Prescribing Practice and Drug Usage*, London: Croom Helm.
Marazagáo, C. & Segall, M. (1983) 'Drug selection: Mozambique', *World Development* 11(3): 205–16.
Melrose, D. (1982) *Bitter Pills, Medicines and the Third World Poor*, Oxford: Oxfam.
Melville, A. (1980) 'Reducing whose anxiety? A study of the relationship

between repeat prescribing of minor tranquillisers and doctors' attitudes', in R. Mapes (ed.) *Prescribing Practice and Drug Usage*, London: Croom Helm.

Melville, A. & Johnson, C. (1983) *Cured to Death: The Effect of Prescription Drugs*, London: Secker & Warburg.

Mosher, E. (1976) 'Portrayal of women in drug advertising: a medical betrayal', *Journal of Drug Issues* 6(1): 72–8.

Muller, C. (1982) *The Health of Nations*, London: Faber & Faber.

Murray, R. (ed.) (1981) *Multinationals Beyond the Market*, Brighton: Harvester.

Norris, R. (ed.) (1982) *Pills, Pesticides and Profits*, New York: North River Press.

OECD (1985) *The Pharmaceutical Industry – Trade Related Issues*, London: OECD.

Patel, S. J. (1983) 'Pharmaceuticals and health in the Third World', *World Development* 11: 3.

Reekie, W. & Weber, M. H. (1979) *Profits, Politics and Drugs*, London: Macmillan.

Scrip (1988a) 'UK script trends 1976–86', *Scrip* 1296: 3.

— (1988b) 'UK tranquilliser legal action discussed', *Scrip* 1286: 6.

— (1988c) 'UK campaign against tranquillisers', *Scrip* 1291: 2.

— (1988d) 'UK tranquilliser action in the autumn', *Scrip* 1337: 13.

— (1988e) 'Wyeth files for half-strength lorazepam', *Scrip* 133: 13.

— (1988f) 'Roche – a renewed force?' *Scrip* 1296: 8.

— (1988g) Scrip 1285:8

— (1989) 'Indicative drug budgets for GPs – UK White Paper on NHS. *Scrip* 1384: 1–3.

Silverman, M. (1977) 'The epidemiology of drug promotion', *International Journal of the Health Services* 7(2): 157–65.

Silverman, M. & Lee, P. R. (1974) *Pills, Profits and Politics*, Berkeley: University of California Press.

Skegg, D. C. G., Richards, S. M., & Doll, R. (1979) 'Minor tranquillisers and road accidents', *British Medical Journal* 1: 917–19.

Slatter, S. (1977) *Competition and Marketing Strategies in the Pharmaceutical Industry*, London: Croom Helm.

Steele, H. (1962) 'Monopoly and competition in the ethical drugs industry', *Journal of Industrial Economics* 5(October): 131–63.

Steele, H. (1964) 'Patent restrictions and price competition in the ethical drugs industry', *Journal of Industrial Issues* 12(July): 198–223.

Taylor, D. (1987) 'Current usage of benzodiazepines in Britain', in H. Freeman & Y. Rue (eds) *Benzodiazepines in Current Clinical Practice*, London: Royal Society of Medicine Services.

Teeling-Smith, G. (1972) *Pharmaceutical Industry and Society*, London: OHE.

Van Der Geest, S. (1987) 'Pharmaceuticals in the Third World – local perspectives', *Social Science and Medicine* 25(3): 273–321.

Waldron, I. (1977) 'Increased prescribing of Valium, Librium and other drugs – an example of the influence of economic and social factors on the practice of medicine', *International Journal of Health Services* 7(1): 37–62.

Wells, N. (ed.) (1985) *Pharmaceuticals Among the Sunrise Industries*, London: Croom Helm.

Weston, J. F. (1979) 'Pricing in the pharmaceutical industry', in R. Chien (ed.) *Issues in Pharmaceutical Economics*, Lexington, Mass.: Lexington Books.

White, E. (1983) 'Cooperation among national drug manufacturers', *World Development* 11(3): 271–80.

Yudkin, J. S. (1980) 'Economics of the pharmaceutical supply in Tanzania', *International Journal of the Health Services* 10(3): 455–77.

Part II

Evaluating the contribution of the social sciences

8 Long-term tranquilliser use: a general practitioner's view

John Horder

I am invited to evaluate earlier contributions to this book from the point of view of the general practitioner of medicine.

Since practice, in some form, is the main focus for the science and art of medicine, usefulness must be the chief criterion. Most doctors value knowledge more highly for being useful than for being interesting – useful for recognizing illness, for understanding what it feels like, why and how it comes about and how it can be prevented, relieved, or supported. I use the word 'illness' deliberately, because it is a wider term than 'disease' – a distinction to which I shall need to return.

It would be a mistake, however, altogether to omit comments about topics arising in the book which are interesting or important without contributing directly to practice. Some will indeed prove to contribute indirectly, others will just be interesting because doctors are also patients and people with general concerns.

To comment from the viewpoint of the general practitioner or family physician is more difficult than might be obvious at first sight. No other group in the medical profession is so varied in the range of its opinions or behaviour. Attitudes towards the many controversial issues which surround the recognition, understanding, and management of psychological and social problems show this variation to the full.

I shall try to deal with this difficulty by offering some generalizations about the role of the general practitioner in countries like the United Kingdom, while also revealing some of my own biases.

In the main part of this chapter I shall test the usefulness of the book to general practitioners by raising a small number of questions to which I believe many among them might be seeking answers and then seeing how far the writers are able to provide these.

VARIATION AMONG DOCTORS

Among the many ways in which general practitioners and family physicians vary, one can be seen in the weight which different doctors give to anxiety and depression compared with bodily pain. Their willingness to recognize these symptoms depends on this; their ability to do so is a further variable (Shepherd *et al.* 1981: 60–5). Especially relevant to the present context is variation in attitudes to the propriety of influencing the mind by using physical agents; indeed this issue can rouse strong feelings of the sort which are more commonly associated with the contexts of morality, politics, or religion.

Nevertheless, alongside these and other variations there is, of course, a vast area of common ground. Efforts to agree broad definitions of general practice, family medicine, or primary care have succeeded – even across national boundaries (Second European Conference 1974). They contain such statements as '[general practitioners] will include and integrate physical, psychological and social factors in their considerations about health and illness'. 'Family physicians provide continuing health maintenance and medical care to the entire family, regardless of age, sex and type of problem, be it biological, behavioural or social' (American Academy and Board of Family Practice 1975: 10).

Such agreements are essential as a basis for training programmes, but they were chiefly stimulated by the challenge of increasing specialization, the success of which seemed for a time to leave no clear role for generalists. The crucial responsibilities which now distinguish the role of the generalist are to be accessible and to offer a high degree of personal continuity; to offer breadth rather than depth of understanding, so that at least an initial response can be made to a very wide range of problems; and to integrate – that is, to hold things together, weighing the relative urgency of different problems and attending to their interactions. These responsibilities are complementary to those of specialists; they are important for all sick people, but not least for those whose problems can be summarized as 'anxiety' or 'depression'.

In English-speaking countries and most of those in western Europe, training for this role has taken increasing account of the psychosocial aspects of medicine. Certainly in the United Kingdom the behavioural sciences and psychiatry have come to occupy a much larger proportion of both the undergraduate and the postgraduate curricula than they did even twenty-five years ago. Nevertheless, the longer history of the physical sciences which contribute to medicine has given them a dominance, particularly in basic training, which is maintained.

The evidence from this book (Gabe, Chapter 2; see also Gabe & Lipshitz-Phillips 1984) suggests that a significant proportion of general practitioners and family physicians do now give due importance to psychological and social influences upon illness and its management. Their situation – living and working fairly closely to their patients, seeing them sometimes in their homes, and dealing with a variety of problems in the same person over a period of time – does at least provide ample opportunities.

But there is a limit to what can be achieved through training in increasing awareness of these influences and in deciding the weight which should be given to them. Doctors inevitably bring the experiences and beliefs of their earlier upbringing into their practice, while the pressures of the job itself may later prevent them from applying the knowledge and skills which their training gave them (Ashbaugh & McKean 1976).

It is particularly relevant to this book that generalists cannot be expected to have a training which simultaneously covers a wide range of relevant topics and also goes deeply into each of them. The challenge to educators is to select what is most relevant and useful, showing how the rest can be discovered when necessary.

PERSONAL BIAS

My own clinical experience has been as a London general practitioner, working mainly within the British National Health Service between 1951 and 1981. I was not alone among my partners in having a special interest in psychiatric and social problems. I tended earlier in my career to value psychological approaches to them; later I was more impressed by physical ones, but always insisted on the supreme importance of keeping a balanced view.

Tranquillisers became available in the middle of this time. We welcomed them as replacing the barbiturates which were used by 4 per cent of our patients (Adams *et al.* 1966). They clearly reduced the risk of successful suicide attempts. They also promised to cause less dependence. I looked after many patients who were chronically anxious and I had reason to give relatively high importance to mental as opposed to physical suffering. Experience with depressed patients taught me that psychotropic drugs must be given in doses which would be effective and that risks must sometimes be taken.

I was even impressed for a time by the notion attributed to the author Compton Mackenzie that 'he had been born two whiskies below par'. In other words, the idea of long-term medication, certainly for depression, possibly for anxiety, seemed in principle to be reasonable. The problem of dependence on tranquillisers was not as obvious in the 1970s as it has become in the 1980s.

THE RELEVANCE OF THIS BOOK TO GENERAL PRACTICE

There are three questions which seem most likely to be uppermost in the mind of a general practitioner or family physician who sees the title of this book and wonders whether it would help with what is a fairly common problem in practice. Are benzodiazepine tranquillisers effective? Should long-term use be avoided? If so, is effective alternative treatment available and practical?

EFFECTIVE? FOR WHAT? FOR HOW LONG?

Anxiety, tension, 'nerves', sleeplessness have always been the leading indications on which general practitioners prescribe tranquillisers. Michael Montagne (Chapter 3) quotes Lennard & Cooperstock (1980) to add that they are prescribed for three types of patients: those who present with an immediate problem that is transient in nature, those who are experiencing 'problems in living', and those with acute or chronic somatic diseases, who need help in dealing with the stress of a debilitating illness. (It is perhaps not surprising that the advertisement 'Whatever the diagnosis . . . there is a place for Librium' appeared in 1969.) These three main categories can be found in the International Classification of Diseases (World Health Organisation 1980) and in DSM III (American Psychiatric Association 1980). Leaving aside the category of somatic illness, both classifications distinguish acute reactions to stress from persistent disorders. Among persistent disorders, both distinguish those with phobic avoidance from those without. Lennard and Cooperstock's 'problems in living' are more or less equivalent to 'persistent disorders'. Further distinctions can be neglected here.

Since anxiety sometimes reaches crippling proportions, any drug which reduces it might seem to offer the possibility of helping a person to cope better with current problems, in addition to giving relief.

SHORT-TERM USE

It was not due merely to the exceptional volume of advertisements (Prather, Chapter 6) that general practitioners in the United Kingdom accepted tranquillisers so easily and prescribed them for so many patients in the first place. These patients themselves told us how effective they were on first use. We ourselves felt safer than when using barbiturates. Taken by day, benzodiazepines appeared to calm without sending to sleep. Taken at night, they might have seemed rather less effective than their predecessors, but an apparently reduced rate of dependence and a reduced risk of a successful suicide seemed more important. The actual risk of dependence at normal therapeutic doses was, of course, not obvious at first, because the evidence of harm took time to accumulate; it became widely known only after 1980, although evidence in writing had been available since at least 1973 (Covi *et al.* 1973).

Is it possible that we were witnessing only the placebo effect? The references quoted by Alan Shiell (Chapter 5) show that there is now some reason for at least questioning even those strong clinical impressions. In particular, a small double-blind randomized trial (East of Ireland Faculty, Royal College of General Practitioners 1983) concluded that 'there was no demonstrable difference between diazepam and placebo' when used in the management of minor conditions in general practice over a period of three weeks. This study receives more recent support from Tyrer *et al.* (1988). In this trial, diazepam was less effective than placebo on all of six measurements over a ten-week observation period.

In contrast to the two trials quoted above, Oswald *et al.* (1982), in a larger double-blind trial of nitrazepam and lormetazepam against placebo, used for poor sleepers, were in no doubt about effectiveness and concluded that benzodiazepines remain effective for at least twenty-four weeks, but that a period of disturbed sleep may be expected after withdrawal. The United Kingdom Committee on the Review of Medicines (1980: 910) found that 'all benzodiazepines were efficacious in the short-term treatment of symptoms of anxiety and insomnia', but not beyond four months of continuous treatment. The Committee on Safety of Medicines (UK) in 1988 issued advice that benzodiazepines should be used in the short-term only (two to four weeks) when anxiety and insomnia are severe (clearly the Committee was not prepared to dismiss the drugs as being either totally without effect or too dangerous to use).

LONG-TERM USE

Williams & Bellantuono (Chapter 4, Table 4.2) have listed seven studies from several countries which all propose one year as the arbitrary dividing line between short- and long-term use. Williams (1983) showed that, of 124 patients who started, twenty-four were still receiving tranquillisers after six months.

There is some evidence about the natural history of minor affective disorders (i.e. anxiety and depression). The findings of Kedward (1969), Mann *et al.* (1981), Cooper *et al.* (1969), and Fry (1960) are represented in the following table from Mann's study. It could be deduced that at least a quarter of the males and a third of the females had not improved after one year. There is clearly therefore a case for treatment in some form.

Table 8.1 Comparison of outcome studies, as determined by 'caseness'

	% still cases at end of follow-up period		
Author	*Males*	*Females*	*Follow-up period*
Fry (1960)	27	43	3 years (acute + chronic)
Cooper *et al.* (1969)	26	43	1 year (acute)
	21	37	3 years (acute + chronic)
Kedward (1969)	25	28	3 years (acute)
	50	59	3 years (chronic)
Present study	48	50	1 year (acute + chronic)

Source: Mann *et al.* 1981.

Do tranquillisers become less effective with long-term use? The United Kingdom Committee on the Review of Medicines (1980: 910) concluded that 'there is little convincing evidence that benzodiazepines are efficacious in the treatment of anxiety after four months of continuous treatment'. But Rickels *et al.* (1983), in an American double-blind trial of diazepam against placebo for 180 chronically anxious patients, conceded that 'a significant number of patients benefit from prolonged diazepam treatment. Tolerance to the anxiolytic effect of diazepam does not develop during a 22-week study period.'

But patients, with the help of doctors, continue to use these drugs for years. This book offers possible reasons, in several of the chapters. One is that the lack of any of three resources important to women – paid work, children and partners, leisure – tends to encourage long-term usage. This is also true if these resources are unsatisfying or unsuitable. Another reason is that the side effects of stopping after continuous use are as bad or worse than the symptoms which originally caused the use of tranquillisers (Cormack & Sinnott 1983; see also Golombok). This book offers yet other explanations—the images and metaphors used to explain the way drugs help or harm (Montagne, Chapter 3), the influence of doctors in medicalizing, mystifying, or exerting social control (Montagne, quoting Koumjian 1981). I find neither of these last two explanations as convincing as either the unpleasant experience of stopping or the fact that the life problems or the constitution of some patients cause the original anxiety to persist. For them the benzodiazepines do indeed seem to be effective and to continue so. People differ. Controlled trials of drugs are seldom able to throw much light on individual differences.

CAN THE USE OF THESE DRUGS BE JUSTIFIED TODAY?

The evidence is inconclusive, so that each doctor must make up his or her own mind. But they would be unwise not to be guided by the current advice of the Committee on Safety of Medicines (1988):

> benzodiazepines are indicated for the short-term relief (2–4 weeks only) of anxiety that is severe, disabling or subjecting the individual to unacceptable distress. . . . They should be used to treat insomnia only when it is severe, disabling or subjecting the individual to extreme distress. Use as a hypnotic should if possible be intermittent.

This advice rules out continuous long-term treatment and calls for a major effort to wean existing continuous users. If I were still in practice, my behaviour in regard to these drugs would have undergone a radical change, but I would not rule out short-term or intermittent usage.

WRONG USE BY GENERAL PRACTITIONERS?

It may be true that some doctors sometimes react with a prescription alone and omit any attempt to identify what is causing symptoms. Hurried practice has, after all, been one of the more common failures of the National Health Service; it is seen in other countries and under other systems also. However, the evidence in this book and in Gabe and Lipshitz-Phillips (1984) suggests that such inadequacy is not the rule.

Unfortunately, time devoted to identifying and discussing a patient's psychological and social problems does not necessarily lead to their resolution. The problems may be too difficult (for example, among women who lack certain important resources). Alternatively, a patient may habitually over-react to problems which others might solve or tolerate without any effect on their physical health or their capacity to cope with the rest of their daily life. In these circumstances tranquillisers do seem to help (confirmed also by Lennard & Cooperstock 1980); they do not seem automatically to reduce a person's ability to face a problem or to work through it to a solution (by creating 'a barrier to thinking' – see Montagne, Chapter 3), they may indeed seem to do the opposite.

Depressed patients are often given tranquillisers by general practitioners. They are too often used, in my opinion, when an antidepressant is actually required (Weissman & Klerman 1977; Rodrigo *et al.* 1988). One explanation is that depressed patients, their energy and ability to cope reduced, become anxious. Molehills look like mountains. The depressive element may not be obvious, yet it is more fundamental than the symptoms of anxiety, needs to be helped and often can be. It is not that tranquillisers are useless in this circumstance, but they are insufficient, offering less chance of shortening the illness or of giving relief. Some doctors fear the use of antidepressive drugs, especially in proper dosage, because patients, unless warned, complain of their initial side effects; but these are usually brief and worth tolerating.

In a similar way, some doctors use tranquillisers for phobic forms of anxiety. Marks, in particular, has provided good evidence that they help here for only as long as they are taken, while other forms of treatment (especially behavioural treatment by 'exposure' and in some cases antidepressants) offer better hope of lasting relief (Marks & Horder 1987).

AVOIDING LONG-TERM USE

Williams & Bellantuono (Chapter 4) estimate, by combining several studies, that 2–3 per cent of the United Kingdom population use tranquillisers for more than one year. The question 'what proportion of this group is dependent (reliant, refusing to withdraw or defaulting from a withdrawal regime)' finds less consistent evidence. Petursson & Lader (1984) propose that 5–10 per cent of patients on continuous clinical doses of benzodiazepines would exhibit difficulty in withdrawal after six months, the proportion rising thereafter to 75 per cent after six to eight years. Lader & File (1987) report that withdrawal can be difficult even after short-term use – indeed occasionally after a single dose.

Although the total number of prescriptions for tranquillisers has diminished in the United Kingdom, the number of individuals on long-term regimes does not yet appear to have decreased. Nevertheless, there have been changes in the attitudes of doctors. Awareness of the risk of dependence has certainly increased. The attitude of some doctors even suggests a crusade (Kraupl Taylor 1989). Because of this it seems very likely that fewer people will recently have entered the long-term group. On the other hand, a survey of fifty-eight practices in Southampton (1984/5) suggested that 10 per cent of the doctors in them believed that benzodiazepines were not drugs of dependence or did not know that they were (Cantopher *et al.* 1988).

Clearly avoidance is desirable and there can be few patients or doctors who would not now be of this opinion. Even long-term users have feelings of disapproval or resentment, while most doctors subscribe to autonomy as an ideal for patients; they often resent those who seem to depend too much on tranquillisers. Most doctors would suspect that there is some impairment of mental functioning from the use of these drugs, even if the actual evidence reported by Golombok (Chapter 1) is inconclusive (not so, however, File & Pellow 1987).

HOW THEN AVOID?

Very short-term use – less than four weeks continuously – is acceptable practice at present (Committee on the Safety of Medicines 1988; Royal College of Psychiatrists 1988). Intermittent use for periods of less than four weeks, with significant gaps, is an obvious move. It offers the possibility of early detection of those who are becoming dependent and showing symptoms of difficulty in withdrawal. There are many 'continuous' users who adopt this plan themselves, simply because it sufficiently answers their needs, but it may still tend towards gradual increase of dependence.

Such a solution is unlikely to satisfy the idealist, whether patient or doctor. So what other methods of dealing with anxiety states have been shown to be as effective as the use of tranquillisers in the long-term?

More careful assessment and reassessment

Looking at the alternatives, one which seems to me most essential – and which should precede any other – is referred to by the writers of this book only indirectly. Surely the essential need is for more thorough assessment or reassessment of the patient's personality, circumstances, feelings, and drug experience? It cannot be assumed that this has been already achieved – *especially* when a patient has been on a doctor's list for a long time. There is a well-known parallel in that the 'regular' doctor is liable not to notice a change in the appearance of a familiar patient who has slowly developed a defect of thyroid function.

It is often valuable for a general practitioner to step back and give time to reassessment, even when the patient does seem well known. Gabe and Lipshitz-Phillips (1984) showed that one-third of the doctors they interviewed said that they felt that running behind time, a full waiting-room, and administrative interruptions combined to increase the likelihood that they would prescribe rather than try to reach agreement with the patient about an alternative course of action. Contrariwise, the studies by Morrell *et al.* (1986, 1987) and by Howie (1989), confirm the importance of longer appointment intervals in the recognition and management of psychiatric problems. Moreover, an important study of the correlates of effective outcomes in primary care (Bass *et al.* 1986) gives pride of place to agreement between patient and doctor about the nature of the disorder; this is something which may need discussion and take time to achieve.

There is, of course, always the other possibility – referral to a psychiatrist. This may serve the same purpose as well or better, especially if the psychiatrist visits a practice regularly, as now often happens in the United Kingdom (Strathdee & Williams 1987).

A valuable contribution in this book is the evidence which it provides about risk-factors for dependence on tranquillisers. Clearly these are to be taken into account in any formal assessment or indeed whenever dealing with anxious patients. Several studies agree that the risk-factors are – being older, being female, showing a high level of emotional distress, having to cope with 'social problems', having a previous history of using any psychotropic drug (see Gabe & Thorogood 1986). Two of these five factors are, of course, among the leading reasons why the drugs are prescribed in the first place. But it remains true, as a report of the General Medical Services Committee points out (1989: Appendix IX), that 'there is no certain guide to the type of patient who is likely to develop dependence'.

In this book, the first alternative actually to be mentioned (Shiell, Chapter 5) is counselling. This can perhaps be regarded as a form of assessment or reassessment, but there can be few counsellors (or psychologists or psychotherapists) who have the proper balance of training to assess all the aspects which need to be considered. For example, in the evidence provided by Williams and Bellantuono (Chapter 4) about risk factors, the presence of physical disorders features importantly. Moreover, in some cases the most appropriate outcome of assessment might involve the use of alternative physical agents.

Assessment could usefully include some enquiry into 'the images and metaphors' (Montagne, Chapter 3) which accompany a particular patient's use of a tranquilliser. But at this point I have to say again that there are limits to the depth of enquiry which any general practitioner can afford to make.

Counselling by the general practitioner

The trial by Catalan *et al.* (1984) defined counselling as 'explanation of the nature of any symptoms and why they had occurred; exploration of underlying personal or other problems and ways of dealing with them; reasons for not prescribing drugs'. The average consultation length was ten minutes.

This form of counselling produced improvement similar and parallel to anxiolytics, without increasing demands on the doctor's time.

'Anxiety management'

The study of Butler *et al.* (1987) showed that twenty-two patients with 'generalised anxiety disorders', treated by 'anxiety management', changed more than a matched group waiting for treatment. In this approach, fears of being unable to cope, of losing control, of illness, or of social embarrassment are allayed by teaching ways of coping with them. Each person's specific fears are identified. The method combines relaxation, reassuring 'self-talk', and practice in the use of anxiety-provoking imagery to induce anxiety, which is then brought under control by relaxation, distraction, and discussion of upsetting thoughts. Emphasis is on active self-help, using a booklet.

The changes were highly significant and were replicated almost exactly when patients on the waiting-list completed treatment. In both cases the effects persisted through a six-month follow-up. At the start of the trial 46 per cent of the patients were taking regular medication; after six months, 13 per cent.

The study by Blowers *et al.* (1987) confirmed the benefit of a similar treatment for twenty generally anxious clients, compared to those on a waiting-list, but not any greater benefit than for a group offered non-directive counselling.

Relaxation alone

Used alone, this achieves short-term reduction in anxiety (Mathews & Gelder 1969; Butler *et al.* 1987). It is unlikely to produce lasting improvement in chronic cases (Raskin *et al.* 1973; Leboeuf & Lodge 1980). It may have a more promising application for tension headache (Canter *et al.* 1975) and for sleep-onset insomnia (Budzynski *et al.* 1973). The method used is important. Special arrangements are likely to be needed in a general practice.

HOW AVOID – CONCLUSION

In contemporary general practice, the most promising alternatives to the use of drugs for patients who are chronically anxious but show no evidence of depression are, in my opinion, *more careful assessment* and *counselling*, as defined by Catalan *et al.* (1984). The two processes are scarcely distinct from each other.

MODELS

Williams and Bellantuono (Chapter 4) quote Box's statement: 'All models are wrong but some are useful'.

This speaks to experience; models are indeed useful, but it is only after the excitement of their discovery or creation has worn off that one realizes how limiting or distorting they can be. The 'medical model', centring round the idea of a 'disease', with standard features related to causes, course, outcome, and methods for cure or relief, does have unusually wide applications and has proved its usefulness beyond dispute. But even in the physical context where it fits most usefully, it can distort by distracting attention away from variations which are due to personality, circumstances, or environment (Querido 1959). Since such variations are even more prevalent when it comes to disorders of thought, feeling, or relationships, the model limits and distorts reality the more; but it is not totally inappropriate or useless, for instance in understanding manic-depressive disorder and thence in offering one way of thinking about the much more common disorder, 'depression' without mania.

Behavioural scientists sometimes criticize doctors for their narrowness, urging them to use models other than the medical one. They see this as being concerned only with objective or physical or technological thinking. But doctors do not see a separate alternative or one which compares in usefulness, given the problems they deal with. Is this simply because they are exposed to no other model in their training? Or because alternatives are expressed in words which are unfamiliar because they depend for their meaning on a background of different training? These reasons do apply, but I believe that there is another one which is less simple, but more important. This depends on the distinction between 'disease' and 'illness'. 'Illness' refers to a lived experience which people feel and suffer; it is partly expressed as symptoms. 'Disease' is a concept, essentially formed and elaborated by trained professionals, as a systematic and useful way of thinking; it enables aspects of the lived experience to be understood and influenced (relieved, cured, or prevented). Although many doctors make every possible effort to force all the phenomena which they observe and treat into some classified system of diseases, there are others who not only see that this is impossible, but also set particular value on attending to the lived experience which patients describe, if only in the form of symptoms. This they see not as an alternative to the medical model, but as an essential first contribution to it; they would not see it even as complementary; usually described as 'history taking', it is integral to it. Three out of four disease diagnoses can be achieved correctly by this means alone (Hampton *et al.* 1975). If it is omitted, the chances of reaching an incorrect diagnosis rise sharply, however many other methods are used. It also offers the earliest and best chance of making a personal relationship through the verbal and visual exchange.

Behavioural scientists are unlikely to accept that the average medical history taking is all that they have in mind when they recommend a 'social' or 'psychological' model. Many doctors would accept this, as I do. There are other insights which can be incorporated and which come from behavioural sciences; they may contribute to the achievement of a disease diagnosis, but they are more likely to contribute to the doctor's understanding of the person and the situation or to the person's understanding of themselves. Curing diseases is not the only way in which doctors can help people to regain or develop their autonomy.

Those for whom the medical model incorporates 'illness' as well as 'disease' will find it easy to include insights due to behavioural sciences within the medical model and they will tend to do so. The definitions of the general practitioner or of the family physician quoted early in this chapter show that leaders in this part of the profession want to incorporate the relevant messages from behavioural science in their practice.

This book has such messages for general practitioners and family physicians about a problem in which they have found themselves entangled.

ACKNOWLEDGEMENT

I am particularly indebted to Charles Medawar and for his help with this chapter. I also acknowledge the help of Clare Harrison.

REFERENCES

Adams, B. G., Horder, E. J., Horder, J. P., Modell, M., Steen, C. A., & Wigg, J. W. (1966) 'Patients receiving barbiturates in an urban general practice', *Journal of College of General Practitioners* 12: 24–31.

American Academy and Board of Family Practice (1975) 'Official definitions', *American Academy and Board of Family Practice Reporter* 2: 10.

American Psychiatric Association (1980) *Diagnostic and Statistical Manual of Mental Disorders*, 3rd edition, revised, Washington, DC: American Psychiatric Association.

Ashbaugh, D. G. & McKean, R. S. (1976) 'Continuing medical education', *Journal of the American Medical Association* 236: 1485–8.

Bass, M. J., Buck, C., Turner, L., Dickie, G., Pratt, G., & Campbell Robinson, H. (1986) 'The physician's actions and the outcome of illness in family practice', *Journal of Family Practice* 23(1): 43–7.

Blowers, C., Cobb, J., & Mathews, A. (1987) 'Generalised anxiety; a controlled treatment study', *Behavioural Research Therapy* 25(6): 473–502.

Budzynski, T. H., Stoyva, J. M., & Adler, C. S. (1973) 'E.M.G. biofeedback and tension headache; a controlled outcome study', *Psychosomatic Medicine* 35: 484–96.

Butler, G., Cullington, A., Hibbert, G., Klimes, I., & Gelder, M. (1987) 'Anxiety management for persistent generalised anxiety', *British Journal of Psychiatry* 151: 535–42.

Canter, A., Kondo, C. Y., & Knott, J. R. (1975) 'A comparison of E.M.G. feedback and progressive relaxation training in anxiety neuroses', *British Journal of Psychiatry* 127: 470–7.

Cantopher, T. G. A., Olivieri, S., & Edwards, J. F. (1988) 'Rates of tranquilliser prescribing in primary care (letter)', *British Journal of Addiction* 83: 969–70.

Catalan, J., Gath, D., Edmonds, G., & Ennis, J. (1984) 'The effects of non-prescribing of anxiolytics in general practice I & II', *British Journal of Psychiatry* 144: 593–602, 603–10.

Committee on the Safety of Medicines (1988) 'Current problems', Bulletin 21, obtainable from the Committee, Market Towers, 19 Elms Lane, London SW8, UK.

Cooper, B., Fry, J., & Kalton, G. W. (1969) 'A longitudinal study of psychiatric morbidity in a general practice population', *British Journal of Preventive and Social Medicine* 23: 210–17.

Cormack, M. A. & Sinnott, A., (1983) 'Psychological alternatives to long-term benzodiazepine use', *Journal of Royal College of General Practitioners* 33: 279–81.

Covi, L., Lipman, R. S., Pattison, J. H., Derogatis, L. R., & Uhlenmuth, E. H. (1973) 'Length of treatment with anxiolytic sedatives and response to their sudden withdrawal', *Acta Psychiatrica Scandinavica* 49: 51–64.

East of Ireland Faculty, Royal College of General Practitioners (1983) 'A double-blind randomized controlled trial of diazepam', *Journal of Royal College of General Practitioners* 33: 635–6.

File, S. E. & Pellow, S. (1987) 'Behavioural pharmacology of minor tranquilliser', *Pharmacological Therapy* 35: 265–90.

Fry, J. (1960) 'What happens to our neurotic patients?', *The Practitioner* 185: 85–9.

Gabe, J. & Lipshitz-Phillips, S. (1984) 'Tranquillisers and social control?', *Sociological Review* 32(3): 524–46.

Gabe, J. & Thorogood, N. (1986) 'Prescribed drug use and the management of everyday life', *Sociological Review* 34(4): 737–72.

General Medical Services Committee (1989) Supplementary report to a special conference of representatives of local medical committees – 27 April, Appendix 9, obtainable from the Committee, British Medical Association, Tavistock Square, London WC1, UK.

Hampton, J. R., Harrison, M. J. G., Mitchell, J. R. A., Prichard, J. S., & Seymour, C. (1975) 'Relative contributions of history-taking, physical examination and laboratory investigation to diagnosis and management of medical outpatients', *British Medical Journal* 1: 486–9.

Howie, J. G. R., Porter, A. M. D., & Forbes, J. F. (1989) 'Quality and the use of time in general practice; widening the discussion', *British Medical Journal* 298: 1008–10.

Kedward, H. B. (1969) 'The outcome of neurotic disorders in the community', *Social Psychiatry* 4: 1–4.

Koumjian, K. (1981) 'The use of Valium as a form of social control', *Social Science and Medicine* 15E: 245–9.

Kraupl Taylor, F. (1989) 'The damnation of benzodiazepines', *British Journal of Psychiatry* 154: 697–704.

Lader, M. H. & File, S. E. (1987) 'The biological basis of benzodiazepine dependence', *Psychological Medicine* 17(3): 539–47.

Leboeuf, A. & Lodge, J. (1980) 'A comparison of Frontalis E.M.G. feedback training and progressive relaxation in the treatment of chronic anxiety', *British Journal of Psychiatry* 137: 279–83.

Lennard, H. L. & Cooperstock, R. (1980) 'The social context and functions of tranquilliser prescribing' in R. Mapes (ed.) *Prescribing Practice and Drug Usage*, London: Croom Helm.

Mann, A. H., Jenkins, R., & Belsey, E. (1981) 'The twelve-month outcome of patients with neurotic illness in general practice', *Psychological Medicine* 11: 535–50.

Marks, I. & Horder, J. (1987) 'Phobias and their management', *British Medical Journal* 295: 589–91.

Mathews, A. M. & Gelder, M. G. (1969) 'Psycho-physiological investigation of brief relaxation training', *Journal of Psychosomatic Research* 13: 1–12.

Morrell, D. C., Evans, M. E., Morris, R. W., & Roland, M. O. (1986) 'The "five-minute" consultation: effect of time constraint on clinical content and patient satisfaction', *British Medical Journal* 292: 870–3.

Morrell, D. C. & Roland, M. O. (1987) 'How can good general practitioner care be achieved?' *British Medical Journal* 294: 161–2.

Oswald, I., French, C., Adam, K., & Gilham, J. (1982) 'Benzodiazepine hypnotics remain effective for 24 weeks', *British Medical Journal* 284: 860–3.

Petursson, H. & Lader, M. H. (1984) *Dependence on Tranquillisers*, Oxford: Oxford University Press.

Querido, A. (1959) 'Forecast and follow-up: an investigation into the clinical, social and mental factors determining the results of hospital treatment', *British Journal of Preventive & Social Medicine* 13(1): 33–48.

Raskin, M., Johnson, G., & Rondesfredt, J. W. (1973) 'Chronic anxiety treated by feedback-induced muscle relaxation', *Archives of General Psychiatry* 28: 263–7.

Rickels, K., Case, G., Downing, R. W., & Winokur, A. (1983) 'Long-term diazepam therapy and clinical outcome', *Journal of the American Medical Association* 250(6): 767–71.

Rodrigo, E. K., King, M. B., & Williams, P. (1988) 'Health of long-term benzodiazepine users', *British Medical Journal* 296: 603–5.

Roland, M. O., Bartholomew, J., Courtenay, M., Morris, R., & Morrell, D. C. (1986) 'The "five-minute" consultation: effect of time constraint on verbal communication', *British Medical Journal* 292: 874–6.

Royal College of Psychiatrists (1988) 'Benzodiazepines and dependence: a

College statement', *Bulletin of the Royal College of Psychiatrists* 12: 107–9.

Second European Conference on the Teaching of General Practice (Leeuwenhorst, Netherlands) 1974 *The General Practitioner in Europe*, obtainable from the Royal College of General Practitioners, 14 Princes Gate, London SW7.

Shepherd, M., Cooper, B., Brown, A. C., & Kalton, G. (1981) *Psychiatric Illness in General Practice*, 2nd edition, Oxford: Oxford University Press.

Strathdee, G. & Williams, P. (1987) 'A survey of psychiatrists in primary care: the silent growth of a new service', *Journal of Royal College of General Practitioners* 34: 615–18.

Tyrer, P., Murphy, S., Kingdon, D., Brothwell, J., Gregory, S., Seivewright, N., Ferguson, B., Barczak, P., Darling, C., & Johnson, A. L. (1988) 'The Nottingham study of neurotic disorder: comparison of drug and psychological treatment', *Lancet* II: 235–40.

United Kingdom Committee on the Review of Medicines (1980) 'Systematic review of the benzodiazepines', *British Medical Journal* 280: 910–12.

Weissman, M. M. & Klerman, G. L. (1977) 'The chronic depressive in the community: unrecognised and poorly treated', *Comprehensive Psychiatry* 1977 (18): 523–32.

Williams, P. (1983) 'Patterns of psychotropic drug use', *Social Science and Medicine* 17: 845–51.

Williams, P., Bellantuono, C., Fiorio, R., & Tansella, M. (1986) 'Psychotropic drug use in Italy: national trends and regional differences', *Psychological Medicine* 16: 841–50.

World Health Organisation (1980) *International Classification of Impairment, Disabilities and Handicaps*, Geneva: WHO.

9 The benzodiazepine controversy: a psychiatrist's reaction

Anthony Clare

This is a difficult time in which to discuss dispassionately the widespread use of the benzodiazepines. In part this is due to the fact that, as Montagne (Chapter 3) reminds us, the deployment of any new drug or brand of drugs passes through three stages. The first is a stage of euphoric enthusiasm in which the new drug is hailed as yet another magic bullet. Then there is a stage of paranoid uncertainty in which the new drug is suspected of being ineffective, counter-productive and even downright dangerous. Finally comes a stage of judicious evaluation in which the now established drug is seen as having a narrow and specifically defined role in the treatment of a relatively discrete cluster of illnesses and a clear-cut series of limitations attached to its use. The benzodiazepines are in the second of these stages. After having been warmly welcomed at the beginning of the 1960s as benevolent substitutes for their much more toxic predecessors, the bromides and the barbiturates, these drugs are now regarded with considerable public ambivalence and unease. They are widely regarded as less safe and/or less effective than was previously believed and are frequently portrayed as an inappropriate treatment for the emotional symptoms and psychosocial circumstances for which once they were heartily recommended. When first introduced, the minor tranquillisers appeared virtually perfect for their role – inexpensive, effective, and lacking any serious or lethal consequences. Thirty years on, they are assailed as potentially addictive, cognitively incapacitating, and morally crippling.

Yet, as several of the contributors to this book implicitly or explicitly confirm, there are other reasons worth examining if we are to understand the waxing and waning in popularity of these remarkable drugs. It is clear that the decision to prescribe a benzodiazepine incorporates a series of judgements and decisions which are in their own way controversial and value-laden. There is the decision to categorize certain kinds of distress and dissatisfaction as morbidity or disease warranting medical intervention, a decision which, as Prather (Chapter 6) points out, is influenced by the pharmaceutical industry which produces the drugs as well as by the doctor who prescribes them and the patient who consumes them. There is the choice of a biological response, a drug, instead of a psychological one (psychotherapy) or a social one (provision of money, a job, a house, a divorce, etc.), which a prescription represents. There is the potential consequence of prescribing drugs in response to unacceptable social situations, namely that individuals will be tranquillized into social conformity. (At the heart of much of the concern about women being more frequently prescribed tranquillisers than men is this suspicion that a sexist, chauvinist society is being maintained in part by little helpers that are not so much mother's as father's, not so much wife's as husband's.)

Related to such considerations is the fact that it is doctors who prescribe and in prescribing anxiolytics and hypnotics they retain a crucial influence on the evaluation and management of a plethora of social forces, interactions, situations, structures which otherwise might well fall outside their professional ambit altogether.

In the midst of this controversy can be discerned five key questions relating to the prescribing and the popularity of the benzodiazepines, questions which reverberate throughout this collection as they do throughout the wider reaches of the controversy within the media and the general public. Why are the benzodiazepines prescribed? For whom are they prescribed? Are they effective? Do their benefits outweigh the deficiencies? Are there alternative therapies which could be as or more effectively, economically, and safely deployed? These are by no means the only questions which relate to the long-term use of these drugs but they are the questions which most frequently recur and to which the representatives of sociology, epidemiology, psychology, communication studies, and economics repeatedly return in their contributions to this volume.

WHY ARE BENZODIAZEPINES PRESCRIBED?

The answer to this seemingly simple question depends in part on who has been asked to answer it. There is the role of the pharmaceutical industry in solicitously ensuring that these drugs are in the forefront of the minds of doctors and patients whenever stress, anxiety, depression, and difficult living situations are raised within the consultation (Prather, Chapter 6). There is the historical fact that people have always sought pharmacological relief for psychological distress and social strain – be it by way of opiates, gin, bromides, or barbiturates – and the development of the benzodiazepines appeared to mark the emergence of a very much safer medication (Montagne, Chapter 3). There is the fact that within health services the current structure of incentives makes it more likely that drugs are prescribed for particular problems while alternative approaches, such as benevolent inaction, counselling, the use of relatively harmless tonics, are discouraged (Shiell, Chapter 5). Ray (Chapter 7) adds the often neglected perspective of the political economist when he reminds his readers that the benzodiazepines are high-technology commodities, mood-altering drugs with addictive properties that are marketed by complex and powerful organizations in pursuit of profit. They are prescribed because companies have manufactured them to fill a need and these same companies, by means of an army of trained representatives and expensive marketing and advertising campaigns, make every effort to ensure that the market remains a lively and an active one.

This reference to market realities also, however, reminds us of the epidemiological facts pertaining to mental health. The work of researchers such as Shepherd, Goldberg, Jenkins, Regier and others, work which spanned the same decades as witnessed the rise of benzodiazepine prescribing, has revealed the magnitude of the pool of anxiety, depression, irritability, sleep disturbance, impaired concentration, and fatigue existing outside the hospital services and within primary care and the community. Remember that in one year the average British general practitioner will deal with around 200 minor emotional illnesses, at least twelve patients will present with severe depression, and approximately fifty-five of his/her patients will be suffering from chronic mental illness and will be living in the community. Remember too the ubiquity of such symptoms as fatigue, anxiety, impaired concentration, and irritability within that same community. For example, Jenkins (1983) in her study of healthy, young, educated male and female civil servants, found that 37 per cent of the men (27 per cent of the women) reported impaired concentration, 29 per cent of the men (37 per cent of the women) reported fatigue, and 34 per cent of the men (52 per cent of the women) reported anxiety within the preceding two weeks.

FOR WHOM ARE BENZODIAZEPINES PRESCRIBED?

One of the saving graces of the entire benzodiazepine controversy is that it has helped focus attention on the valuable role played by good, detached, impersonal epidemiological research in clarifying the various factors involved. In recent years the assumption has grown that the benzodiazepines, precisely because they are relatively cheap and seemingly innocuous in terms of side effects, are being prescribed in an indiscriminate way to middle-aged people of both sexes, who are locked within difficult personal and/or social situations and who don't really want or need such inappropriate therapies. Such an assumption, Gabe (Chapter 2) points out, is hammered home within the media and is reinforced by consumers of benzodiazepines who are ambivalent about their use. However, Williams and Bellantuono (Chapter 4), reviewing the available research, suggest that such an apocalyptic view is not supported. There is, for example, no evidence that over the past decade the number of people taking these drugs on a regular basis has increased. What has increased is the proportion of benzodiazepine consumers who are taking them for a lengthy period of time – a finding which is itself a cause for concern but which does not support the notion of an escalating epidemic of drug use.

Nor is the prescribing haphazard. Long-term users tend to be older rather than younger, physically ill rather than healthy, socially isolated rather than integrated. Female long-term users tend to have social problems and few social supports. There is, in short, an identifiable pattern to benzodiazepine prescribing and precious little evidence to suggest doctors behave in a random or cavalier way when prescribing. These are important findings for, as Williams and Bellantuono (Chapter 4) and Gabe (Chapter 2) emphasize, their identification leads on to a more sophisticated examination of such issues as the higher consumption of benzodiazepines by women and the kind of social stresses such women manifest.

But as Ray (Chapter 7) reminds us, the situation is not as sanguine in the developing world. The fact that, as he points out, the sums spent on diazepam and thioridazine at a Dar es Salaam hospital would have provided malaria prophylaxis for 350,000 children not merely emphasizes the distortion that can occur when certain drugs are commercially pushed but indicates the extent to which the indications for drugs are gradually expanded to include all manner of complaints, significant and trivial, in addition to the symptoms and conditions for which the drug was originally shown to be reasonably effective.

ARE THE BENZODIAZEPINES EFFECTIVE?

While the position concerning the effectiveness of the benzodiazepines when taken on a short-term basis for the release of acute attacks of anxiety seems reasonably uncontroversial, the argument for the effectiveness of long-term use is a good deal more problematic. As Rickels (1987) has pointed out, there is a rich literature describing the pharmacokinetics of the benzodiazepines and the positive results of short-term clinical trials but 'long-term efficacy data are sparse'. In two prospective studies conducted with diazepam and clorazapate, anxiolytic efficacy was maintained for a six-month treatment period. In these studies, tolerance to the drugs' anxiolytic effect did not develop but there was evidence of physical dependence. Rickels (1987) has gone on to argue on the basis of his reading of the literature that certain patient populations may benefit from, and even require, prolonged anxiolytic therapy. Included are patients with chronic, year-long generalized anxiety disorder, panic disorder, and anxiety secondary to chronic physical illness.

The fact that many patients cannot conceive of living without regular (or access to regular) consumption of a minor tranquilliser must not of course be taken as evidence of their effectiveness. Yet, as Higgitt's study of the effects of withdrawing long-term consumers from their drug shows, the results can be catastrophic (Higgitt *et al.* 1987). Three of the ten patients in that study became agoraphobic on withdrawal to the extent that they were completely housebound. When long-term users have been asked to specify the ways in which benzodiazepines and other tranquillisers are beneficial, many frequently mention aspects of social functioning and performance. We know that many users have difficulties in social functioning, experience reduced social support and increased social stress; in the absence of effective and equivalently cheap alternative therapies, the benzodiazepines seem one of the few cheap therapies available.

Tyrer (1988) has emphasized the relative safety of the drugs as a long-term benefit on the grounds, which some might question, that if people are going to take an anxiolytic on an intermittent or long-term basis then of the anxiolytics commonly available – benzodiazepines, barbiturates, alcohol – the benzodiazepines would seem the safest. It is, in other words, a question of the least obnoxious poison. Pharmacological Calvinists may well wonder why so many people need to have recourse to mood-altering drugs at all but, as Montagne (Chapter 3) pointedly reminds us, there is nothing very novel about any of this. Drugs have exercised a potent attraction for humans throughout recorded history, a fact particularly true for mood-altering drugs. In such circumstances, it is hardly surprising that those who call for the abolition of all anxiolytic drugs on the grounds that reliance on such drugs saps one's psychological and physical resilience should find themselves confronted by an equally convinced group arguing that, since drugs, like poverty, will always be with us, the sensible thing to do is to find the safest forms and discard the more dangerous. It is to this latter group that the benzodiazepines appear a genuinely progressive development for the very simple reason that, when compared with their predecessors, the opiates, belladonna derivatives, bromide salts, barbiturates, propanediols, and carbamates, the benzodiazepines appear to represent a remarkable advance. They may not be the safest anxiolytics – but they are the safest thus far discovered.

DO THE BENEFITS OUTWEIGH THE DEFICIENCIES?

Amid the many shortcomings attributed to these drugs, two seem particularly identified by the contributors. The first is the suggestion that the medicalization of problems inherent in the prescription of a benzodiazepine removes the incentive to change an unacceptable situation. Gabe (Chapter 2) directly confronts the issue of tranquillisers as agents of social control. If his analysis is correct, it would appear that the key protagonists within the social drama – the doctor and the long-term user – do not believe this to be the case. It is patients rather than doctors who seem most inclined to seek a single cause for problems. If gender stereotyping is indeed at work it would appear to affect patients rather than doctors in that women do more frequently present with psychological problems to their doctors than do men.

The second major deficiency is dependence. Within a few years of their development, clinical studies had demonstrated that diazepam (Hollister *et al.* 1963) and chlordiazepoxide (Hollister *et al.* 1961) taken for a month in dosages two to three times the maximum recommended daily therapeutic dose produced physical dependence and a clinically significant withdrawal syndrome. Some twenty years later, researchers began to suggest that the long-term use of benzodiazepines taken within the usual range of therapeutically prescribed doses could also result in physical dependence (Lader 1983; Winokur *et al*. 1980).

Golombok's (Chapter 1) own study involving the assessment of the effect of long-term use on responses to a wide battery of psychological tests confirms that the persistent use of high doses of these drugs is potentially harmful, although even in this careful account we cannot be sure just what the impaired ability to perform tasks of visual-spatial ability and sustained attention amounts to in real life. But exposure is important; in Golombok's words, 'As with alcohol, the effect is cumulative – the higher the intake, the greater the risk'. At the same time, as she acknowledges, for all the concern about the benzodiazepines and the dangers of dependence, there is surprisingly little evidence of escalation of dose and the phenomenon of tolerance is not particularly well documented.

Leaving aside the moral doubts about the wisdom of relying on drugs long term to cope with or solve problems, one is tempted to inquire as to what all the fuss is about. Why, given the world-wide tolerance of moderate to heavy regular alcohol consumption for example, has so much anxiety been aroused by the widespread prescribing of anxiolytics? Are they actually any more toxic and undesirable than aspirin? Given the ubiquity of the common psychological symptoms of distress and the relative safety of the benzodiazepines, would it not make better sense to concentrate on teaching people how to use them more effectively, efficiently, and safely than morally to disapprove of their use and condemn those who prescribe and use them?

ARE THERE ACCEPTABLE, EFFECTIVE, ECONOMIC ALTERNATIVES?

The question of economics is confounded by the fact that the benzodiazepines are exceedingly cheap unless artificially overvalued. Taylor (1987) pointed out that while the benzodiazepines represented some 3 per cent of the total NHS medicine costs (in manufacturer's prices) and 0.3 per cent of all NHS spending, they were contained in 8 per cent of all the prescription items dispensed by the British family practitioner services. They are cheap (particularly when compared to other health service inputs – medical and equivalent professional labour costs being around £15 per hour). He points out, not unreasonably, that this fact 'rather than some hypothesized draining of health service resources due to benzodiazepine purchases, may lie at the bottom of any failure of the NHS to provide alternative/complementary provisions' such as GP-attached counsellors or social workers or psychotherapy.

Behaviourally trained nurses, social workers, and psychologists on a sessional basis are among the professional interventions that have been assessed with a view to shifting the emphasis from pharmacotherapy in general practice. Really watertight cost-benefit analyses are still lacking, although attempts have been made to show an impact on drug prescribing. It is difficult, however, to compete on financial terms alone with the minor tranquillisers.

But, of course, one acceptable, effective, and economic alternative might be no treatment at all. Catalan and his colleagues (1984) suggested that very brief counselling for patients with low to moderate levels of anxiety was every bit as effective as benzodiazepine therapy. Non-specific curative factors, such as supportive contact with a doctor, patient expectation, and the passage of time, may have become undervalued with the headlong rush to pharmacotherapy.

Bound up with arguments in favour of no therapy or very brief therapy are certain assumptions about the problems for which benzodiazepines are prescribed. Some critics are in danger of appearing to suggest that the problems for which benzodiazepines are prescribed are not *real* problems, the suffering they are prescribed to ease is not *real* suffering. The work of Williams and Bellantuono (Chapter 4), Gabe (Chapter 2), and others reminds us that this is not so. The problems for which the benzodiazepines are prescribed are, for the most part, significant and substantial.

SUMMARY

From their different perspectives, the contributors to this volume emphasize the extent to which the prescribing of the benzodiazepine group of drugs is no mere doctor–patient transaction undertaken within the confines of the consulting rooms. It is a complex cultural and social process with political, economic, moral as well as medico-social implications. The controversy concerning the use and abuse of minor tranquillisers may appear related to such worrying adverse consequences as impaired cognitive function and physical dependence and, indeed, it is largely conducted as if this were indeed the case. In fact, there is much more at issue. There is concern about the possibility that in the development of this group of drugs we have arrived at an illusory position of a pill for every social ill, that complex social and interpersonal problems are being squeezed into a pseudo-disease category for which such drugs are presumed, mistakenly, to be indicated and that money and effort tied up in the production, dissemination, and consumption of such drugs could be better spent. There is concern, justified it would appear, that such drugs are being carelessly, some might argue mischievously deployed in Third World countries with deforming effects on health care service development. There is concern too that in the very process of marketing and advertising such drugs, a need is being artificially stimulated which only the drugs can meet.

But there is another side to the coin. The benzodiazepines are only the latest in a long line of drugs which men and women have used to ease psychological distress and help them cope with adverse life circumstances and, for all the problems associated with their use, they are the safest to date. Those who use them are more often ill than well (physically as well as mentally), old than young, poorly supported than supported. For the most part, doctors and patients know full well tranquillisers are not the panacea for personal and social ills and, largely no doubt as a consequence of media concern, also know that the relief brought with their use does exact its own price. The doctor's decision, therefore, to prescribe or not to prescribe a benzodiazepine and a patient's decision to consume or not consume the drug represent a particularly subtle and complex risk–benefit judgement. We are only now subjecting this process to an appropriately thorough analysis.

REFERENCES

Catalan, J., Faih, D., Edmonds, G., Ennis, J., Bond, A., & Martin, P. (1984) 'The effects of non-prescribing of anxiolytics in general practice', *British Journal of Psychiatry* 144: 593–610.

Higgitt, A., Golombok, S., Fonagy, P., & Lader, M. (1987) 'Group treatment of benzodiazepine dependence', *British Journal of Addiction* 82: 517–32.

Hollister, L. E., Motzenbecker, F. P., & Degan, R. O. (1961) 'Withdrawal reactions from chlordiazepoxide', *Psychopharmacologia* 2(L): 63–8.

Hollister, L. E., Bennet, J. L., Kimbell Jr., L., Savage, C., & Overall, E. (1963) 'Diazepam in newly admitted schizophrenics', *Diseases of the Nervous System* 24: 746–50.

Jenkins, R. (1983) 'Some epidemiological observations of minor psychiatric morbidity', MD thesis, University of Cambridge.

Lader, M. (1983) 'Dependence on benzodiazepines', *Journal of Clinical Psychiatry* 44(4): 121–7.

Rickels, K. (1987) 'Antianxiety therapy: potential value of long-term treatment', *Journal of Clinical Psychiatry* 48: 12 (Suppl.): 7–11.

Taylor, D. (1987) 'Current usage of benzodiazepines in Britain', in H. Freeman & Y. Rue (eds) *The Benzodiazepines in Current Clinical Practice*, London: Royal Society of Medicine Services.

Tyrer, P. (1988) 'Benefits and risks of benzodiazepines', in H. Freeman & Y. Rue (eds) *The Benzodiazepines in Current Clinical Practice*, London: Royal Society of Medicine Services.

Winokur, A., Rickels, K., Greenblatt, D. J., Snyder, P. J., & Schatz, N. (1989) 'Withdrawal reaction from long-term, low dosage administration of diazepam: a double-blind controlled case study', *Archives of General Psychiatry* 37: 101–5.

10 Long-term tranquilliser use: a health policy perspective

Helene L. Lipton and Lisa A. Bero

INTRODUCTION

Long-term tranquilliser use is a complex issue. What are the factors contributing to long-term tranquilliser use? What are its outcomes and treatment? This volume examines in detail the various social, psychological, cultural, and economic factors that contribute to long-term tranquilliser use. The current chapter will analyse the policy implications gained from these social science perspectives by considering patient, physician, and societal contributions to the problem. We will discuss the factors at each of these levels that lead to or inhibit long-term tranquilliser use and describe areas where more information is needed to understand the problem. Our comprehensive policy recommendations will be directed at all levels including changes in individual and societal attitudes towards drug therapy for anxiety, physician prescribing practices, and government regulation of the pharmaceutical industry and drug treatment. A multidisciplinary approach to the problem of long-term tranquilliser use, such as that offered in this book, is essential to the understanding of this drug use phenomenon.

Before the problem of long-term tranquilliser use can be discussed, a consistent definition of 'long-term' must be agreed upon. In this text, some authors refer to 'continuous' use; others refer to use exceeding twenty-one days; still others consider long-term use to mean a year or more. Gabe notes that 27–45 per cent of tranquilliser users are dependent, indicating that physical dependence is a problem with long-term use. However, intermittent use of low-dose tranquillisers does not produce physical dependence, whereas continuous, long-term use of tranquillisers does produce a true physical dependence and withdrawal syndrome. Therefore, long-term intermittent use is appropriate according to pharmacological guidelines for prescribing. Policy makers need information to further define whether or not intermittent use of tranquillisers to deal with task-specific stresses is socially acceptable compared to long-term compulsive drug-taking behaviour. In this chapter, we will define long-term tranquilliser use as intermittent or continuous use for one year or more. This chapter will concentrate on policy recommendations related to long-term use.

THE CONTRIBUTION OF THE PATIENT TO LONG-TERM TRANQUILLISER USE

Patients' attitudes toward tranquilliser use – and their beliefs about the safety and efficacy of these drugs – help determine patterns of drug use. We are beginning to understand the characteristics of patients 'at risk' for long-term tranquilliser use; however, much more needs to be learned. The greater use of drugs by women is an additional patient-centred issue. Patients' attitudes also affect their ability and willingness to learn non-drug coping strategies and their perceived effectiveness of drug or non-drug therapies. Each of these issues will be discussed in this section.

In considering the patient, an important question arises: what are the characteristics of patients 'at risk' for long-term tranquilliser use? In a major study, three significant factors were identified: 1) history of psychotropic drug use (the presence of such a history decreased the likelihood of discontinuing treatment); 2) an interactive effect of sex and social problems (such that women in whom the general practitioner identified social problems were less likely to discontinue treatment than were either women without such problems or men); and 3) the passage of time – the longer the duration of treatment, the less the chance of stopping tranquilliser use (Williams 1983, as cited in Williams & Bellantuono, Chapter 4). However, subsequent studies did not confirm the presence of all these predisposing factors. Therefore, more rigorous research is required to identify subgroups particularly vulnerable to long-term use. Once these subgroups are identified, they can be targeted for educational and policy interventions. As noted by the authors, one intervention could involve the development of a checklist for general practitioners in which the factors predisposing to long-term use are specified, thus helping physicians identify patients at risk of becoming long-term users.

The studies reviewed report higher levels of psychotropic drug use among women than among men. This finding is consistent even after symptomatology and frequency of physician consultations have been taken into account. Studies reviewed by Gabe (Chapter 2) suggest that the tendency for women to be given tranquillisers more often than men can only partly be explained by theories on gender differences in physician behaviour. The patients' structural position in the household and the resulting amount of social support and stress experienced also need to be considered. Thus, there is a need for more research to determine exactly why women use more psychotropic agents than men. It is possible that: 1) it is culturally more acceptable for women to report emotional problems and seek medical treatment; 2) women are more susceptible biologically to anxiety; 3) advertising of psychotropic agents targets women and influences physicians' prescribing (as discussed in detail by Jane Prather, Chapter 6); 4) as women increasingly enter non-traditional (formerly male) professions, their social roles become more stressful and time-constrained, precipitating the desire for psychotropic drug use; and 5) women may be more likely to have certain illnesses and conditions (e.g. hypertension) that are associated with psychotropic drug therapy. These are provocative hypotheses, worthy of more investigation, as noted by Lipton and Lee (1988) in their recent review of this literature.

A significant theme expressed through all the chapters is the importance of examining patients' attitudes and cultural preferences regarding tranquilliser use. The authors note that patients tend to express ambivalent attitudes towards the use of psychotropic drugs. In fact, in one study cited by Gabe (Chapter 2), a significant proportion of patients stopped using these drugs. We need to know more about how and why some patients terminate tranquilliser use and whether their ambivalent attitudes play a part in drug termination. To what extent is the ambivalence genuine? Conversely, to what extent is patient ambivalence a reflection of patients' beliefs that it is socially undesirable to respond that they are totally satisfied with their use of mood-altering medications? If patient ambivalence is genuine, then, possibly, physicians and other health professionals can use patient ambivalence creatively, that is, as a motivational lever to shift patients to consider non-pharmacological approaches to the treatment of anxiety.

The main alternative to conventional treatment of anxiety through prescribing tranquillisers is psychological counselling. In clinical practice, counselling tends to supplement drug therapies rather than replace them. It is important to identify what counselling adds to conventional treatment by way of cost and benefit. But it is difficult to assess the value of different therapies, given the shortage of studies quantifying both costs and benefits.

Counselling has the potential to reduce long-term dependency on tranquillisers if patients are willing to participate and perceive that the counselling is effective. For example, in certain cultures, talking directly to a health professional about one's problems is not considered a socially acceptable way of dealing with stress. Evidence suggests that counselling from general practitioners (Catalan) or nurse therapists (Marks) is cost-effective in treating new cases, but there is little evidence that counselling alone reduces long-term levels of tranquilliser use (Shiell, Chapter 5) because most studies analyse counselling as an adjunct to drug therapy, rather than a separate treatment. It is possible that counselling prevents patients from becoming long-term users. This hypothesis is worthy of investigation. Indeed, longitudinal studies of patients' drug use over time – the conditions under which tranquilliser use is initiated, terminated, resumed, and sustained – would be illuminating.

Effectiveness of various therapies is really dependent upon the outcome being measured. Studies are needed that include drug use as an outcome – levels of tranquilliser use as well as concomitant use of other drugs. Additional patient-centred outcomes that need to be explored in a cost-benefit analysis include quality of life, reduced absenteeism from work, and improved performance at work.

The expenditure of time is a 'cost' of counselling that is not usually assessed because of problems inherent in placing a value on time. Nevertheless, time as a resource cannot be underestimated. Several authors in the book maintain that there is a societal preoccupation about saving time. Drug therapy can represent a 'quick fix' and may be preferred over the time commitment of counselling by working men and working women – populations that are relatively under-studied in research about tranquilliser use. When patient preoccupation about time is combined with physicians' scheduling pressures, the result may be a joint preference for chemical solutions to stressful life situations. One resulting policy implication is the need to educate patients about the benefits of non-pharmacological approaches to long-term tranquillisers. Patient education should be directed away from the notion of a 'quick fix' and towards the alternative notion of changing behaviour by adopting individual coping strategies. Incentives to provide this treatment would be enhanced were physicians and other health professionals to receive adequate training not only in pharmacological approaches to treating anxiety but also in patient counselling methods.

THE CONTRIBUTION OF THE PHYSICIAN TO LONG-TERM TRANQUILLISER USE

Like patients, physicians play a critical role in determining whether and to what extent tranquillisers are used. The appropriateness of physicians' prescribing practices, the nature of their interactions with patients in the area of drug use, and their ability and willingness to apply non-drug alternatives all contribute to patients' drug-taking behaviours. Each of these issues is addressed in turn.

Long-term tranquilliser use should be distinguished from misuse because both of these problems can result from poor physician prescribing practices. While excessive duration of use can pose problems, other types of inappropriate prescribing of tranquillisers by physicians can present equally serious health hazards. A specific example would be prescribing a tranquilliser for the wrong indication. Williams and Bellantuono note the widespread prescribing of tranquillisers for the treatment of depression as well as for the treatment of chronic physical illnesses (Chapter 4). While these patterns of use may be inappropriate, it is important to note that physicians often prescribe drugs for unapproved uses and sometimes these uses ultimately find acceptance in clinical practice.

Other misuse problems include therapeutic duplication; excessive daily dosages; inappropriate frequency of administration; inappropriate choice of a particular tranquilliser given the patient's concomitant conditions; and/or physicians' failure to consider non-drug treatments – all of which can create grave clinical problems for patients.

The fact that these inappropriate uses of tranquillisers are left largely unaddressed by current research should not imply that all current short-term uses of tranquillisers are accepted. A view of tranquilliser use as an 'all or nothing' phenomenon is oversimplified. More useful would be a careful examination of the conditions under which the prescribing of tranquillisers is appropriate. Policy recommendations differ for misuse and long-term use problems. For example, to reduce misuse, specific educational interventions regarding dosage, scheduling, and indication could be targeted towards physicians. Government surveillance of the number of prescriptions for tranquillisers, or stricter government control of pharmaceutical industry practices, could be used to reduce excessive, long-term use.

The patient's ability and willingness to use non-drug treatment alternatives can contribute to a patient's long-term tranquilliser use. Treatment programmes designed to eliminate or reduce tranquilliser use are analysed by Golombok (Chapter 1). A review of psychological theories of addiction is presented and their implications for treating tranquilliser dependence is noted. When stressful situations or unpleasant withdrawal symptoms become cues for taking tranquillisers, patients must learn alternative coping strategies. It is important to note that these coping mechanisms have been identified and refined through behavioural and cognitive approaches to the understanding of tranquilliser use. For treatment programmes to be successful they need to include a gradual drug withdrawal programme as well as training in the use of psychological coping mechanisms (e.g. anxiety management techniques). In other words, in order to achieve permanent withdrawal from tranquillisers, it is important that patients not only gradually reduce their intake but also learn to cope with stressful situations in ways other than by using medication. One policy recommendation flowing from this work is that out-patient treatment programmes need to incorporate both medical and psychological components in order to be effective. Also demonstrated is the need for tranquilliser treatment programmes to be made more generally available and their effectiveness evaluated across different population groups, different treatment settings, etc. Government agencies are in a unique position to fund such efforts and to examine their applicability to programmes concerned with drug dependence in general (including programmes targeted towards users of illicit drugs).

Many authors in this book assume that tranquillisers are acceptable 'first line' therapies and that short-term treatment with tranquillisers constitutes conventional prescribing practice. One could seriously question whether this is really the most appropriate prescribing practice or whether consideration should instead be given first to non-drug therapies. (These might include biofeedback, meditation, exercise, and counselling.) However, these drug-free alternatives are inherently labour intensive and time consuming. Physicians, like patients, are preoccupied with saving time. They may prescribe tranquillisers rather than behavioural alternatives because drugs are perceived as 'quicker' than non-drug approaches. Further, even if physicians are motivated to provide non-drug therapies, they may be unwilling or unable to do so because of lack of training in how to administer these approaches.

Specific types of physician–patient interactions may contribute to the use of long-term use of tranquillisers by patients. There is a great deal of variability in physicians' prescribing of tranquillisers and much research has been devoted to determining the reasons. Williams and Bellantuono describe a study in which the differences among the physicians with regard to the prescribing of psychotropic agents is explored. The differences in patients' duration of tranquilliser use were not due to differences in the characteristics of the patients, in the patients' clinical status, or between specific aspects of treatment. But the impact of the passage of time on the likelihood of stopping drug therapy did vary among physicians, 'suggesting that some doctors interact with their patients in such a way as to encourage, albeit not consciously, long-term use of tranquillisers and other psychotropic drugs' (Williams (1983) as cited in Williams and Bellantuono, Chapter 4). This hypothesis is worthy of investigation and is best examined through longitudinal studies of physician–patient interaction. Such studies could also determine whether patients seek out physicians who meet their prescribing needs, whether patients request or even demand tranquillisers over their physicians' objections, or whether patients' demands for tranquillisers are created primarily by inappropriate physician prescribing.

THE SOCIETAL CONTRIBUTION TO THE PROBLEM OF LONG-TERM TRANQUILLISER USE

A recurring theme throughout the text is the medicalization of social problems and consequent long-term use of tranquillisers to treat problems of everyday life. It has been postulated that the prescribing and use of tranquillisers functions as a form of social control. The use of tranquillisers redefines social problems, such as loneliness and marital discord, as medical problems. This redefinition causes patients to deny the social origins of their distress and, hence, reduces the chances for social change. Gabe and Lipshitz-Phillips (1984) found limited support for the hypothesis that tranquillisers represent a form of social control. Their data suggest that the initial factors motivating a patient to begin tranquilliser use might not be the same factors that sustain them in their use. Long-term studies of a group of tranquilliser users would help clarify the dynamics of use over time. In some instances a patient's anxiety may be so acute, and the patient rendered so dysfunctional, that social relations cannot be changed until the patient is rendered functional enough to confront and deal with problematic situations. For these patients, treatment with tranquillisers could promote recovery. Therefore, policies regarding recommended indications for tranquilliser use should focus more on the individual patient, rather than regulating tranquillisers as a form of social control.

A pressing policy question related to the medicalization of social problems emerges from Ray's discussion of the political economy of long-term tranquilliser use. Which do we need to regulate or modify – the activities of the international pharmaceutical industry or the restructuring of social attitudes? Are the drug manufacturers really initiating use or are they just profiting from the medicalization of social problems?

Studies assessing the impact of pharmaceutical marketing on the prescription of tranquillisers suggest that advertising is associated with an increased number of new prescriptions. For example, Prather, in her chapter 'Decoding advertising', concludes that the marketing of Valium and other tranquillisers by pharmaceutical companies has contributed to the increased use of these drugs. However, no studies have examined the influence of advertising on the appropriateness of prescriptions for tranquillisers, especially regarding their duration of use. Advertisements for tranquillisers do not give the impression that these drugs should be prescribed only for an acute episode of illness. Limits for the duration of therapy are not stated explicitly. Further studies are needed to determine if advertising promotes the inappropriate use of medications, as well as increased use. In addition, the indications for which tranquillisers are prescribed should be scrutinized. Tranquillisers have been marketed for the treatment of 'new' diseases created by the medicalization of stress and social problems such as tension and anxiety. Because these psychological disorders (e.g. anxiety) are not defined precisely, and because we lack widely accepted, clear-cut medical guidelines for the prescribing of these drugs, the prescription of a tranquilliser for an inappropriate indication could be triggered by advertising.

Although most developed countries have regulations governing drug advertisements, the regulations are often ill defined and ineffectively enforced. Developing countries in particular have been the victims of misleading drug advertisements by pharmaceutical companies who exploit the lack of regulation in these countries. But are strictly enforced government regulations sufficient to stop the influence of drug advertisements on prescribing? We feel that policy recommendations regarding 1) government regulations, 2) the publication of drug advertisements and educational promotions in medical journals, and 3) physician education would more effectively reduce the influence of drug advertising on the inappropriate use of medication.

As suggested by Prather (Chapter 6), government regulations should focus on the abstract symbols and visual messages in advertisements as well as their content. Advertisements for psychotropic drugs have been criticized for their sexist content and misleading claims. Advertisements should be restricted to conveying accurate information about the marketed drug; both the benefits and adverse effects of the drug should be presented in close proximity in the same advertisement. More recently, advertisements have been featuring women and men in stereotyped roles which, through suggestive symbolism, promise the patient or prescribing physician benefits ranging from higher self-esteem to increased sex appeal. Most significantly, these symbolic advertisements do not impart any scientific information about the drug.

The predominant marketing format for pharmaceutical companies is the medical journal. Drug promotion could be regulated by restricting the publication of advertisements. Both journal editors and government agencies could take an active role in the scrutiny of drug advertisements. The major argument against limiting drug advertisements in journals is that the drug companies subsidize publication of the journal. Increased subscription rates would be the consequence of more professional publications.

A decrease in advertising in medical journals could produce an increase in other methods of marketing by drug companies. Office visits from pharmaceutical sales representatives, free samples, direct mailings, television advertising, 'educational' symposia sponsored by drug companies, and marketing directly to patients could increase. Therefore, a primary strategy to reduce the influence of pharmaceutical marketing on prescribing is to improve physician education about pharmaceuticals. Physicians should be capable of evaluating the information provided by pharmaceutical companies. Education in medical school should include the development of problem-solving skills and the knowledge base needed to assess new therapies for each patient. In addition, physicians should learn how to use non-biased sources of information that are available to them, such as drug bulletins, computer-assisted prescribing programmes, or pharmaceutical services. Enlisting the help of experts in drug therapy, such as clinical pharmacologists and pharmacists, could also aid physicians in making informed decisions about drug therapy.

Even if the influence of pharmaceutical companies on the prescribing of tranquillisers was reduced, sociocultural influences would still promote the use of these drugs and other 'chemical comforters'. During his discussion of the culture of long-term tranquilliser users, Montagne (Chapter 3) describes how societal norms and cultural beliefs contribute to long-term use. Patients and physicians have constructed cultural norms that make medication an acceptable method of coping compared to non-drug alternatives. Although some societal norms indicate a conflict between the biomedical disease model for psychological problems and the belief that dependence on medications is a sign of moral weakness, in general society has accepted medication as an appropriate way of dealing with the stresses associated with social change.

An understanding of the social acceptance of tranquillisers as a treatment for the problems of everyday life suggests policy recommendations for promoting the appropriate use of these drugs. One obvious way of eliminating inappropriate use would be to reduce the societal problems that precipitate the need for tranquilliser use. Then our overburdened social services and welfare systems would be able to help people deal with societal change without the benefit of 'the safety net of medical care'. More realistically, society could redefine an acceptable level of anxiety or nervousness that would not require drug treatment for a number of life's everyday problems. The development of coping mechanisms would be one way to deal with these problems. Another strategy for prevention is to encourage non-drug alternatives for dealing with stress and anxiety. Because substance abuse is a culturally defined problem, drug dependency on tranquillisers could be considered an unacceptable method of coping. Physicians and patients would have to accept the social stigma of condoning tranquilliser use for social problems.

SUMMARY OF POLICY RECOMMENDATIONS

The problem of long-term tranquilliser use is low on national policy agendas for many reasons. Gabe notes that there is a reluctance to challenge physicians' prescribing patterns. Additionally, long-term use is seen as a problem of 'otherwise respectable' middle-aged women, not as a problem of groups like working-class youth who are seen as a threat to law and order (Chapter 2). But in our view, there are other considerations: tranquillisers are viewed as legitimate therapies to combat bona fide psychiatric disease; there are relatively small numbers of long-term users (2–3 per cent according to Williams and Bellantuono, Chapter 4); and the use of tranquillisers is not seen as 'costly' to society – in terms of dollars or in terms of violent crime. There are no 'headline grabbers' that call attention to this issue.

One reason for the lack of attention paid to tranquilliser use is that we lack full knowledge about the problem. More research is required in this field, and key unaddressed issues will be summarized in this section. Another reason for the low priority assigned to the issue of tranquilliser use is a reluctance by the government to put needed policy reforms into practice. Policy recommendations – discussed throughout the chapter – will be summarized here. It is important to note that our suggestions – including the need for an expanded research agenda – are targeted at the level of the individual (physician, patient) as well as the society (government, pharmaceutical manufacturers, health professional organizations, etc.).

Research agenda

Key unanswered questions that need to be addressed at the level of the patient include:

(1) What role does patient ambivalence towards tranquillisers play in the process of becoming a long-term tranquilliser user? More specifically, what are the patient factors that contribute to *sustained* use? Are these factors different from those that *initiated* use?

(2) What are the characteristics of patients 'at risk' for long-term use? We know that women use more psychotropic medications than do men but the reasons are only imperfectly understood. In addition to gender, other patient factors need to be examined, such as medical history, prior history of tranquilliser use, and socio-economic status.

(3) In order to evaluate the effectiveness of various therapies to treat anxiety (including drugs), patient outcomes need to be assessed. These include but are not limited to: patient satisfaction with treatment; patient quality of life; use of health care resources (physician visits, use of casualty services, or hospitalizations); health and functional status; the presence or absence of dependence on

tranquillisers; and the use of other mood-altering medications (including alcohol and nicotine).

(4) The benefits and costs to patients of prolonged prescribing of tranquillisers are not fully known. There may be some patients who continue to receive benefits with minimal costs even after prolonged treatment with tranquillisers, but current data do not adequately inform us about who these patients are. We need to get away from the notion that long-term tranquilliser use is inherently injurious under all conditions and for all patients. The focus instead should be more patient-specific: under what kind of conditions, and for what particular patients, should specific types of therapies – or combinations of therapies – be administered to combat anxiety and other problems for which benzodiazepines are prescribed?

A number of questions regarding the physician's contribution to long-term tranquilliser use also need to be addressed. Key research issues at the level of the physician will now be discussed.

(1) An epidemiology of tranquilliser misuse is needed. What are the incidence and prevalence of various types of prescribing problems? Is long-term tranquilliser use the most serious and most prevalent problem? Or are other types of prescribing problems more compelling, such as therapeutic duplication, inappropriate indication, or excessive daily dosages?

(2) Besides chronicling the types of prescribing problems, we need to delineate the settings in which they are most likely to occur and to discover why these settings are so problematic. In the United States, nowhere is the long-term use of tranquillisers so pervasive and inappropriate as in nursing home settings. The reasons for this problem and the strategies to overcome it are crying out for solution. Since health care resources are so limited world-wide, we need to allocate them to those settings where patient need is greatest.

(3) We need rigorous, prospective studies of doctor–patient communication to determine how physicians encourage or discourage tranquilliser use. Such studies would enable us to determine whether patients select physicians who meet their prescribing needs; whether patients request or even demand tranquillisers over their physicians' objections; or whether patients' demands for tranquillisers are created primarily by inappropriate physician prescribing.

(4) Finally, what qualities characterize physicians who prescribe tranquillisers for long-term use? Knowing the answer to this question, we can begin to create effective educational strategies designed to encourage physicians to explore additional therapeutic modalities.

Policy recommendations

In addition to the need for an expanded research agenda, major policy recommendations include the following:

(1) Physicians and patients need to learn more about drug-free therapies for the treatment of anxiety and other problems for which benzodiazepines are prescribed. Principles underlying behavioural approaches, and methods of administering them, should be incorporated into medical school curricula. National education campaigns to educate the public should be mounted as well.

(2) Multidisciplinary collaboration among health professionals needs to be encouraged. Collaboration between physicians and psychologists would enable physicians to add anxiety management coping skills to their repertoire of treatment possibilities available to patients. Much also could be learned by working with anthropologists who could sensitize physicians to patients' cultural beliefs and how best to work within patients' value systems to assure safe and effective medication use.

(3) Stronger regulation by national governments of tranquilliser approval and marketing is clearly warranted. Advertisements should be restricted to conveying accurate information about the marketed drug; both the benefits and adverse effects of the drug should be presented in close proximity in the same advertisement. Since the predominant marketing format for pharmaceutical companies is the medical journal, drug promotion could be regulated by restricting the publication of advertisements. Both journal editors and government agencies should take an active role in the scrutiny of drug advertisements.

(4) Physicians need sources of information about drugs other than those provided by pharmaceutical manufacturers. These information sources include unbiased reports of advances and current status of drug therapeutics such as publications like the *Medical Letter*, published in the United States, and the *Drug and Therapeutics Bulletin*, published in England. Information from other knowledgeable health professionals such as pharmacists and pharmacologists could also help physicians make informed choices regarding drug therapy.

(5) Additional treatment programmes for combating long-term tranquilliser use should be funded. Such programmes should incorporate psychological (i.e. coping skills) as well as medical components. A critical dimension of the programmes should be a systematic and rigorous evaluation plan. The measurement of a variety

of clinical outcomes and cost-benefit analysis should be a part of the evaluation effort.

REFERENCES

Catalan, J., Gath, D., Edmonds, G., Ennis, J., Bond, A., & Martin, P. (1984) 'The effects of nonprescribing of anxiolytics in general practice', *British Journal of Psychiatry* 144: 593–610.

Gabe, J. & Lipshitz-Phillips, S. (1984) 'Tranquillisers as a social problem', *Sociological Review* 36: 320–52.

Lipton, H. L. & Lee, P. R. (1988) *Drugs and the Elderly: Clinical, Social, and Policy Perspectives*, Stanford, CA: Stanford University Press.

Williams, P. (1983) 'Factors influencing the duration of treatment with psychotropic drugs in general practice: a survival analysis approach', *Psychological Medicine* 13: 623–33.

Name index

Subject index